KT-210-882

GILLIAN TINDALL

Three Houses, Many Lives

VINTAGE BOOKS
London

Published by Vintage 2013

2 4 6 8 10 9 7 5 3 1

Copyright © Gillian Tindall 2012

Gillian Tindall has asserted her right under the Copyright, Designs
and Patents Act 1988 to be identified as the author of this work

This book is sold subject to the condition that it shall not,
by way of trade or otherwise, be lent, resold, hired out,
or otherwise circulated without the publisher's prior
consent in any form of binding or cover other than that
in which it is published and without a similar condition,
including this condition, being imposed on the
subsequent purchaser

First published in Great Britain in 2012 by
Chatto & Windus

Vintage
Random House, 20 Vauxhall Bridge Road,
London SW1V 2SA

www.vintage-books.co.uk

Addresses for companies within The Random House Group Limited
can be found at: www.randomhouse.co.uk/offices.htm

The Random House Group Limited Reg. No. 954009

A CIP catalogue record for this book
is available from the British Library

ISBN 9780099547037

The Random House Group Limited supports the Forest
Stewardship Council® (FSC®), the leading international
forest-certification organisation. Our books carrying the FSC
label are printed on FSC®-certified paper. FSC is the only
forest-certification scheme supported by the leading
environmental organisations, including Greenpeace.
Our paper procurement policy can be found at:

HEREFORDSHIRE LIBRARIES	
223	
Bertrams	06/06/2013
942	£9.99
LM	

Contents

List of Illustrations

The maps and plans, based on a variety of different sources and on personal observation and surmise, have been composed and drawn up by the author. Reworking and lettering by Rosie Collins.

And yet they think their houses shall continue for ever, and that their dwelling-places shall endure from one generation to another: and call the lands after their own names.
Psalm XLIX, verse 11

Houses have their own ways of dying, falling as variously as the generations of men.
Howards End, by E. M. Forster

. . . Snow fell, undated. Light
Each summer thronged the glass. A bright
Litter of birdcalls strewed the same
Bone-riddled ground. And up the paths
The endless altered people came.
From 'An Arundel Tomb' by Philip Larkin

If you faign my name would know
In letters plain I will you show . . .
. . . This Book shall my name have
When I am Dead and Laid in Grave
When Groady worms my Body has eat
Then you may see my name Compleat.
Margaret Hardin, wife of George Harding, Clark.
(Margaret Harding, wife to the parish
clerk of Limpsfield in the mid-eighteenth
century, wrote this and other comments
on blank spaces in an outdated register.)

Chapter I

'FOR THEE WAS A HOUSE BUILT'

For thee was a house built
Ere thou wast born –

I see it in memory now. The handwriting was late Victorian or Edwardian, the time of my grandparents' youth, when people with leisure on their hands kept what were called commonplace books, and copied into these books poems or sections of prose they wanted somehow to possess.

I did not of course read it in the original hand of the writer, far, far further back in time: a blackletter form that would in itself have been impenetrable to me, even if it had been in any language I could understand. The copier adopting it for himself in his commonplace book – long-dead great-uncle? distant cousin? one of those wraiths referred to by grandmothers as 'dear Bunty' or 'poor Harold' – had at the bottom of the column noted pedantically: *'Translated from the Anglo-Saxon original by HWL.'*

I was perhaps nine years old, and Anglo-Saxon meant to me only the two baffling characters in *Through the Looking-Glass* who struck Anglo-Saxon attitudes. Nor, I am sure, did I read most of the poem, which had seemed hard to decipher and anyway discouragingly long. I was mildly bored, on my own on a Sunday afternoon in a house in the country, pulling out bound volumes of old *Punch* and other fat books from my grandfather's shelves. It was enough, for that afternoon, that the first two lines gave me a small but distinct thrill of pleasure.

For thee was a house built . . .

Someone, before I even existed, in that mysterious time known as 'before the war' or even 'before the *last* war', had built a house for *me*. So everything was destined, everything organised ahead – for me and, as I presently worked out, for everyone else as well. Houses had been planned for us, uncounted numbers of them, but each one assigned for a particular future occupier to make his own. As I grew up, I would just have to learn how to find it, my house, that was, somewhere, already there, waiting for me.

. . . The house is not highly timbered,
It is unhigh and low . . .

That will do me nicely, I thought. Children spontan-eously make houses for themselves, under the table or behind the sofa or in a big cardboard box. The genes that led their remote hunter-gatherer ancestors to create the first shelters are at work in a three-year-old mind. Later, for the luckier ones, come camps at the end of the garden, or in woods, or among acres of bracken whose feathery tops can be tied together to make mini-ature tents. Growing up on the edge of Ashdown Forest, I knew about bracken-houses. I had noticed that grown-up people sometimes made them too, though exactly why I wasn't sure. Were these couples playing? They didn't seem to want to be disturbed, but then nor did I once I had got my little house for that afternoon neatly hollowed out, among the hum of insects and scent of crushed fronds.

There was another house on the edge of Ashdown, a full-sized one this, that I and another child had found when out for a walk with our attendant mothers. It had been near-invisible during the summer, when the hawthorn bushes surrounding it were impenetrably green and oaks and birches reared overhead. But on this cold afternoon, winter's rains, or the casual attentions of a woodman from the broomyard, had beaten down some of the invading gorse and brambles. We could see the moss-covered tiled roof through the twigs, and the high brick chimney and the dark-paned upper windows. It was only a small house, a cottage put up a hundred or so years before on a strip of common land, by someone with a respectable reason to be there.

Beneath a twisted arch of hawthorn we found a rotting wooden gate and forced it wide enough to squeeze past. Bracken, dead now for the winter, a brown mat of stems, covered the remains of a paved path and what must once have been a vegetable garden: old pea-props sagged, potato plants had turned into creepers invading the remains of an empty chicken run. Rose bushes grown wild and scrawny grabbed at our arms. A bird called in faint alarm and warning, sighting people unexpectedly in its territory.

The front door was locked, as if someone had planned to return. But we worked our way round to the back, where the remains of autumn's apples rotted under gnarled trees and there was a water butt and a rusting enamel bucket on its side and a hoe abandoned against a wall. Here was another door, and this one stood slightly ajar, wedged on a broken hinge.

Of course we went in. And explored the whole place, in spite of faint grown-up interjections about being Careful, and how there might be holes in the stairs and Don't Touch anything – because you never Know . . . But the cottage, though open to any passing stranger, seemed undisturbed. It had been abandoned in some year there was no one left to compute, with all its basic furniture: a kitchen table, wooden chairs and stools, a dresser fixed to the wall, a kitchen range stiffened with rust but with old pots still stacked on it, fire irons and a coal scuttle. In a dark larder invaded through its small window by ivy, more pots, a wire meat safe and rolling pin. In a lean-to, whose sagging roof warned mutely of the dissolution that would, one day, overtake the whole house if someone did not recognise it for his own and rescue it, stood a low, pockmarked yellow pottery sink with one tap. There was also another devastated enamel bucket, a broken chair and a mangle. Up the creaking stairs – Careful, children! – were two small attic bedrooms, one containing a hollowed-out bed and a wrought-iron child's cot, both without mattresses, and the other a small pile of sacks in which were traces of a mouse's nest. Droppings littered the floorboards.

The room where the beds were had one of those tiny fireplaces with a grate hardly ever used that the Victorians installed in bedrooms as a minimal gesture toward comfort. But this one had been lit – perhaps to warm someone in his or her last illness – not long before the house was left to its silence. For in the rusty grate was a pile of dank, black ashes, through which, in natural disobedience to what the mothers had said, we ran our inquisitive fingers.

On a narrow mantelshelf was a small, clouded mirror, and a picture from a calendar of a girl looking over her shoulder: crimped hair, black-rimmed eyes, a feeble rosebud mouth and a yellow waistless dress.

Of course we begged to adopt the place as our own – 'It's *empty*, Mum. No one wants it. We could make it nice.'

'We could bring some blankets . . . I know! Daddy's army sleeping bag . . .'

'We could camp here for the night. There's even a lavvy.'

There was too, between the back door and the apple trees. A hut like a sentry box, with a hole in the seat over a deep pit from which well-nourished plants were now sprouting. Still hanging on a nail were torn squares of faded paper that had once brought news of distant wars and foreign revolutions. Being country children of the 1940s such lowly conveniences were not unfamiliar to us.

'Oh *do* let us make it our house, Mummy. We could ask Mr Killick to scythe the garden.'

But our mothers, amused though not really paying attention, smoking Player's Weights and talking between themselves in the garden, well wrapped up in their camel-hair coats, were firm. The place was dirty. ('But we could clean it! We could bring proper buckets and a broom . . .'). You couldn't tell who'd Been in it – 'And darlings, it isn't ours. It must belong to someone. And anyway, it's time to go home for tea. Come *along*.'

Many years later I went back, to find this first house I had recognised as mine before I had even read the poem promising me such a place. The location was exactly as it had been, including the surrounding hawthorn hedge, now reduced back to a manageable height and whitening with another spring. A remembered cuckoo called.

But the cottage was gone. In its place was a different, tidy house, new but of traditional Sussex brick and tile, taller than the old one but otherwise of much the same dimensions. Planning regulations are strict these days in such Protected Areas. No one, now, can build a snug home for himself on an empty bit of waste by a Royal Forest.

By that time, I knew that houses rise and fall, are loved, looked after, altered, but continue, then decay and are replaced, even as people are. Houses last longer than human beings, usually much longer. To the Venerable Bede in the eighth century a human life was like the flight of a bird in at the window of a hall-house, across the lighted, occupied space and out again into the dark. By contrast with the brief human span the building represented permanence. Unlike the human body, as the house ages it can almost always be repaired, given the will and the funds. But without these it sags and weakens, till one soaking day or wind-battered night its decay is perceived to be irreparable. The one-time refuge, warm meeting-place, has like failing flesh and bone, become a burden. And then an emptiness, a silence. By and by those for whom it was once filled with intricate memories are all gone, and it is eventually demolished by strangers who know nothing of the life it contained. 'Death comes for stones,' wrote the seventeenth-century antiquarian John Aubrey, echoing Cicero, 'as well as names.'

But often a new house rises on the same site, and so the life cycle of home and shelter continues. Very many of the houses in the villages and towns of Britain, Europe and other long-lived-in parts of the world are simply the current occupants of parcels of land that have been used and reused for many centuries. London terrace houses still reflect the standard widths, 12, 16, 20 and 24 feet, that came about through the practices and limitations of medieval builders. Many French farmhouses, stalwart nineteenth-century constructions from the first period when small landowners prospered on new markets and new fertilisers, stand in the footprint and on the foundation walls of one-storey dwellings that were raised there in a time so remote that it is useless to seek any written evidence of them. Yet other evidence may be found. Houses known to have been built only within the last two hundred and fifty years sometimes harbour beams and roof timbers that, on analysis, turn out to have come from oaks felled and sawn several centuries earlier. These houses have inherited the bones of their ancestors, even as humans do.

And then there are some houses which, like some

human beings, go through extraordinary transformations: several different lives are lived end to end. A medieval hall-house, built for a world dependent on the land and its produce, will have started out as one large space with a central hearth whose smoke rises up into the roof timbers, and one flimsily screened smaller room at each end. But, if it survives, it will grow in time in status as well as size. A hundred years or so after it is first built the fire is moved to one side, and later again a proper fireplace and chimney are constructed over it. The end rooms develop sleeping chambers above them, then a gallery to connect the two ends. By and by the whole of the one-time smoke bay beneath the roof is closed by an upper floor.

Another generation again adds further rooms and a second chimney. More time passes, and a new owner, perhaps enriched by the sixteenth-century Reformation, raises the roof and constructs a whole, gabled second floor, jettied out on fresh beams. He replaces the old, small windows and their wooden bars with larger ones containing expensive glass panes, just as he replaces the rush-strewn dirt floor downstairs with good, clean stone. It is a wealthy Elizabethan merchant's house that stands there now, with a street of other houses extending each side and a vegetable and fruit garden behind.

But a hundred years, a Civil War, a king's destruction and a Restoration later the fine, timbered house is looking old-fashioned beside its newer brick or stone-fronted neighbours. It is divided up among several families, and tradesmen and artisans move into the ground-floor rooms. Yet another half-century later its social decline is arrested. The small town in which it now stands has flourished and grown wealthy with the eighteenth-century coach trade. The innkeeper in the building next door acquires the old house to extend his own place with rooms fit to feed and lodge travellers. To enlarge his stabling and yard, he paves over the garden. He leaves the inside of the house essentially as it is, but below the old-fashioned protruding top floor he slaps on a fine new, straight-up-and-down brick and stucco façade, with new twelve-paned sash windows.

Another century passes. The town that was so prosperous in the days of stagecoaches and rented post-chaises is now a backwater. Rich businessmen, along with the railway companies, have gone elsewhere. The inn is once again serving local farmers and labourers. The building that started life as a hall-house is presently let out to a fishmonger and a dealer in coal and lamp oil, with a large number of tenants on the upper floors. Washing hangs out of the windows. Children play in the open gutter, for drainage has not yet reached that little-regarded part of town. The one-time garden at the back is now covered in sheds where scrap metal is stored. It can only be a matter of time, say the more influential citizens sitting in the late-Victorian town hall, before the whole ramshackle run of buildings is replaced by something decent and modern. With terracotta dressings . . .

So easily then might this house, like so many others of its time, have become nothing but dust and grit in the wind, a space soon filled, a few vanishing memories, perhaps one sepia photo as the background to a celebratory parade that is now in itself quite forgotten.

But time and chance and another distracting war intervene, and somehow the house survives. By the 1920s distinguished visitors to Stratford-upon-Avon are 'undressing' the houses Shakespeare might have known, removing two hundred years of cladding, and the vogue for exposed timbers spreads through the towns and villages of England. By the 1930s the dilapidated house has been acquired cheaply by an antiquarian book dealer as a place to keep his extensive stock. By and by, he strips away layers of accreted stucco and plasterboard, unblocks concealed Tudor fireplaces, discovers carved lintels. He moves on, and in the 1950s the place is the flourishing Olde Tea Rooms ('Elevenses, light Lunches, pastries a Speciality'), decorated with a spinning wheel in the window and flowery curtains.

By the 1980s, renovated further and now with fragments of its long-vanished incarnation as a hall-house, as well as its Elizabethan architecture, carefully exposed, it is a Listed Building. It is on the circuit of the Historic Town Tour organised by the newly opened local museum. At the back, where the filthy old sheds have been pulled down, a knot garden is currently planned.

– Thus, any really old house in any ancient town: a classic case.

The rest of this book concerns three different, real and specific old houses and their past lives, in three very different places in southern England. Each is in busy modern use, but each has, at its core, the remains of a home built long ago for the world that we have lost. In the centuries intervening since the first roof timbers were raised each has undergone remarkable physical changes and also transformations in use and meaning.

One is in a village in the Cotswolds, on the border of Oxfordshire and Gloucestershire, a place still deeply rural in appearance but crucially altered by the social changes the twentieth century has brought. Another is where Surrey merges into the Kentish Weald just below the North Downs. Once entirely rural, this is today a consciously preserved enclave with crowded commuter towns near at hand. And the third one, built long ago as an isolated country retreat for a City merchant, has for the last hundred years been swallowed up in one of the least picturesque districts of London's enormous spread.

None of these three houses has anything extraordinary about it: that is why I have chosen them. None figures on a tourist map. They are all in disguise, for none, at a casual glance, looks as old as it really is. I could have chosen three other houses in other parts of the country. Or three hundred. Each one therefore must stand for many others. I have picked these particular houses because I have, at one time or another, had a relationship with each of them, and because each house seems to me to exemplify in its own way something about the everyday history of England over the last three hundred years.

None has been the home of anyone truly famous, though each has known occupants who were, in their own time, people of substance and renown. They led busy lives in the public eye, they were conscious of their social standing, they were forceful and made things happen, they were unique to themselves and to each other – and then they were gone, and others took their place.

> *For thee was a house built*
> *Ere thou wast born.*

Not till I was grown up, and rediscovered that Anglo-Saxon poem, did I realise that it was not, as I had thought as a child, about some benign destiny creating a house just for me. It is about the transience of human life as opposed to earth's permanence. The 'house' referred to is a house of clay '. . . *doorless, And dark within*' where human life is eventually laid to rest.

It is to recover traces of lost people, and to decode the marks that their full but fleeting lives have left on their enduring houses, that I have made this account.

Chapter II

ANY BOARDING SCHOOL

The child who wanted to adopt the derelict cottage on Ashdown Forest is now several years older. The days of long Sunday afternoons in the bracken, or poking round her grandparents' house, are ending. She is to go to boarding school. Mummy had 'loved' her boarding school, apparently. So the child is supposed to as well.

A slow car journey from Sussex into Surrey with a new, heavy school trunk sticking out of the boot. A new, heavy sinking feeling in the stomach under an unfamiliar green serge garment.

'It's a lovely old Elizabethan manor house . . . And with central heating in the dormitories, you lucky little thing.'

We pass through suburban Oxted, up a hill lined with neat, gabled houses in gardens, turn yet another corner and suddenly this is Limpsfield and we park. A high, intimidating wall of pink bricks with an iron fire escape zigzagging down it. Looks like a hospital, the child thinks. Or a prison. To one side, between this building and an older stone wall that drops down to the road, is a great pile of coke.

'The old bit of the house is further on – I think.' Mummy, always bad at recognising places because she doesn't like wearing her glasses, is a shade nervous now, perhaps realising belatedly how the place will actually look to the child.

Past the pink bricks and the coke, the road runs alongside another large section of building in older brick, with ivy. Then, joined to the other end but set back, is a quite different-looking frontage of white painted stucco. Semi-circular steps up to a door under a bell-shaped porch. Polished brass. Then a narrow, blue-carpeted hallway, another step up and, beyond, a much bigger hall with a wide old fireplace with a great beam across it and an inglenook with a spinet standing in it. This, thinks the child, is more what she has been led to expect.

And the headmistress, when fetched by the maid who opened the door, has a tinkling, insincere laugh and bracelets on her plump wrists, and seems more like the sort of grown-up you might meet in a drawing room. We are indeed briefly ushered into a drawing room, with chintz armchairs and Chinese lacquered cabinets, looking out on to rolling lawns and a huge ilex tree that looks good for playing in, with a view of Limpsfield village church. But very soon we are despatched into the care of Sister, a grimmer figure in nurse's starched uniform, who escorts us through a labyrinth of narrow corridors and ill-lit stairs to a room with a collection of old beds in it and a view of the coke pile far below, but no apparent central heating.

Here Sister abandons us, having told us the trunk will be brought up 'later, when the other girls arrive', and given instructions for regaining the different world of the front hall. We attempt the journey, get lost among steps up and down, dead ends, basins and pegs, bare floors and cracked linoleum, but finally stumble by chance back to the blue carpet and the spinet. The headmistress has clearly been waiting.

'Ah, there you are. Say goodbye to your mother now, child.' A moment of awful realisation of what life was

now to be, searing desolation – and then suddenly
Mummy isn't there any longer, and the headmistress is
saying:

'You can run up those front stairs just for now. Ordinarily you mustn't use them.'

The child runs.

She was never to use those stairs again, never to cross
the blue carpet for years, except on Sunday evenings
when carrying sewing things to the drawing room for
Sunday Reading, or when summoned there on dreadful
occasions to be told she was underhand, vulgar, a disgrace
to the school or some other reproach for a minor misde-
meanour as seemed to the headmistress appropriate. She
was never to play on the lawns or under the ilex tree
either, as all that part of the grounds was Out of Bounds
to the girls, except once a year when they were lined up
there to have the annual photograph taken, and for
Parents' Day.

Only when she was older did the child, now a chronically wary and frustrated teenager, realise that if she
furnished herself with a suitable excuse ('Miss Reich has
asked me to take these papers to the school secretary')
she could venture out of the cold, grubby, ramshackle
corridors, away from the smell of ink and unwashed
female bodies and stale bread, through a one-time
external doorway and into that Other Place where the
blue carpet lapped the old flagstones round the great
Tudor hearth. Under an arching beam a small door with
linenfold panelling on one side of the fireplace led to a
yet more forbidden place – the Private Sitting Room
where the two headmistresses (for there were in theory
two of them) went when they 'didn't want to be disturbed'.
The teenager longed to see into that room, further into
this secret Other house that seemed to be existing apart
from all the rest of the buildings, but she never managed
to.

She did wonder vaguely why the headmistresses

needed so much space for themselves (for they had a dining room too, and of course their bedrooms upstairs) when there was so little space anywhere else? No common rooms, no library, no gym, nowhere to go after supper except the echoing, unfurnished Assembly Hall or the comfortless classrooms most of which were wooden sheds built out over the one-time garden. Nowhere to keep anything of your own except the crowded bedrooms, which were Out of Bounds till bedtime.

The school had been opened (the prospectus preferred the word 'founded') in the stucco-fronted, Georgian-looking house in 1897, with just a handful of pupils. The three Misses Lyon, who owned it and did most of the teaching, were those classic figures of the late-Victorian era, the unmarried daughters of a father who had speculated unwisely. The emphasis seems to have been on such ladylike subjects as Social Etiquette and French. By 1901 there were twenty pupils boarding, aged between fourteen and eighteen, and a hall had been built on to one side of the original house. This served for morning prayers and as a dining room, and there were four big bedrooms above. It was a fairly pleasant neo-Queen-Anne addition in brick with tall chimneys. Oddly, no bathroom seems to have been included, but a little later three bathrooms were fitted into the already-much-altered back of the older building.[1] By 1920 the school had forty-odd girls, mostly boarders, some of whom were lodged in another house up the High Street. It was still a manageable number with which to run a small, informal establishment with scope for individual attention. The boarders were required to provide their own umbrellas for walks, and changed into 'neutral shan-tung silk dresses' every evening – though one Old Girl did remember, a lifetime later, 'that there were some very smart girls who put on bright red lipstick and

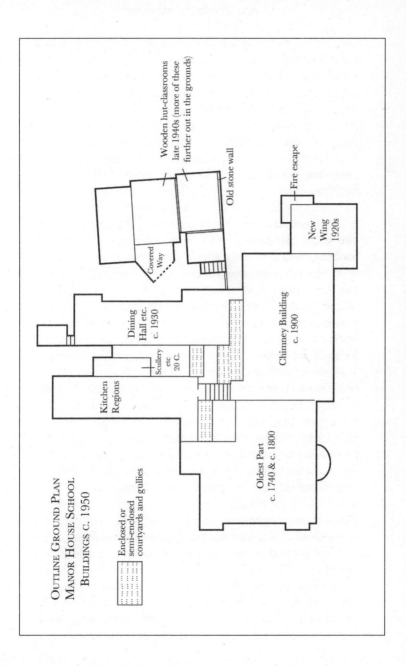

OUTLINE GROUND PLAN
MANOR HOUSE SCHOOL
BUILDINGS c. 1950

Enclosed or semi-enclosed courtyards and gullies

Wooden hut-classrooms late 1940s (more of these further out in the grounds)

Old stone wall

Covered Way

Fire escape

New Wing 1920s

Dining Hall etc. c. 1930

Scullery etc 20 C.

Kitchen Regions

Chimney Building c. 1900

Oldest Part c. 1740 & c. 1800

smoked cigarettes when they could.'² There were also illicit 'escapes' into the village.

Possibly the Misses Lyon began to feel they could no longer cope with the Modern Girl, for in 1923 they sold the place. It was was bought by someone who seems – I was surprised to discover from a cache of old papers that eventually found their way into the County archive – to have been one of those gifted teachers who can invigorate any school. She evidently managed to raise the intellectual level, for by 1933 there were seven girls who had recently left and were at university in either Oxford or London, and two at the Royal College of Music. Tennis courts, a gym and a small swimming pool were built, and a laboratory equipped for science lessons. A room was set aside as a library, with 'comfortable chairs for silent reading'. The further front wing also appeared, quickly built during one summer holiday: three storeys in cheap pink fletton brick with an obtrusive fire escape and no pretension to the elegance of the chimney-stacked building next to it. Here were two new classrooms, a cloakroom, and bedrooms on the floors above. A new entry was constructed through what had now become an enclosed yard, and for the first time the house had more than one staircase. Presently a new, bigger dining room was built out at the back, alongside the kitchens, in the plywood-beamed mock-Tudor style then spreading far and wide along England's suburban road network. But the school roll was still only about seventy pupils, many of them day girls from the expanding suburb of Oxted. There seems still to have been scope for outdoor summer lessons under the ilex tree, and impromptu trips to Sussex beauty spots, and these continued under the next head, who took over in 1936.

In 1940, the first and worst full year of the Second World War, the numbers went abruptly down to sixteen. In the autumn of 1939 various London schools had been evacuated to Limpsfield as a 'safe area', but now there was a realistic fear that Surrey might find itself invaded by German tanks. In the leaflet which replaced the usual school magazine in July 1940 the head wrote: 'a rapidly changing world has not left the Manor House unaffected, and financial pressure compels me to give up my school which has given me such joy'. It was at this low point that Mrs P. and Mrs M. acquired the place, surely at a knockdown price. Both were assistant teachers on the staff, and their status as married women was rather notional. Mrs P. had recently married a retired vicar, who died a few years later, while Mrs M., at this time, was still Miss Hurran and a concert pianist.

The invasion-scare subsided. Numbers rose again and went on rising. By the early 1950s they had doubled from the pre-war figure: there were almost seventy boarders and as many day girls. The library room, the gym and the lab had disappeared, sacrificed apparently to cram in more pupils. No one, now, was educated up to university level. Yet by the end of the decade the school roll was 167. Somehow, the overall inadequacy of the buildings and the amenities to such numbers was blandly ignored by the two headmistresses, the ostentatiously uniformed Sister and the gullible parents. These last, in any case, were rarely shown anything now beyond the lawns with the ilex tree, the tennis courts, and the stagnant swimming pool which was only cleaned and made temporarily bright blue for the yearly Parents' Day. These were the features of which much was made.

Because the stucco-fronted Georgian house had once been a gentleman's residence the grounds were large. Useless in winter, except for the dreariness of obligatory hockey and netball – and anyway Out of Bounds on dark evenings – in summer they provided a breath of space and freedom, a chance to be alone, or to play hopscotch on a dusty path under pine trees with one chosen friend, or even to sit and read uncomfortably but poetically on the sagging branch of a rhododendron. Sometimes, at dusk, rounding the corner of the vegetable gardens from which you could see, over a very old wall, the forbidden lawns and the ilex tree and the church tower beyond, the girl would feel an unaccustomed impulse of simple happiness. The bell-ringers practised on Friday evenings, pealing and pealing out into the sunset sky till you could feel the sound within you, and a hazy perception reached her that the church and the old, forbidden heart of the house were somehow allied. They were clearly nothing to do with the ugly collection of disparate buildings that had grown up around the house like giant toadstools, leaving foetid inner yards and gulleys with choked drains, cut off from their original purpose.

People, real people – not boring, stupid, giggling, bullying girls or lying teachers – had lived here once. They had been christened or married in that same church; perhaps some of them now lay in the churchyard. She vaguely wished she knew about them but there was no one to ask. She could not go and mooch around the churchyard to read the names on the graves because, until you were in the sixth from, you were never, ever allowed outside the school gates except in a crocodile.

'An old Elizabethan manor house . . .'

In fact, the property never was a manor house. That name was a piece of mid-nineteenth-century affectation. Earlier, it had been known as 'Stanhopes' and that is the name now once again bestowed on it – or rather, on the private housing estate that today, when all the dank toadstools have been demolished, occupies its grounds. Behind that name is an arresting story, amusing for a moment and then, on reflection, tragic. But although Stanhope was the name of one of the three school divisions spuriously called 'houses' to which the girls were assigned for competition purposes, they were never told its origin, or the story. Possibily the two headmistresses were themselves ignorant of it, for all their trappings of culture. (Mrs P., with her bangles, fat wrists and attendant Pekinese dog, was given to lecturing the girls on Gracious Living in contrast with their own Disgusting Habits; while her meeker companion, Mrs M., concentrated on music and seemed inclined to leave most school matters to others.)

It is possible also, unlikely as it seems, that they were unaware that for several years in the early 1930s, in its brief intellectual heyday, the school had had as a boarder someone whose eventual death was heroic. Diana Rowden had spent her earlier childhood in France, and returned there as a young woman. She joined the WAAF in England in 1941, but her bilingual skill brought her to the notice of the Special Operations Executive, which was being formed to help the French Resistance against the Nazi occupation. Parachuted into France, she spent much of 1943 there, acting as a messenger between agents, and took part in the sabotage of an armaments factory. Near the end of the year, she was betrayed and arrested. She was interrogated for two weeks, then sent to the notorious prison at Fresnes, and the following May to a concentration camp in Germany. In July, having been moved to another camp in Alsace, along with several other SOE agents she was put to death. She was posthumously awarded the MBE and the Croix de Guerre. Her name is on the memorial at the site of the death camp, and also on the soaring monument near Valençay in central France. A watercolour of her and her companions hangs in the Special Forces Club in London.

It would have been good to have known about Diana Rowden while struggling to grow up within the Manor House's stunting confines, with its nunnery feuds, its endless petty and punitive rules and its restricted syllabus. That might have bestowed some confidence that there was a wider world elsewhere, and not one that might only be accessed by going on to secretarial college or by Getting Engaged at eighteen – the generally shared ambition.

But although the much-publicised story of another wartime heroine, Odette Hallowes, was well known by the 1950s, no one ever mentioned Diana Rowden to us. Instead, the chosen Model Old Girl was the youngest daughter of Winston Churchill, the one who, as Lady Soames, went on to lead a scandal-free life, unlike her two sisters. She had attended the school in the 1930s because her family were living nearby at Chartwell. When I spoke briefly to her a lifetime later she had benign memories of the school but explained that she had been a day girl, so free from any sense of imprisonment. In those easy-going days she was allowed to ride her own pony to school and back again. Twenty years later her name was regularly invoked as part of the Morning Assembly lecture on Gracious Living and the importance of Getting Back to Pre-war Standards, though these did not apparently include any relaxation of the school's close confinement policy. Meanwhile, year by year, with no capital outlay, the standard of living within the school quietly declined: china mugs were replaced by squashy plastic beakers, the kitchens became visibly dirtier, there were outbreaks of septic spots and impetigo. More and more beds, of any old date and condition, were fitted into the upstairs rooms, though the number of operative bathrooms remained at three. (There were two others, apparently just for show, as they had no hot water plumbed to them and even the cold water was intermittent.) No operative bedroom basins, nowhere to wash or dry underclothes. Six lavatories for over sixty boarders. No changing rooms for games, no showers at all.

This was just one, unremarkable school. There were others something like it at the time, both for girls and for small boys, all over the British Isles. They marked a peculiar period, between the end of the nineteenth century and the third quarter of the twentieth, when upper middle-class parents felt it was normal, and indeed desirable or even somehow socially necessary, to relinquish responsibility for the upbringing of their own children for nearly three-quarters of the year. No one has ever been able to explain the phenonomen satisfactorily except by reference to the necessary training of Empirebuilders, and this would hardly have been relevant to girls. The system never existed to the same extent in any other country. Nor, except in the well-endowed, wellestablished Public Schools, mainly for teenage boys, did boarding necessarily ensure a good education.

The model is now broken. Such private boarding schools as survive today, a tiny fraction of those functioning fifty years ago, do not think it part of their remit to sequester their charges from normal life, let alone to dictate when their parents may or may not see them. Nor do most parents so complacently abandon their offspring for months on end without asking a few questions about the range of subjects taught, the exam results, or even the arrangements for having baths. During the 1960s a social sea change, which probably had as much to do with changing class structures as with new patterns of family life, meant that, in the space of a few years, the traditional small schools began to shut down all over Britain. Because their fees had been kept low enough to attract large numbers of parents, their finances had always been delicately balanced, dependent on packing in as many pupils as possible without further outlay on buildings or staff. When numbers fell, the tipping-point that turned a fat profit into a loss was soon reached. The Manor House School shut down in 1969.

One would like to think that, in its declining, depleted state, and with Mrs P. and Mrs M. long retired, the place returned in its last years to something nearer the easygoing community that it had apparently been between the wars. A sentimental plaque now fixed to the roadside wall would seem to suggest this.

Chapter III

LETTERS AND DEEDS

B ut who was the never-explained Stanhope?
The Stanhope family was, and is to this day, a well-known aristocratic family that has proliferated through the generations over several centuries, producing a mass of family letters and, from time to time, such an eccentric and flamboyant a figure as Lady Hester Stanhope, the trousered traveller in the Middle East and niece to William Pitt. By the seventeenth century one branch were Earls of Chesterfield: the fourth of these, who lived through much of the eighteenth century and died three years before the celebrated Lady from the branch of the Stanhope Earls was born, was also flamboyant in his way though far more calculating. Whig Member of Parliament, diplomat, orarator, schemer, pamphleteer, Secretary of State, sometime friend of both Johnson and Voltaire, keenly intelligent, witty but argumentative, selfish and cynical: this was Lord Chesterfield. He was a well known figure in his own time. He would now be utterly forgotten but for a packet of letters that he certainly never expected anyone but the recipient to read, let alone to print. These were letters he wrote to his illegitimate son, Philip Stanhope.

He was determined to shape this, his only child, whose mother had been a French governess, to follow in his own footsteps. He sent him to Westminster School, and then on the Grand Tour to Italy, all the time posting him missives full of well-intentioned instructions and parental hope:

> I am not now preaching to you like an old fellow upon either religious or moral texts . . . I am advising you as a friend, as a man of the world, as one who would not have you old while you are young, but would have you take all the pleasures that reason points out and that decency warrants . . . A *commerce gallant* insensibly formed with a woman of fashion; a glass of wine or two much unwarily taken in the warmth and joy of good company, or some innocent frolic by which nobody is injured, are the utmost bounds of that life of pleasure which a man of sense and decency . . . will allow himself . . .

One cannot help noticing that Chesterfield must have gone further than he intended in either decency or an innocent frolic to have produced Philip, but then complete honesty was not what he himself habitually advocated:

> Dear Boy, I recommended to you in my last an innocent piece of art – that of flattering people behind their backs, in presence of those who . . . will not fail to repeat, and even amplify, the praise to the party concerned . . .

A star in his own world, he was determined that Philip should shine too:

> It is in Parliament that I have set my heart on your making a figure . . . This means that you must be a good speaker there; I use the word *must* because I know you may if you will . . .

By 1750 Philip was in Italy, and his father, now fifty-six, was still on the same themes, including the import-ance of 'little things . . . too material for me to omit':

> How go your pleasures in Rome? Are you in fashion there; that is, do you live with the people who are? . . . Are you domestic enough in any considerable house to be called *le petit Stanhope*?
>   . . . Do you use yourself to carve, eat and drink genteely, and with ease? Do you take care to walk, sit, stand and present yourself gracefully? Are you sufficiently on your guard against awkward attitudes, and illiberal, ill-bred and disgusting habits; such as scratching yourself, putting your fingers in your mouth, nose and ears? Tricks always acquired at schools.
>   You seem to like Rome . . .

Quite unknown to his father, Philip had then just met in Rome an obscure woman called Eugenia Peters. Vari-ously said to have been someone's illegitimate daughter herself, or 'of humble origins', she was also 'plain almost to ugliness' but well-educated and accomplished. He was eventually to make her his secret wife. Secret? Yes, because during the long years when Philip, who persist-ently failed to develop Lord Chesterfield's gifts and flair for the wordly life, was fulfilling minor diplomatic posts in German principalities, his loving father did not cease to bombard him with good advice. Philip must take his time about marrying, and be sure to pick a wife of the right sort of family and fortune, who would advance his career. To marry unwisely was the greatest folly in a man of the world and always led to repentance . . .

Evidently the crucial moment, at which Philip might have admitted where his affections lay, had been allowed to pass. After that, it became increasingly impossible to tell the truth. The fact that Eugenia was for a long time not technically his wife suggests that he vaguely went on hoping he might yet get round the problem. Two sons were born to them, Charles and another Philip, before he finally married Eugenia in Dresden in 1767. Never in good health, he died the following year in eastern France, seemingly of kidney failure ('dropsy'), aged just thirty-six. Only then did Lord Chesterfield learn of the marriage and of the existence of his grandsons.

The death, and the realisation that his son had, after all his efforts, learnt the art of duplicity all too well, and had been a stranger to him in such an essential way, was heart-breaking for Lord Chesterfield. He rallied, however, did 'the decent thing', brought the bereaved family to England, made friends with the little boys, who were then about eight and six, and paid for them to go to school – 'for,' he wrote to his newly-met daughter-in-law, 'I do not intend that, from this time forwards, the two boys should cost you one shilling'. It seems he was staking a claim. Evidently Eugenia had some means of her own, either from her husband or from her nebulous forebears. Lord Chesterfield appears to have been on reasonable terms with her, and to have taken a genuine interest in the boys' progress and individual characters: 'Charles will be a scholar, if you please; but our little Philip, without being one, will be something or other as good, though I do not yet know what.' He did not live long enough to find out. When he died, in 1773, he left £100 a year to each of them, which was enough to keep them as schoolboys, plus the then-enormous sum of £10,000 when they should reach adulthood.

He left Eugenia nothing. Presumably she was disappointed by this, and she took the view that she did not have enough to live on. All the letters Lord Chesterfield had written to his son over the years had ended up in her possession, and she sold them to a publisher for fifteen hundred guineas (£1,575). This ensured her a comfortable life for the ten years that remained to her. Her action created a scandal, some regarding it as treacherous, for the publication of personal letters was a novelty then, while others were more shocked by the letters' intimate and amoral tone. This naturally increased their sale and led to reprints for the next hundred years. It was an ironic bestowal of posthumous fame on a man who would never have wanted this kind of exposure.

Once Eugenia had come into money she acquired a house suitable for a widowed lady in easy circumstances, who wished for country quiet combined with ready access to London. This was the stucco-fronted house with a porch in Limpsfield, Surrey, that much later came to be called the Manor House, but was known from Eugenia's time as Stanhopes.

It is, however, unlikely that Eugenia's house had then yet acquired either porch or stucco. It certainly had fine brickwork, and a commanding position on raised ground at the bottom of the village High Street, near to the church, and some land attached to it. But, as we know, it had at its centre one of those wide, great-beamed open hearths typical of the Tudor period, or of rather later country farms and cottages, but not of new-built Georgian architecture. Something, or more than one thing, had happened to the house already, long before Eugenia lived there, just as many other trans-formations and distortions were to happen to it in the two centuries after her death. To discover what, requires a trip into the archives.

As with most picturesque English villages, a few people have written on 'Old Limpsfield', but not extensively and with varying levels of research. The single High Street is a patchwork of old, interesting and much-altered build-ings; and the district contains a number of well-preserved

Wealden houses, including some that were, in their original form, medieval hall-houses. These have been fairly well documented, and are almost all now in the hands of people who appreciate and care for them. But an old structure that is much more heavily disguised tends to slip through the antiquarian nets.

When public concern about the post-war destruction of established buildings began to gather impetus in the late 1950s, the oldest part of the 'Manor House', along with some other buildings in Limpsfield High Street, was hastily Listed by the local authority. The Listing description reads 'House. Late eighteenth century, possibly by Samuel Savage, with early nineteenth and twentieth century extensions to rear.' This partly true but essentially inaccurate summing-up has been repro-duced down the years, and has gained the status of received fact. The name 'Samuel Savage' appears in local history booklets and on a scrappy internet page, as if he were a well-known figure and/or a local builder.

However, Savage does not seem to have been a local man. He gave money to Limpsfield church in 1764 for a new pulpit and some communion plate, but maybe this good deed was insurance for the afterlife, for he did not play a part in village affairs and there is no evidence of him living there. He was a London-based speculator in property much like those we have today. He lived in Hanover Square. His only significance, as far as the evolution of Limpsfield is concerned, is that his financial interest in the place demonstrates the way in which, by the second half of the eighteenth century, this once purely rural hamlet tucked under the North Downs had become a place worth investing in.

One of the ways of trying to find out about properties and their tenants long ago is by looking at the annual Land Tax returns, perhaps in conjunction with the Church Rates and the Poor Rates, when these have survived. However, the Land Tax was imposed only from

1780 onwards, and we know that by that time Eugenia Stanhope was living in the house. (She was assessed at £5 Land Tax per annum, while occupants of more modest dwellings paid only a few shillings. The largest sums, £58 and £24 respectively, were paid by the two people who each owned multiple properties and extensive acreage: one was the current lord of the manor and the other the vicar.)

Much more information about actual houses can be got from their Deeds – when these can be found. The original Deeds of very many houses have long since disappeared into the strongrooms of extinct firms of solicitors or mortgage brokers, or lie irretrievable in dusty lofts or forgotten trunks, have been destroyed by bombs or ignorance, used to clean guns or line pie dishes or have been made into lampshades. But with Stanhopes-alias-the-Manor House I am in luck. In the middle of the nineteenth century, the house together with its accumulated grounds was acquired by the resident Lord of the Manor. Actually, that parcel of land had been owned by the same family (the Greshams) long before, but they had let it go in the mid-eighteenth century, when a spendthrift, gambling Gresham, Sir Marmaduke the Younger, was forced to hand over the manor, with its lands and houses, to trustees. After his early death, when his eventual heir was still a minor, the trustees sold up to clear the debts. The lordship of the manor changed hands a number of times in the late eighteenth century, as if it had become no more than a Stock Exchange commodity, but near the end of the century it was bought back again, along with much of the land, by Marmaduke's son, Sir John Gresham, who had married an heiress. He died in 1801, but three years later his only daughter married one of the wealthy Leveson-Gower family, which made it possible to buy back yet more land. Eventually the family also purchased Stanhopes, plus several other holdings in Limpsfield that the Stanhope descendants had in the meantime acquired, so the Deeds to Stanhopes came to rest in Leveson-Gower possession. They evidently took care of all these bulky parchment documents, and finally, in the late twentieth century, entrusted them to the Surrey County Archives, where I found them.

Bundles of Deeds, being talismanic objects that are rarely read right through, are not usually found stored in chronological order. In addition, since it is in the nature of such legal documents to recapitulate the past manoeuvres in the property's ownership, each lengthy screed tends to resemble a verbal cat's cradle, unpunctuated and full of 'the said So-and-So, heretofore referred to' and 'the said adjoining tenement late in the occupation of N and M or one of them previously as stated in the occupation of the aforementioned X . . .' Putting Deeds in logical order and disentangling the facts from the multiple reiterations therefore takes some time.

It also takes effort to read the elegant but opaque Chancery hand to which lawyers' clerks remained faithful long after everyone else had begun to employ a more readable copperplate. Possibly this was why Samuel Savage was mistakenly seized upon by an earlier researcher as the 'builder' of the house 'about 1775'. A copy made of the document setting out the sale of the land to Samuel Savage, dating from 1771, happens to be the earliest one in an easy-to-read hand. But as it also mentions on the land 'all that one messuage or tenement . . . heretofor erected and built by Marmaduke Mills' I don't think the researcher can have read very far.

The earliest Deed in the bundles proved to date from 1707 – 'the fifth year of the reign of our sovereign Lady Anne by the Grace of God, of Great Britain and Ireland Queen . . .' It is a smaller chunk of parchment than the later Deeds and the most lavishly decorated, with an elaborate royal crest and an enormously embellished heading, and written in a highly ornate form of Chancery hand. It appears only to relate to a relatively small stretch of land near the High Road:

> – **Between** Elizabeth Lone of Limpsfield in the county of Surrey spinster of the one part and William Gresham the older of Limpsfield aforesaid Esqr. of the other part **Witnesseth** that the said Elizabeth Lone for and in consideration of the sum of five shillings of lawful English money to her in hand paid . . . by the same William Gresham . . . therefore present doth demise, lease . . . [illegible] unto the same William Gresham . . . his Administrators and Assigns **All** that stable adjoining and being at the North End of a Barn now or late in the occupation of Nicholas Constable and Elizabeth Lone or one of them . . . with all ways and paths, passages, profits and commodities thereunto belonging. And also a poire or parcel of land at the south end of the stable of the said William Gresham in the occupation of John Mills . . .

There follow further provisions regarding William Gresham's right (and that of his Heirs and Assigns) to pace the land out, and also to throw 'dung or compost' out from the stable.

The Gresham family, originally from Norfolk, had acquired the manor in the sixteenth century, shortly before the Reformation, when they were already in process of becoming a wealthy merchant dynasty. A Marmaduke Gresham a hundred years later had supported the Royalist cause and was made a baronet by Charles II when he was restored to the throne. I think that the 'William Gresham the older' referred to in the Deed of 1707 was a brother of the current baronet and Lord of the Manor, Charles Gresham. Evidently there was a Gresham clan around Limpsfield, a tradition observable down the generations.

Of Elizabeth Lone I have been able to discover

nothing. She was presumably in a humble way of life, though literate enough to sign her name clearly, even elegantly: her signature appears at the bottom of the Deed. I have not found her baptism in the parish register, although she may have been related to a John Lone, Lane or Loan who kept the White Hart pub in Limpsfield during the late seventeenth century. Nor have I found her burial in the parish, though the next Deed, of 1735, refers to her as 'deceased'. What her exact arrangement was with Nicholas Constable is anyone's guess.

The significance in the earliest Deed lies in the reference to buildings on the land. There is a 'stable' adjoining the north end of a 'barn', and reference to another stable further to the south-east already in the possession of William Gresham. The tithe map indeed shows this configuration of buildings on the site. Yet there is something more. On a scrap of paper attached to the Deed, in a much more recent, probably late-nineteenth-century hand, someone has written: 'A cottage supposed to be part of the Manor House'.

In other words, one of the buildings on this land, probably the one adjacent to the barn, even if it had descended to use as a stable by the eighteenth century, had originally been in human occupation. I believe that this is where the secret heart of Stanhopes – alias the Manor House – lies.

I think that when I first came through the Georgian porch and front door, and then up another step that opened into a wide hall with a great old-fashioned fireplace, what I was walking into was the remnant of a fifteenth- or sixteenth-century cottage that had been turned, by Elizabeth Lone's day, to lowly farming use. I think its great brick chimney and beamed hearth were later used as a central core round which another dwelling was constructed.

In the next Deed, that of 1735, the essential property is still described as 'a stable and a piece of ground in

Lympesfield'. Now it is being leased by William Gresham for ninety-nine years to Samuel Savage – to all appearances, a building lease.[1] The name John Mills as the occupant of the other building near at hand also appears again. John Mills, incidentally, was the parish clerk, and so a man of some standing in the village. That same year he recorded in the parish register the burial in the churchyard of 'Mr William Gresham, gent.'

The next surviving Deed dates from 1743, and here an actual house is mentioned. Samuel Savage seems to have sub-leased the building rights to Marmaduke Mills,[2] whom I believe was a son of John and was a blacksmith. The Deed records Marmaduke Mills leasing to John Bignall (who was a thatcher) 'all that one Messuage or Tenement (being one of the Messuages or Tenements lately erected and Built by the said Marmaduke Mills . . . on garden or orchard ground purchased from Sir Marmaduke Gresham'. Marmaduke, not William? Yes, because the Gresham family remained the ground landlords at this point, and presumably the improvident Marmaduke had inherited from William. So this dates a proper house on the site, built around the remnant of a very old one, to about 1740. A further Deed of 1748 mentions a mortgage taken out by Bignall – and here again, on the outside of the parchment, someone has written in a later hand '2 cottages in Lympesfield'.

So what was the house built by Marmaduke Mills like? A blacksmith was a skilled man with investment in relatively expensive forge equipment. By the 1740s, with commercial horse traffic increasing and coaching routes opening up, blacksmithing could be a highly profitable trade. The dates, and the involvement of Savage, would suggest that Mills built the house not to live in but as an investment. But it is highly unlikely that a blacksmith would have planned and built a fashionable residence. And the external style of the house, as we view it today, does not suggest a time as early as the 1740s: its façade is the sort of thing that was applied at a slightly later date.

We know that Mills incorporated into the centre of his building a traditional rural fireplace, with a wide, bulky chimney stack, of a kind by then unknown in smart new houses. His was, I surmise, a good, foursquare house, with a deep cellar, ground floor, first floor and attics. But not a grand house. It had a brewhouse and a wash house, possibly an ice house, all useful rural appendages, and a barn still standing alongside, but no extensive kitchen and back premises for servants as yet: these came considerably later. Mills may also have sunk the well, outside to the south-east, the side where the other stable lay, as it is not mentioned in previous descriptions of the land. Yet there is a village legend that once this site was known as Joan-atte-Wells, which does at least provide further circumstantial evidence that Mills's house was not the first one on this ground.

Subsequently he let the house to the thatcher, and then (1765) to John Jarret, a yeoman farmer from a family still well known in Limpsfield today. Jarret in turn sold his lease on it to William Langridge for £70. Langridge may have been in funds, but he was a 'husbandman' (a small farmer) and could only sign his name shakily. None of these men would have set up home in a gentleman's house with a pillared porch.

Ultimately documents can only tell one so much: sometimes it is the building itself that contains further clues. In the summer of 2010 the stucco-covered house was, for only the most recent of many times in its long life, in the hands of builders. I was able to poke round it.

This confirmed what I had long begun to suspect – that the straight-up-and-down front, with its porch and pedimented top, was a subsequent addition to a building that was originally simpler. It also became clear that the rear-addition (site of the extensive drawing room used by the headmistresses) had once been only half the present length. A string course stopping abruptly, a slight misalignment in the wall at that point, similar evidence in the roof and the faint indentations in the brick walls of older, smaller windows, long filled in, indicated that at some point significantly later than 1740 the house was enlarged, given a general facelift and new twelve-paned windows. This revamp was Georgian, that much is true. But it was probably late Georgian, dating from after Eugenia's sojourn in the place.

In 1771 William Langridge sold his interest in the house back to Samuel Savage, who, the same year, appears to have acquired the freehold. By 1779 Savage was dead, and his executor and heir, a Thomas Douglas Esq. of Manchester, sold the property to Eugenia Stanhope – 'All that one Messuage or Tenement and the Yard, Garden and Outhouses thereunto belonging . . .' She would hardly have had time to do extensive works on the house herself, as she died in it in 1783. She naturally left it to her sons, by then young men who had recently come into their inheritance from their grandfather. They bought more land adjacent to it, as well as other properties in the area. Both were educated as lawyers, which may be another reason that most of the documents relating to Stanhopes were preserved so well.

We shall return to the Stanhope family, whose name has remained attached to some part of their property to this day, but whose personal imprint on this earth did not last. Young Philip died, like his father, before he had reached the age of forty, in 1801. His only surviving daughter, though married, died without issue. Charles lived a long life but eventually died as a childless widower. Neither brother apparently went in for the kind of unofficial union favoured by both their father and grandfather.

It is time to examine another house whose stuccoed exterior also hides an ancient core, but whose popular myth of origin is quite different.

Chapter IV

BOMBS AND FANTASIES

In the mid-1950s boarding school was over. Sussex was over, and Mummy was over too.

London was where the girl now went exploring. Several districts presently became clear in her mind – Hampstead, Oxford Street, the area round Victoria station – but they were unconnected by anything but the diagrammatic tube map, where names were just beads on a string. The thought of all those uncharted hinterlands yet to be fitted into the jigsaw was daunting but also stirring. So many people, millions of them, all with their unknowable lives. In the fatigued London summer evenings she walked and walked, in a billowing cotton skirt and small flat shoes.

It was still the London of bomb sites. She had seen blitzed houses on visits there ever since she could remember, and they therefore seemed to her a normal part of the townscape, just as food rationing had seemed, till recently, an ordinary and permanent part of life. A sliced-open interior wall, amputated of its floor but still with its patterned wallpaper, rain spotted, a blackened hole of a fire-grate high up and the remains of a broken mirror hanging above it, did not speak to her of a fresh horror but rather of something bleak but permanent. Now she discovered sites already a dozen or fifteen years old, their rubble covered with bushes and flowering weeds that turned desolation into beauty. St Paul's, seen from the river side, reared up above a sea of rosebay willow-herb covering blackened basements. Weather-beaten signs painted on walls still said 'Air Raid Shelter' or 'ARP post' or 'Static Tank', but there were small prefabricated houses on cleared spaces and cranes and cement-mixers in many streets. The war was ages ago, when she had been a small child.

She acquired an unsuitable boyfriend with whom she rolled around, along with many other equally blatant but constrained couples, on the tired summer grass of Green Park. He was a Greek Cypriot, four years older than she was. In years to come, with the influx of black-skinned people from the Caribbean and brown-skinned people from the Indian subcontinent, the pale-skinned Greeks would merge like chameleons into the mass of native British, indistinguishable Londoners except for their foreign surnames. But in the 1950s they were seen as dark, alien and not very welcome; potential enemies, even. British National Servicemen – anybody's son between eighteen and twenty-one – were being killed in Cyprus, where the army was supposedly keeping the peace. The British were trying, with as good grace as they could muster, to relinquish their Empire.

Adam (for that was his name) lived in a district called Finsbury Park, which he described as being up the Seven Sisters Road. It sounded distant and faintly sinister, but with an exotic resonance, like Hackney Marshes or Dalston Junction. She was living, for the time being, in a house perched picturesquely though inconveniently on the edge of Hampstead Heath. A single-decker bus ran one way to suburban Golders Green and the other way to Finsbury Park via Archway. She always got off at Archway, a windswept junction of five main roads, to take the tube to central London and the A-level course she was supposed to be attending. One day she decided to stay on the bus all the way to the remote land of Finsbury Park to see what it was like.

She would not attempt to visit Adam. He might not like that. She just wanted to see where he lived. She understood that he, like huge numbers of Londoners at that time, rented a room in a terraced house occupied by many other people. She was not even sure he had the room to himself: he mentioned the 'friends' he lived with, other Greeks. Once he had taken her to a small restaurant with paper tablecloths near St Giles-in-the-Fields, where the Centre Point tower had yet to be built. It was the first time anyone had taken her to a restaurant (except Daddy) and there was wailing music, and a stout, effusive man with gold teeth who talked with Adam in Greek, and was Adam's uncle.

She longed to know more about his life, but felt inhibited by not being able to reveal much of her own to him. It would be awful if he realised she was posh.

At Finsbury Park station ('All change!') there were multiple iron railway bridges, booming overhead, and a yard with trolleybuses. After wandering first into the Seven Sisters Road (which seemed, disappointingly, not sinister but unremittingly noisy and ugly), she finally found the way past a billiard hall, a cinema with Gregory Peck's enormous face and an embankment with some hoardings advertising Guinness and Cremola, into the Stroud Green Road. Somewhere off this road, with its rows of small shops, Adam lived.

Intimidating. That was her overwhelming impression of the side streets she began to pass. Cracked stucco, blackened yellowish brick, broken or missing front walls where the railings had been wrenched off for supposed wartime uses. Some houses were boarded up, or had gaping dark windows. Here and there were what she knew must be cleared bomb sites, dusty expanses of nothing but occasional piles of rubbish. Children sat on kerbs or played with old pram wheels attached to wooden boards. Dogs barked. Mid-Victorian architecture was then generally considered hideous. 'Scabrous' was a word often used to denote its peeling dilapidation, as if the buildings had been diseased people.

Then, as she went further, the run-down plain-fronted houses gave way to more elaborate ones, with bow windows and steps up half-basements, front porches with terracotta decorations, and dwarfish pitched roofs. If the earlier houses were regarded as sick, the brave pretentiousness of these and their ornamentation put them beneath contempt. 'Debased' or 'degenerate' they were called, again as if some moral fault were implied. To the girl's eyes, these harmless late-nineteenth-century houses, once the pride of their first owners, looked almost daemonic in their ugliness.

The area was hemmed in by railway lines in each direction. Many trains were then still pulled by steam engines. Soot lay like a faint black rime in every crevice in the walls, every hopeful stone curlicue of the porches, every joint of brickwork, every windowsill, as if a giant had gone round enhancing the detail with charcoal. It impregnated the limp net curtains that occluded the windows. It coated every leaf on every bush in the neglected front patches, it ran in streaks down the trunks of plane trees. It got grittily under your nails when you touched anything. The air you breathed smelt of it, like hard-boiled eggs.

She had veered away from the main road now, avoiding a big corner pub where a group of men were waiting for opening time, and two of them whistled at her. Ahead was another portcullis railway arch, streaked with green damp and trailing creepers. On the left, two shops, one derelict, were supported by heavy timber props, as if a bomb had shaken them loose. Then there was a space; not a bomb site, no, more like somewhere that had once been a garden. There were two or three big trees with drooping arms like the Limpsfield ilex, so that you expected grass and flower beds around them, but instead there was just mud and cinders and two cars parked. At the end of it was a house bigger than all the others, set end-on to the road. It, too, looked sooty, covered in greyish stucco, but it had a foursquare porch and other buildings to the back of it. A faded sign said 'Stroud Green Conservative Association'.

Goodness. Here? Conservatives in Sussex had been men with dark suits and loud, confident voices, and their wives had had pearl necklaces and nice scarves and asked you whether you were thinking of joining the Young Conservatives because they had Such Fun? She tried, and failed, to imagine any of them in Stroud Green. She wouldn't have expected any of them to know Stroud Green existed, but in any case this place looked to her an extremely unlikely setting for them, as if it had come from a different version of reality: indefinably strange, vivid only like a bad dream.

A woman in a wrap-around pinafore came out from the porch with a mop in her hand and stared inquisitively but kindly at the girl.

'Looking for someone, are you, dear? There's no one here just now. I'm just the caretaker, see.'

'No – not really. That is – I . . .' She was going to name the road where Adam lived, which was the pretext for her expedition but that she was not sure now she wanted to find. Adam was, in some way, hers, or so he seemed to think. He was very handsome. She did not, after all, want to picture him here.

'Um – what's this road called, please?'

'Stapleton Hall Road, this is. Called after this house, you see. Though it goes all the way up the hill.'

This didn't quite make sense, but the woman beamed at her, obviously about to impart a favoured piece of information.

'This is a very old house, dear. Once it was a palace.'

The girl looked at the house's grey porridge coating,

at the porch with its heavy embellishments and its dust-filled stone flowerpots, and back at the mud and the cars under the trees. She had a sudden vision that these things were some sort of stage setting, that concealed behind were turrets and an inner courtyard with a proper garden and a fountain, like at Hampton Court. She remembered plays she had been taken to, where what appeared to be a solid wall was abruptly penetrated by light, or simply floated upwards into the dark.

Politely she said: 'The house must have been a lot bigger when it was a palace.'

'Oh well, I suppose so, dear. There's a nice bit of carving in the room at the back. Mr Jordan would be the person to tell you all about that. He's in charge, but he's not here just now . . . I suppose it'll all be coming down some time soon. Shame, really.'

'Coming down?' She thought of the tumbled, flowery ruins of the bomb sites. But the woman couldn't mean that. The bombs were over. Perhaps none of the buildings round here were quite real, but somehow insubstantial, trembling on the verge of extinction, and could at any time be dismantled in a night, like cardboard scenery, leaving behind – what? More mud? Acres of rough grass? Another Hampstead Heath, with ponds . . . Sand, like a shore?

I shall go back to Finsbury Park station, she said to herself, and get on a tube and find my way back to real London, to the one I know about. But the woman was still talking:

'. . . Oh, a lot's coming down round here, they say. All round Campbell Bunk too – that's what they call it, it's Campbell Road really – and lots of other roads. Tollington Park way. Redevelopment, see.' She pronounced the word with the same imposing emphasis with which she had pronounced 'palace'. Redevelopment was clearly something prestigious.

Idling back down the Stroud Green Road (the men

had disappeared into the pub now) the girl passed a fish-and-chip shop and plucked up courage to buy some soft, fatty chips in a cornet of newspaper. Eating them as she walked, soothed by their vinegary taste, she thought about what the woman had said. If all these streets of houses and shops, these aching miles of bus routes, were going to be knocked down, was that what people meant by 'slum clearance'? But this didn't really look like her image of a slum. It was, she thought, more like one of those places you only read about in a newspaper where something awful had happened: a fire, a strike and a riot, or a murder. And then people said it was 'that sort of area'.

Although she did not then know it, her view of such districts as part of an amorphous, alien wasteland, was commonplace then, even among people who had lived in London for many years. The sustained inflation in property of the second half of the century was only just, inconspicuously, beginning, among the battered Georgian terraces of Islington. To most people living in the few areas outside the centre that were recognised as 'good' – Kensington, St John's Wood, Hampstead, Chiswick – great intervening tracts of the rest of London were mentally consigned as having 'gone down' or even as being 'slummy'. The term was used more and more subjectively, so that a 'slum' came to be almost any area lived in by people lower down the social scale than the speaker. By this reckoning, almost the whole of inner London was off-limits, and this, it was assumed, was the natural destiny of most urban districts. Decay was thought to be endemic to them, as to the human body. Metaphors from disease, such as 'cancerous growth' and 'leprous walls' were freely applied. War damage was seized upon as a further pretext for removal. In local government circles extensive demolition plans were being drawn up for a whole new townscape that owed nothing to the population's own tastes.

The impending reality of this was not yet fully realised by the huge numbers of ordinary people who called these despised districts home. They would have been distressed and insulted to hear their own familiar, intricate territory, the houses that sheltered them and the everyday peacetime life for which they had been told they were fighting, dismissed as fit only for knocking down. In time, many *were* distressed, or were temporarily fooled or browbeaten into thinking that they should accept the planners' visions, and be grateful for high-rise flats set in windy no-man's-lands of 'green spaces'.

In the end Stapleton Hall escaped destruction, against all the odds. But it was a close-run thing.

In time, as more and more people aspired to own their own homes, planners' dreams of mass public ownership became discredited. From the 1960s the price of houses rose, and went on rising, with only the occasional stalling point, for decade after decade. The steam trains had gone, as had the coal fires in several million sitting rooms, and London became abruptly cleaner. The 'scabrous' Victorian terraces of Paddington, Fulham, Lambeth and Camden Town were repaired and painted and discovered to be charming period properties.

In time, the demands of the market colonised more and more swathes of once-despised houses in places like Finsbury Park and Stroud Green. The appeal of 1890s moulded decorations, stained-glass panels, Edwardian pitched roofs and turreted dormers once again became apparent. What had been built as houses to rent to respectable city clerks and their families, then had steadily descended, via genteel lodgings, into multi-occupied working-class accommodation, by the late twentieth century had become desirable homes for a newer, monied middle class. Neglected gardens once again blossomed. By the time the girl was old, her own grown-up children were to make their home in these streets, which now seemed leafy and pleasant and redolent of a London that no one wished to see pass away.

One evening at dusk near the beginning of the twenty-first century, going up Stapleton Hall Road on the top deck of a bus: a brief view into the lighted interior of the house, that had earlier been the Conservative Association, showed unmistakable old beams.

The history of Stapleton Hall is a fugitive and patchy one and, like that of many old houses, is marked by fantasy retellings.

The core of it was probably constructed in the building boom that took place under Elizabeth I, then enlarged and improved in the reign of her successor, James I, as a country retreat for a wealthy man with interests in the City of London. It seems to have started out as a classic T-shaped, timber-framed house of the time, the main part one room deep but with a projecting wing at the back. It had a ground floor, probably stone-flagged, a first floor and attics above, each floor with several rooms. When built, and for a long time after, it would have stood almost alone among green fields, well out of the already increasing smoke of England's prosperous capital.

There was already then an established tradition of such retreats. In the early fifteenth century the first Garter King of Arms had built himself a substantial house near the hamlet of St Pancras, north-west of London, where he once entertained the Holy Roman Emperor of the day. (All trace of it has long gone.) Hackney, north-east of the City, was also a favoured place for such houses. Late fifteenth-century Brooke House survived there till the mid-twentieth century, when bomb damage, compounded by the London County Council's desire to place a traffic roundabout on the site, finally annihilated it. Sutton House chanced to fare better and, after many vicissitudes, stands in central Hackney to this day, its Tudor panelling and windows at last carefully restored.

Further north again, a sixteenth-century retreat, Bruce Castle, embellished with a mock-fortified tower that was probably a grand dovecote, evokes a lost woodland past among the suburban sprawl of Tottenham. Today it houses a museum and the local archives – including, it turns out, mementoes of Stapleton Hall. Just north of Hornsey village, too, in the same borough, stood another sixteenth-century house known as 'Brick Place', from the era when bricks were still a sign of grandeur. It was owned by City merchants, but was demolished in the eighteenth century after storm damage, and all trace of the moated site later disappeared under a railway embankment.

These last three houses were all built after the Reformation and the seizure of monastic lands, which Henry VIII then bestowed on his favoured men. The same is true of Stapleton Hall which, while never as grand as these examples, was in the same mould. It was one of those 'many fair and comely buildings' described by Norden, the Elizabethan cartographer – 'especially of the Merchants of London, who have planted their houses of recreation not in the meanest places . . . invironed with Orchards of sundrie delicate Fruits, gardens with delectable walks, arbers, allees . . .' It was a place to which to ride out with friends on fine Sundays for a little duck or snipe shooting, to send your family to spend the summer when plague visited London yet again, a staging post on a journey north, and for gatherings at Michaelmas, Christmas and Candlemas with mulled wine and big log fires . . .

> *Where Tom bears logs into the hall*
> *And milk comes frozen home in pail.*
> *When blood is nipped and ways be foul*
> *Then nightly sings the staring owl . . .*

The story of Stapleton Hall, as habitually recounted over the last two hundred years, seems to derive from a rogue reference to it in the *Gentleman's Magazine* in 1784, that was picked up and embroidered by an Islington anti-quarian called John Nelson in 1811.[1] Since then, succes-sive commentators have reiterated the misinformation in good faith, apparently without noticing that the assorted proffered 'facts' do not actually fit together. In particular, the name Stapleton has accrued a legend around it, just as the name Samuel Savage has in relation to the house in Limpsfield, Surrey.

Even the normally well researched and authoritative *Victoria County History of Middlesex* has fallen into this trap. The Hornsey volume of this work traces, correctly, the family names of those who held the one-time medi-eval Brownswood manor, in which Stapleton Hall was situated.[2] It concludes that the Stapleton name came in only when an early eighteenth-century daughter descended from the manorial family (the Brays) married a Sir William Stapleton, Bart. She inherited the house, and it was subsequently passed on to her son, Sir Thomas Stapleton. However, in the next paragraph, we read 'A house mentioned in 1577 was extended or rebuilt in 1609, apparently by Sir Thomas Stapleton, whose initials appear on the datestone above the door and on internal panelling. Known as Stapleton Hall, it stands near the north-west end[3] of Stapleton Hall Road and presumably was occupied by Stapleton as a tenant.'

Clearly, if the first paragraph is right, the second one cannot be.

One sees why some local myth of a Stapleton presence as far back as the Tudor period was happily seized upon. A renowned Catholic scholar and priest called Thomas Stapleton, who wrote the first biography of his friend Sir Thomas More the martyr, went into exile on the continent under the reign of Elizabeth – though this, in itself, should be a fair indication that he is unlikely to have been building himself a house just outside London at the same period. Then there was an Irish soldier of fortune called William Stapleton in the late seventeenth century, who was rewarded for his services in foreign wars by being made Governor of the Leeward Islands in the West Indies and a baronet, and died rich in property. He is such an archetypal figure of the seventeenth century, that period of great change and social mobility when the first fortunes were being made in foreign investment: it would be attractive to link him with the house in Stroud Green. He was in fact an ancestor of the Stapleton who married a connection of the Bray family in the following century, but he has no physical link with the house.

And actually none of the Stapletons do, neither the later William nor Thomas his son who inherited the property. There is not a scrap of evidence that any Stapleton ever lived in the house at Stroud Green, or in that area. Although a fair chunk of land there, and with it the house, came to bear their name, they were absent landlords. By the eighteenth century, manorial lands and lordships were being bought and sold like any other commodity. The notion that each area by then still had a lord of the manor actually in residence as a 'squire', in the big house, running the lives of his tenants (as the Greshams and, later, the Leveson-Gowers really did in Limpsfield) owes more to folklore than to reality.

Furthermore, the whole idea on which the story has been built, that a Thomas Stapleton left his initials carved into Stapleton Hall, turns out to be untrue. The idea of a datestone above the door seems to have been an invention. There *is* a crudely carved wooden panel, dated 1609, preserved in a later frame as if it were at some time cut from a lintel and inserted elsewhere. I was beginning to doubt the very existence of this object before I finally ran it to earth, hidden away in storage in Bruce Castle museum at the other end of the borough. But the combined efforts of more than one fellow researcher have thrown up compelling evidence that the intials DTS, in a triangular arrangement with the D at the top and the T and the S below, are not those of any Thomas Stapleton, but of a man whose initials were TD with a wife whose name began with S.

There was a family of prosperous London merchants and brewers called Draper who are known to have held land on Brownswood manor, as well as other extensive holdings north of London, in the Elizabethan and Stuart periods. In 1612 one of this family, a 'Thomas Draper de Stroud Green' was buried in St Mary's church, Islington, the large parish on whose boundaries Stroud Green fell. His wife was called Sarah.

Their five children seem to have been born just before 1600 and in the first years of the new century. This Thomas Draper stands out as the most likely person to have occupied the only house in that place known to have been on the site in 1577, and to have improved it in 1609 and put his own stamp on it with panelling and carving. All over England at that time merchant families who had done well under the relatively peaceful reign of Elizabeth, with new markets opening in distant parts of the world, were embellishing and rebuilding England's houses. Stapleton Hall, which eventually gave its name to a whole crossroads, and then to a residential street winding up the hill to a ridge of high ground, should really have been Draper Hall – though one sees that this might have created confusion with the City livery company of Drapers. The Stapletons arrived well over a hundred years later, and then only in name.

Thomas Draper left his copyhold estate to his three sons. Draper family members two generations later were still concerned with an Islington church charity. The Stroud Green house and lands remained with the family for much of the seventeenth century till they were assigned to a Sir William Paul, who appears to have been connected with the manorial Bray family. It was his daughter Catharine who eventually married a Stapleton. Four years before William Paul's death in 1686, we get what seems a sudden small view of the house, like an attractive print seen at a distance. The place was apparently being offered without the farm land:

> To be Lett or Sold, Upon Stroud Green, towards Hornsey, in Islington Parish, is a delicate House to be lett containing five rooms on a floor, and all manner of Conveniences, Outhousing as Barns, Stable, Coach-house, Dove-house, etc. A Garden walled in before the House and another Garden about one acre.[4]

So, a gentleman's residence, not apparently occupied by the same person who farmed the land, although a barn and other rural buildings had by now been added to it. There was no other house of that kind on Stroud Green, which was an isolated country spot.

The conflicted fantasy history does not end with the appearance on the scene of the genuine eighteenth-century Stapletons as landowners. Although there is intermittent documentary evidence from for-sale-or-let advertisements from the 1740s to the 1770s of 'Stapleton Hall Farm' as a 'good grass farm' with 80 or 81 acres,[5] this has not stopped the dissemination of a further folk tale that goes more or less like this: 'In 1765 the house was licensed as the Stapleton Hall Tavern, having previously been known as The Green Man. The name had been changed by the widowed landlady after her husband died in a fall from his horse while riding home from Islington in 1759. For many years it had the inscription above the door "Ye are welcome all – To Stapleton Hall".' Cue here for a paragraph on Georgian pleasure-grounds and tea gardens.

It is true about the landlord and his horse – the story made the local paper[6] – but what house are we really talking about? It is said to be here that meetings were held of a satirical dining club, which parodied the ceremonies and feasts of the London livery companies. This called itself the Ancient Corporation of Stroud Green, and had a mayor and officers and splendid badges of office depicting St George and the dragon. (One still survives – in the Victoria and Albert Museum). It is said that this club met on occasions in Stapleton Hall between 1750 and 1780, until 'by the late eighteenth century Stapleton Hall had become a private residence again'. A landlord called William Lucas is then mentioned as improving the place. Several supposed nineteenth-century pictures of the house have regularly been reproduced, only one of which bears any resemblance, in its general form and arrangements of windows, to the house standing today.

These various tales are incompatible one with another. A house cannot at the same period be a residence occupied by a baronet's family, a cow-farm with barns and a stock-yard (depicted in one picture), and a slightly riotous inn. A closer look at the assembled scraps of evidence, written and pictorial, makes it evident that what we have here are several different buildings near to one another at the point where, today, the Stroud Green Road reaches a steep ascent and turns up Crouch Hill. That, indeed, is what the Enclosure map of the early nineteenth century shows.

It seems clear that there was an old but once rather fine house dating from 1609, probably a rebuild of an earlier one. This was the one that had become known as Stapleton Hall and that William Lucas did up. But at the same time as this renovation one side of the original T-shape was used to form a separate dwelling, along with the rustic buildings that had been added to it by the late seventeenth century. This created a second house of simpler style than the main one, part weatherboarded, with a yard and various outbuildings. This was the home farm, properly known as Stapleton Hall Farm. There was also a third, barn-like building, which may at one time have been used as a dwelling place. At various times all these buildings may have been in the charge of the same tenant, but in the first proper censuses, taken in 1841, the separate nature of the three different habitations becomes readily apparent.

As for the so-called Stapleton Hall Tavern (aka the Green Man) a comparison of maps and builders' estate plans from different periods and up to recent times shows that this was a quite other building that stood right on the turn of the lane that became the Stroud Green Road. As the Green Man, it was an ordinary alehouse, dating from the early eighteenth century. The fact that for a while it confusingly rechristened itself 'Stapleton Hall' simply indicates, I suggest, that by that time the whole crossroads that was beginning to develop at the north end of Stroud Green had come to be known as 'Stapleton Hall', in the same way that many other London landmarks such as Charing Cross or Knights' Bridge have given their names to whole districts.

The tavern was eventually rebuilt on the same site in the early twentieth century as a large and brash town pub, with a billiard room and a dining room to accommodate ninety-five at tables and a hundred on the dance floor. Today, after a decade or two in which it was called the Larrick and there was an emphasis on night-life, it has been redecorated as a traditional pub with food and is calling itself 'Stapleton Tavern'.

We can forget about the much-mentioned Ancient Corporation of Stroud Green and their ponderous frolics, except insofar as their presence indicates that the Islington parish, on whose edge Stroud Green sat, was by the second half of the eighteenth century a suburb of London. It is perhaps a pointer to Stroud Green's later development that it was already regarded by then as a place where pomp and circumstance could not be taken too seriously, as Potters Bar or Purley would be today. But the inn bean-feasts are not relevant to the already variegated life story of the real Stapleton Hall which, like that of Stanhopes in Surrey, mirrors the changing needs, fortunes and demands of the human lives that passed through and round about it.

Chapter V

LONDON'S COUNTRYSIDE,
WHERE HOUSES GET FACELIFTS

Where exactly is, or was, Stroud Green?

It would be nice to imagine a rough triangle or hexagon of daisy-sprinkled grass, once the territory of munching cows, still surviving between the street patterns as at Islington or Paddington or Turnham Green. However, Stroud Green was never such a focal point. It was simply a long strip of rather marshy common land that ran from Blackstock Lane, a little to the south of the present-day Finsbury Park station, and proceeded northwards almost exactly a mile to the foot of steep Crouch Hill. Since common ground belonged to the community and anyone could walk across it, a footpath developed along its length. This ad hoc right of way was later dignified as 'Stroud Green Lane' before eventually being broadened and surfaced as Stroud Green Road.

It was just a piece of scrubland where people – who were originally supposed to be manorial tenants – cut turf and furze and dug out loam and grazed their animals. It also formed, in an imprecise way, the boundary between the old, spread-out parishes of Islington and Hornsey. When these were transformed in the nineteenth century into the boroughs of the same name the boundary remained in place, and was later made clearer and more precisely delineated by the presence of the road. So, as time and chance and bureaucratic decisions absorbed Islington and the south part of Hornsey into London proper, but left most of Hornsey in Middlesex, the Stroud Green Road finally became the dividing point between the jurisdiction of the London County Council (LCC) and the autonomous suburbs that lay beyond. In this way Stapleton Hall and the adjacent buildings spent their whole life, till the mid-1960s and the coming of the much-extended Greater London Council, on a frontier, neither fully of one place nor of another.

The old parish of Hornsey into which Stapleton Hall arguably fell (though the Draper family evidently found Islington church more convenient) covered almost 3,000 acres. It had always been a spread-out, incoherent collection of hamlets. The only one of any size, before the nineteenth century, was Highgate, at the south-western limit of the parish, which, as it was on a main road north out of London, developed the sort of settlement that such staging places attract. It also developed its own chapel of ease, since both St Mary's Hornsey and St Mary's Islington were too far over muddy, rutted tracks for easy access.

Hornsey village itself, several miles away over on the opposite (north-eastern) side of the parish had a church since the early fourteenth century and possibly before, but for a long time had little else beyond a sprinkling of cottages along the track that led down from that side of Muswell Hill. When the eighteenth-century antiquarian Daniel Lysons was writing his monumental *Environs of London* (1796) he noted that there had been 'about 40' new houses built in the preceding fifteen years, but that even so, over the whole parish of Hornsey, there were only 'about 420, of which 90 are in the village of Hornsey, 264 in the hamlet of Highgate, 23 at Crouch End and 20 at Muswell Hill'. So Muswell Hill, high in the north above everything else where Alexandra Palace stands today, was tiny. Its origins lay in an early medieval chapel, and then in dairy farm which was established there to supply a house of Augustinian nuns in Clerkenwell that sold milk to Londoners. Crouch End – properly 'Cross End', either from a wayside cross or from the fact of its being a crossroads – was geographically at the centre of the parish, but it was very small too, buried damply in the valley between Crouch Hill and Muswell Hill. The whole population of Hornsey parish, according to a survey made in 1801, was only about two thousand, five hundred.

Another hamlet is unmentioned by Lysons, because it really belonged to Islington and Hackney and, later, to Stoke Newington, but it crops up in Hornsey records because the parish owned a detached piece of land there. The hamlet in question was Newington Green, southeast of Stroud Green, nudging the corner of Hornsey parish. Henry VIII is said to have had a hunting lodge there. After the Restoration in 1660, when Dissenters were tolerated but not welcome within the confines of London itself, it became a favourite place for Quakers and other Nonconformists to set up their chapels, a character it long retained.

And then there was the small group of buildings at Stroud Green, on the parish boundary, too few to constitute a hamlet and so not even named by Lysons, but significant enough by their position to figure in local folklore.

The reason for this oversized, awkwardly constructed parish of Hornsey was the extraordinarily precipitous nature of the terrain – what T.S. Eliot, in the grime-darkened early twentieth century, called the gloomy hills of London. These steep slopes and boggy valleys lengthened journeys, creating obstacles and winter difficulties. But essentially the heavy clay out of which they were formed was not well suited to crops, which is why the area did not attract much early settlement. It remained a rural backwater long after districts such as Islington and St Pancras were being colonised by city folk. The soil was, however, good for trees. The few patches of precious woodland that remain today, mainly concentrated in Highgate Wood and Queen's Wood, are the last remnant of the once Great Forest north of London, the hunting grounds of bishops and kings. In the Middle Ages a very large part of the parish was still wooded, though by Tudor times much of the timber had been cut to supply London's growing need for building and firewood.

At this time a part of the cleared land of both Hornsey and Islington was probably used for crops: manorial copyholders (long-lease tenants with a familial security of tenure) would have planted wheat, barley and rye. But by the Elizabethan period, if not before, most of it is recorded as being grass. The meadows could be mown for hay several times a summer, in this way providing essential fuel for London – hay for the horses, on which all population centres relied in the days before the internal combustion engine. Some meadows would also be used directly as pasture, for grazing those same horses and also the large number of cows that provided London's milk and butter. There was, too, a need for temporary pasture for meat still on-the-hoof that had been driven down from the Home Counties of England and was now being fattened for slaughter. In the days before refrigeration all meat, unless salted or pickled, was freshly killed, and none came from remote corners of Britain, let alone from across the seas.

The hilly fields stretching on all sides around the isolated clutch of buildings centred on Stapleton Hall may have *looked* like unspoilt country well into the nineteenth century, but in reality their use had been modified for centuries by the presence of London, that murmuring, ever-expanding metropolis just two or three miles distant.

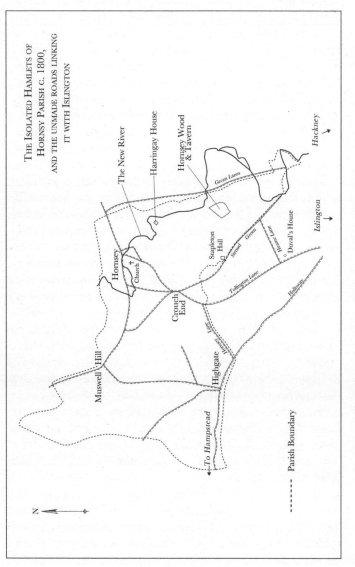

THE ISOLATED HAMLETS OF
HORNSY PARISH C. 1800,
AND THE UNMADE ROADS LINKING
IT WITH ISLINGTON

The New River

Harringay House

Hornsey Wood
& Tavern

Hackney

Green Lanes

Hornsey

Church

Stapleton
Hall

Stroud
Green

Heame Lane

Duval's House

Islington

Tollington Lane

Holloway

Crouch
End

Muswell Hill

Highgate

Highgate
Lane

To Hampstead

N

-------- Parish Boundary

Hornsey parish in the early nineteenth century, still almost entirely rural in aspect.

Soon after Sir William Stapleton acquired the land adjoining Stroud Green through his marriage to Catharine Paul in the 1720s, the holding was described as 'a barn and sixty acres of pasture and woodland . . . three closes [hedged meadows] of pasture amounting to 17 acres . . . and a further thirty-two acres of meadow and pasture'. By 1748, when the tenant farmer had got into financial difficulties, his holding to be relet was slightly smaller (80 acres). Almost exactly the same acreage (81), which one must therefore presume was the same farm, was relet in 1773 as 'a grass farm', and again as Stapleton Hall Farm in 1776. The unexpired remainder of this lease was further advertised in 1779, when it was said to include a good farmhouse with barns, stables and all suitable offices.[1] Clearly, whatever vicissitudes individual farmers had gone through (perhaps their rents were too high?) the hay business continued to flourish. When Thomas Milne produced his beautiful and obsessionally researched land-use map of London's environs in 1800, he showed the land to be very largely down to grass as far out as Finchley, and much further in the north-west. Due north of the City at Hackney, and running up to Dalston, there were patches of arable land, and some more in Tottenham, but that is a long way to the north of the Hornsey district that was eventually to acquire the confusing name of Finsbury Park. A detailed map of Islington parish of five years later than Milne's marks just one large cornfield a little below the southern end of Stroud Green (also marked by Milne) exactly where, for most of the twentieth century, Arsenal football ground was to lie.

Another eighteenth-century sign of the effect of London on the apparently rural backwater of Stroud Green was the ongoing argument about roads. In early medieval times a recognised route north had led from Islington up what is now the Hornsey Road, down into Crouch

End and onwards, but by the Elizabethan era it was said that the way was unusable through the winter months on account of flood water from streams on the heights of Highgate. This was why an alternative route had been developed in the fourteenth century, up what is now the Holloway Road and over Highgate Hill, where the Bishop of London, who owned all that land, put toll gates top and bottom.[2] However, the Highgate route went rather far west, and the Green Lanes route on Hornsey's eastern border was too far in the other direction: neither provided a direct route to or through Hornsey.

Until well into the nineteenth century, the main body of local administration in every district was the parish council, known as the Vestry because that is where it traditionally met. It was down to each local Vestry, or rather to its appointed surveyors of highways (who were local worthies, often doubling as churchwardens) to see that the roads in the parish were maintained. The two Vestries concerned with the roads northwards, Islington and Hornsey, spent much of the eighteenth century bickering with each other. Islington was by then, unlike Hornsey, a true suburb of London, prosperous, fashionable and self-important, full of men with City interests. Its parishoners seem to have been more concerned with being allocated pews suitable to their social standing, and hounding a vicar for his Wesleyan Methodist leanings (Wesley's own chapel was just down the road), than with taking decisions about the state of the adjacent highways.

The constant bone of contention, throughout most of the century, was the highway known to us as the Hornsey Road but confusingly referred to in various minutes as 'Tollington Lane' (because it ran through an estate held by a family of that name), occasionally as Duvals/Devall's Lane, or as Hornsey Lane. The last name sometimes seemed to include within its compass the Hornsey Lane of the present day, which runs at a right angle to the north end of Hornsey Road, in the direction of Highgate. This bit formed the northern boundary of Islington parish, so one can understand why there might have been a dispute over who was to maintain it, but the rest of the highway being argued about lay squarely within Islington.

The problem is clear. The road was Islington's responsibility, but since it might be said to be chiefly used by the parishioners of Hornsey, including those at Highgate, Islington shirked its duty. The matter came before the local Justices of the Peace in 1726, and again in 1730 when the surveyors of Islington were ordered to join with the Hornsey surveyors to tip loads of gravel on to the lane. The Islington Vestry were not pleased – 'When considered by the inhabitants here present, it appears that those repairs have time out of mind been done by Hornsey, and that Islington had never been charged for it.' A further fuss ensued in 1735 and again ten years later. In spite of all this Islington at one point agreed with Hornsey to share a workhouse, to be established at 'Stroud Green'. I wonder exactly where the site was, for sometimes Stroud Green seems to refer just to the strip of common land, and sometimes bestows its name on the fields immediately around it. Clearly this little-inhabited area was just the place you might want to have the poorhouse, out of sight and out of mind for both Vestries. However, the plan seems to have been abandoned, Hornsey developed its own workhouse in Hornsey village, and Islington's was established well within the parish, roughly at the point where what is now Liverpool Road joins the Holloway Road.

Seven Sisters Road, which was eventually to run off the Holloway Road as the main artery through the new district of Finsbury Park, did not then even exist. Or rather, only part of it existed, as Hem or Heame Lane running from Hornsey Lane/Road to the lower end of

Stroud Green. A further footpath through fields led from there to Hornsey Wood House where, in another scrap of ancient woodland, stood an old farm that by the eighteenth century had become a tavern. It was a place for clay pigeon shooting, cock-fighting and occasional duels. Complaints about the state of Hem Lane crop up in the Vestry minutes; as do alarms, especially in the 1740s, about highwaymen and footpads frequenting this isolated area and committing 'diverse robberies and great cruelties'. (It is said that the name Duval sometimes attached to this section of Hornsey Lane/Road derives from the highwayman of legend, Claude Duval, but more myth-making seems to have gone on here. A house attributed to the Devil is recorded in this place long before Claude Duval's Restoration heyday.)

Later in the eighteenth century this worry about crime fades into more general urban preoccupations with law and order, mad dogs, the cost to parishioners having to contribute to the new turnpike roads (especially the one that became the Euston–Pentonville Road), and new requirements for street lighting. There were also complaints about the 'great increase in heavy wheeled conveyances', though one might think that the Islington inhabitants' own coaches and travelling habits contributed not a little to this.

By this time it looks as if the Hornsey Road route was at last being kept in some sort of repair, but attention had shifted to the Hem Lane–Stroud Green location as another and more logical route out of London northwards. Islington Vestry was finally sued for doing nothing about it. Independent surveyors had 'estimated the charge of making a road over Stroud Green at £700 and upwards, which being so large a sum was the reason nothing had been done'. The Vestry claimed that Stroud Green had always been in the same state, and that it had been the practice only to throw down 'a load or two of dry rubbish now and then, to dry up the Sloughs or prevent Cattle from sinking . . .' There was mention of several brick drains having been constructed with earth over them, but not necessarily in the right places to form a roadway. You might suppose that Hornsey parish was just as much involved as Islington since Stroud Green lay along its boundary, but it seems that the wasteland there was technically Islington's. Hornsey parishioners were not keen on a new road through Stroud Green anyway. Another opinion was that if a road had to be made over the waste there 'it may be done by laying down pipes and filling up the Sloughs with drift'. An unnamed local farmer was brought in to declare that he had known Stroud Green for forty years and that it had always been much the same – that the odd brick culvert had been built there not for road-making but 'to stop cattle being drowned'. I wonder if that farmer was from Stapleton Hall Farm?

In the end the case went to the High Court, where the Lord Justice, Lord Mansfield, the possessor of a huge house and park at Kenwood, just beyond Islington's borders, found against Islington. A road across Stroud Green had to be made.

This was in the 1780s. By this date, even had the ancient common land of Stroud Green escaped a road across it, another fate would have befallen it. The need to enclose 'unproductive' pieces of free land was the great topic of the times. In the mid-seventeenth century, a generation after Thomas Draper had left his carved initials on his renovated country house, there were apparently still about 600 acres of common land in different parts of Hornsey parish. Over the next hundred and fifty years this was to be diminished to 200, most of that in the far north of the parish beyond Muswell Hill. Presumably the rest had been eroded by a mixture of piecemeal enclosure by local landholders and unauthorised cottage-building by the landless, but now the end of age-old common rights for the people was approaching more directly. John Middleton, a land surveyor who worked for the Board of Agriculture, was a firm proponent of the Enclosure of commons, heaths and so forth. He wanted to see even straggling pieces of waste such as Stroud Green enclosed and made to grow food, since 'the increasing size of the metropolis demands that every acre near it should be brought into a state of active cultivation'. Common land, which had historically always provided grazing for the animals of the poor, in his view encouraged these same poor to settle there free of rent: 'it gives their minds an improper bias, and inculcates a desire to live . . . without labour, or at least with as little as possible'. (This complaint is clearly of all time, resurfacing today as the insoluble debate about those living on benefits.)

Middleton's motivation, however, was far removed from that of the brutal, grabbing landlord of popular tradition. Other evils he listed were the poor's own 'half-starved' cows and donkeys living on commons scrub, and the way common land attracted 'gipsies, strollers and other loose persons'. Indeed there was a Gipsy Lane just south of Stroud Green, running off Blackstock Lane. Middleton thought that all such land was 'capable of being improved, so as to produce large crops of all the vegetables usually cultivated, and to rear and support a very highly improved breed of cattle'. He deplored that food (he meant chiefly grain) was imported from abroad while 'so many acres of good land are lying waste', and painted a utopian future in which food supplies might be much increased and 'beggary and robbery' correspondingly lessened. (He could hardly have foreseen the Corn Laws which, at the end of the Napoleonic wars, successfully cut foreign imports but were to drive bread prices up to intolerable levels.) He also thought that if 'stagnant water' on low-lying commons were to be drained off, and copses cut down, 'thus removing every obstruction to a free circuit of air' the climate itself would improve (*A View of the Agriculture of Middlesex*, 1798).

The general Enclosure Act for Hornsey came in 1813. Although Stroud Green would seem to have been a perfect example of flat wasteland full of puddles, it escaped enclosure since the road got there first. A local commentator a generation later wrote: 'Stroud Green has been by the enclosure of the waste on both sides much narrowed to the width of a well made road with quickset hedges on both sides; its ancient width can yet be traced by the elms that grow in the irregular line of the old hedges, which have not been thrown into the newly acquired extension of ground.'[3] No houses as yet. The marshy state of the old Green evidently persisted on both sides, for flooding remained a problem. Builders were deterred by this till new drainage arrived in a new era. Today, the remains of the old elm-lined waste has been subsumed into the pavements and the projecting shopfronts of the present-day busy thoroughfare. The creation of the road, incidentally, at last clarified the vague boundary between parishes, putting Stapleton Hall unequivocally in Hornsey.

In the course of the nineteenth century almost all the sizeable common lands round London, with the outstanding exceptions of Blackheath, Hampstead Heath and Wimbledon Common, fell victim to the desire for 'improvement' (frequently by house-building) or else were drastically reduced in size. Often this loss took place at the very same period when, elsewhere in the growing conurbation, parks were being laid out that people might walk on grass and admire the beauties of nature.

Two other features marked Hornsey parish in its rural days, both of them similarly related to the presence of London close at hand.

One was the New River, which wound its way into the north of the parish where it looped round the village of Hornsey, continued in picturesque meanders through the fields, then disappeared into a wooden aqueduct for a section of 78 yards south of Stroud Green where it was augmented by a cut from the river Lee, through sluice gates. Open to the sky again, it finally made its way westwards to and through Islington, to end at reservoir pools and the 'Water House' (a pumping station) near Sadlers Wells. Although it appeared as a natural stream, chattering over pebbles, a drinking place for cows, with people fishing for minnows, bathing naked or extolling its rustic charm according to class, it was in fact a wholly artificial river. Its circuitous course through Hornsey parish seems to have been partly determined by a seam of brick-earth at that point.

Completed in 1613, it was the brainchild of two Elizabethan citizens, one visionary and the other more hardheaded and mercenary,[4] who conceived the idea of bringing a supply of fresh water to the metropolis from some springs at Amwell, near Ware in Hertfordshire. The river, though hidden, is still there, and still providing some of London's water, running from Wood Green through the modern borough of Haringey, through Hornsey, Finsbury Park, Stoke Newington, Hackney, Canonbury and Islington. In the mid-nineteenth century its wandering course round Hornsey village was diverted into a straight channel, and much of the river was encased in large iron pipes. The New River Company was acquired by the Metropolitan Water Board in 1904, and is now part of Thames Water. However, a section of the river remains open as a canal to this day. Through the otherwise prosaic grid of streets on the eastern edge of old Hornsey borough that is known as the 'Harringay ladder',[5] where once stood a gentleman's house and park, it flows under a series of bridges. It is hidden to casual public gaze, but is a haunt of ducks and swans and a source of pleasure to those living in the houses that now hem it in.

The second feature relating to London was the villas. By about 1800, the era when Lysons and Middleton were writing and Thomas Milne was producing his land-use map, one further characteristic would have indicated the influence of London on Hornsey more clearly than any other. That was the significant amount of land (coloured pink by Milne) that was occupied by gentlemen's residences standing in their own large gardens.

Highgate was thick with them. So was Crouch End. There was a sprinkling at Hornsey village, a few more at Muswell Hill, and the seat with the New River through it grandly called Harringay House, built *c*.1790, which would be overtaken a century later by the ladder of modest streets referred to above. There was plenty of pink in Highbury, to the south, and a ribbon of it further north-west running up from Hackney through Stamford Hill. Stapleton Hall, in its garden close, was not marked pink, presumably because at that date it was occupied unpretentiously by whoever was the tenant farmer of the land.

This was only the beginning in Hornsey. The next generation was to see many more substantial houses built, mostly by men who had made recent fortunes in commerce. (Harringay House was said to have been the work of a 'linen-draper', a classic snobbish gibe of the time, though linen had provided the fortune that bought him a collection of fine art and antique books, greenhouses full of rare plants and a large staff to maintain it all.) The heights of Crouch Hill, re-baptised during the eighteenth century as Mountpleasant, were also particularly favoured. A local historian has recently written: 'One unintended effect of the enclosures was to make more land available for building.' [6] But was it so unintended? In the early 1800s 'civilisation' was a watchword, and a private drive planted with trees leading to an elegant house could be seen as embellishing the landscape. Even Middleton, with his utilitarian passion for growing food, wrote in his book on the desirability of enclosures: 'From Muswell Hill . . . there is a most enchanting prospect over Hornsey, Clapton, London and the beautiful river Thames. There are many points in this situation that as much deserve to be adorned with elegant villas as any other spot . . .'

Alas, the villas came to spot, and then to cover, the fields of Hornsey, destroying the very charm that their inhabitants sought. This was the perennial conflict played out with variations through the eighteenth and nineteenth centuries and into the twentieth, between the virtues of a 'pure' pre-industrial, pre-lapsarian rural life, and the equally shining concept of Progress – progress which, in practice, led to increasing ugliness and hence to social decline. The word villa itself, which originally suggested, to generations reared on Latin, a high Roman functionary surveying his estate, became debased by use till it has, in our own day, become a term of contempt for something cramped and tasteless.

This was to be the overarching story of the London suburbs. Already, around 1820, when Cobbett was reporting on the state of the countryside in his *Rural Rides*, he perceived that London was 'a great Wen', devouring land. A similar metaphor from the body was used by William Morris much later in the century: he wrote of the growth of London as a 'spreading sore . . . swallowing up in its loathesomeness field and wood and heath without mercy and without hope'. The image is that of a malign natural force, unstoppable and uncontainable. To E.M. Forster, writing a generation later again in *Howards End*, 'London's creeping' was like a red rust stain appearing over the green hills far to the north of the town. The red rust had by that time (before 1910) more or less covered the meadows, hills and valleys of Hornsey – yet 'the country', that holy place of unspoilt lanes was still only a short walk away. The vast twentieth-century expansion of Tottenham, Edmonton, Wood

Green, Finchley and so many more previously rural areas was still not realistically envisaged. Nor was the irony of what came to line the new arterial roads of the 1920s and '30s, which was a wholesale explosion of mock-Tudor cottages with stuck-on timbers, in a clumsy, wistful re-creation of all that had been lost.

But what of the genuine timbers of Stapleton Hall itself?

We know that when an old house there on Stroud Green was rebuilt or refurbished in 1609, Thomas Draper was sufficiently proud of it to have his own and his wife's initials carved into a fireplace or a lintel; that the Drapers were a presence in the location for much of the century; and that when a house that sounds like the same one was advertised in 1682 it was still a gentleman's residence with walled gardens and 'all manner of conveniences'. We know that the house and farmland became part of the widespread property holdings of the Stapleton family through a marriage in the early eighteenth century. There is also evidence that in 1735 some further refurbishing and rebuilding was being done on the site. Exactly two hundred years later, in 1935, a large old barn that had earlier been part of the general Stapleton Hall collection of buildings, was pulled down because Hornsey Council regarded it as unsafe. (It had been in use as a timber store, with someone else's garage-workshop at one end.) The workmen who demolished it found a coin of 1735 set into the foundations – which did not stop the *Hornsey Journal*, which published and elegant little piece on 'the loss of Hornsey's oldest building', from declaring that the tiled roof dated from 'the days of James I' (i.e. the carved date of 1609 within the house itself).

The workmen also found the remains of old floral wallpaper with metallic paint covered up on part of the barn walls, indication that at some period the place had been used as living space, perhaps for a farm worker and his family.

We do not know who exactly occupied Stapleton Hall at the various dates in the mid- and late eighteenth century when the tenancy of the farm changed, but it seems reasonable to suppose that the Hall itself had by then slipped down the social scale to the status of a large farmhouse. Standards of middle- and upper-class comfort had risen considerably since Tudor and Stuart times, and what had been a fine timbered house for a Jacobean city merchant was no longer quite appropriate for a genteel residence. However, by the end of the eighteenth century there appear on the scene a family called Lucas who were to remain in evidence through several generations and were eventually to play a key role in the transformation of the whole Stapleton Hall crossroads.

In 1796 a Mr Lucas already held, as a manorial tenant, part of what had been the Stapleton estate. Later, the rest was acquired, for when John Nelson published his *History of Islington* in 1811 John Lucas was one of the subscribers to it,[7] and he is described as being the holder of 80 acres. It may indeed have been Mr John Lucas (with a nice social nuance, he is listed thus – grander than tradesman but not yet dignified with 'Esquire') who recounted to Nelson the fantasy history of the house that has persisted for so long. If Mr Lucas was then busy setting up as a gentleman-farmer rather than one of the old-fashioned hands-on sort, naturally he would like a self-aggrandising story about the house having been built by the rich Stapletons themselves two centuries before.[8]

By 1823 John had been succeeded by William Lucas, and this was the owner who went to work to bring the property up to nineteenth-century standards. A building boom had taken place after the end of the Napoleonic wars, and houses conforming to what had become the classic urban model were springing up, individually or in short terraces, all over the new suburbs of Hackney, Highbury and St Pancras. A local commentator wrote of Stapleton Hall twenty years later: 'Mr William Lucas, a late occupant of the premises, converted it into two houses, one of which has a handsome stuccoed front, and wears quite a modern appearance.'[9]

That division into two is what seems to have produced such confusion among later commentators. A painting of the place, now in Bruce Castle museum, apparently copied from a now-lost watercolour of the 1820s, shows indeed a house with a stuccoed front and regular twelve-paned windows that is recognisable, bar a change of porch, as the Conservative Association of a hundred years later. But abutting onto it and facing east rather than south is another construction of a rustic, irregular, part weatherboarded kind, along with outbuildings. This is evidently Stapleton Hall Farm. One or two other pictures of what are clearly these same buildings exist and have been reproduced in recent books and labelled 'Stapleton Hall'. These buildings were never Stapleton Hall itself – and they are now long gone.

'A handsome stuccoed front' . . . At much the same period, or a little earlier, old timbered houses all over England were being gentrified in this way. In addition, their small windows were enlarged, their panelling was plastered over, more elegant, closed-in fireplaces were installed in the principal rooms, which were now carpeted. Upholstered furniture, replacing the old, carved chairs and settles, had become the norm. A water supply was laid on in the kitchen, and sometimes one of the newfangled, odour-free flush lavatories was put in, though as yet these could only be installed on the ground floor.

Far out of London, in Surrey, the house in the High Street, Limpsfield, underwent just the same transformation.

I do not know for certain who was responsible for giving the Limpsfield house its facelift, but my guess is that it was done by the Stanhope brothers when they came into the fortune left them by their grandfather, Lord

Chesterfield. Eugenia, their mother, died in 1783, having lived in the house for only four years: there is a memorial tablet to her memory in the north-west corner of Limpsfield church and her handsome gravestone can still be seen, for she is in a vault under the floor in a part of the church that later nineteenth-century alterations turned into the Vestry. On their mother's death both sons were over twenty-one, and it may be that they had the works on the house done immediately with the intention of renting the place out on a long lease, as was the habit in those days. It looks as if, apart from Eugenia, the Stanhopes of Limpsfield, like the Stapletons of Stroud Green, never actually *lived* in their substantial property, but in both cases their illustrious names became permanently attached to the buildings.

The renovate-to-let plan evidently worked. By 1787 Stanhopes was occupied by a Mrs Strong, at a rent of £50 a year. She was by then already married to Mr Clement Samuel Strong, a marriage that was to produce two sons, both clergymen, and endure for decades, so why it is her name rather than his that figures on the Land Tax accounts for 1787 I do not know. Neither were youngsters; she was a Streatfeild, a family that was going to burgeon locally in the next century and produce several eminent clergymen of its own. Possibly it was the Streatfeilds who arranged the lease on the house, but in any case Clement Samuel was soon securely in residence too. He was to live there till his death, forty years later, in 1827, at the age of eighty-four. His wife died twelve years after him, aged eighty-five 'having resided fifty-two years in this parish', as it says on their joint memorial tablet – one of a number of Strong family tablets that line the south wall of the church. Indeed, her name crops up till the year of her death in all the other places you would expect for a comfortably off widow established in a large house. She is there paying the Church Rate and the Poor Rate, and giving money regularly every Christmas . . .

That was how permanent a leasehold could be, in the nineteenth century.

But it is time to move right away from London and its far-reaching influence out into the Home Counties, and to look at a third house. Like the other two, its core is very old, like the other two it has undergone considerable changes and shape-shifts in the course of its long history; like them it has at different periods been despised, revamped, given a new face, neglected once more, rediscovered. But its history has one thread of stability and permanence the other two lack. It is a vicarage.

Chapter VI

Into Oxfordshire and the
more distant past

'The village' occupies a totemic status in the British imagination which grants it almost supernatural powers. Far more than merely a chance arrangement of pond, post office and old church yew, the village has become the place where the British imagination resides, even while the body is mostly squeezed into a semi on an arterial road somewhere south of Croydon.[1]

Thus, the apt perception of one modern commentator. The mindset being described, however, is far from new. Already, in the 1820s, with the industrial revolution only partway accomplished and the rural population still substantially larger than that of the towns, William Cobbett, the passionate denouncer of rural poverty, was pushing his own view of what village life should be. Despite Cobbett's reputation as a dangerous radical, his ideal was largely traditional, indeed almost feudal. A kindly landowning squire, who knew his peasantry as individuals and understood the nature of their toil, was to rule over a village community both self-supporting and static. Cobbett was vehemently opposed to new methods of doing things, particularly to turnpike roads, frequent coach routes, and anything else which encouraged native countrymen to take their labour elsewhere or newcomers to move in. He had a special scorn for 'Squires of 'Change Alley' – that is, men whose financial interests lay in London but who bought country estates and set up as local gentry: 'a gentry only now and then residing at all, having no relish for country delights, foreign in their manners, distant and haughty in their behaviour, looking to the soil only for their rents . . . unacquainted with the cultivators, despising them and their pursuits . . .'

Essentially the same complaint is heard to this day, stigmatising 'incomers', 'weekenders' and 'second-homers' who occupy many of the houses in ancient villages. The only difference today is that great swathes of England that were, in Cobbett's day, much too far from London or any other urban centre to attract such settlement, are now easily reached and colonised.

The problem is intractable, because both those who complain and those who are complained of are possessed by the same rural dream and always have been. Cobbett's idyll of unchanging village life was actually no different from that sought by the 'Squires of 'Change Alley' and 'stock-jobbers' that he so derided, and no different from the rural yearnings of bankers, lawyers and pop stars today. We all, it seems, or nearly all, wish to leave our modern semi on a road south of Croydon (the epitome of transience) and join a magic circle of old cottages round an unchanging village green.

As a young child, I had first-hand experience of the dankness and solitude of country life in winter, as the dark settles down on another wet, cold afternoon. Yet evidently the village idyll had imprinted itself even so on my consciousness, as one of my favourite toys was my 'Cotswold Village', painstakingly made, with adult help, from a cut-out cardboard kit. Toys were still in short supply in the years after the war. I had a square of tweedy cloth as the village green, and a piece of broken hand-mirror as a duck-pond in the middle of it. (The ducks on the pond, like the sheep on the green, were from my pre-war toy farmyard and were slightly out of scale with the houses. This bothered me subliminally, till I eventually hit on the idea of having them in the foreground, with the houses further off. Lying on the floor to squint sideways at this arrangement produced a convincing effect of perspective.) The Cotswold houses were slightly different shapes, with the church as their centrepiece, but all were in a pleasing design of honey-coloured stone pattern with brownish-grey roofs. The chimneys and dormers had been particularly fiddly to glue. There was a vicarage, rather bigger than the other houses, a post-office-cum-shop, an inn with a signboard (also fiddly, but a triumph) and a school. My only regret was that I had no people tiny enough to populate this desirable world. I thought the whole thing very beautiful and satisfying, and I dare say I should think the same if I could see it again today.

Many years later some cousins of mine called Milner lived in a cottage on a green just under the lee of the Chiltern hills where you descend the escarpment from Buckinghamshire into Oxfordshire. In those pre-motorway days, when hitch-hiking was not yet regarded as louche or dangerous, I used to hitch a lift easily from Oxford along the A40. I would get whoever had picked me up, High-Wycombe-bound van driver or London-bound academic, to drop me off at the Lambeth Arms, and then walk the mile or so to Kingston Blount as travellers had been doing for centuries. There the green in front of the cottage was rough grass, on which my cousins pastured their rabbits in wire-netting runs, and little hay-houses appeared in high summer.

Today that green is mown to a smooth lawn, and someone (the present owner of the cottage?) has put white chains hanging from low posts round it, as if making their own bid at Enclosure.

A few years later I was married, and living in London, and my cousins were, courtesy of the BBC, in Delhi. When they returned to England, their four children had grown so much bigger that they seemed, in the small cottage, like the animals in my cardboard village, slightly out of scale. Their feet stuck out of the ends of the bunks their father had constructed for them in the cottage's attic crevices, and it was quickly decided that something bigger must be bought. Much bigger. The Milners looked to the other side of Oxford, out into the Cotswolds, at villages that were all versions of my beloved, long-forgotten model. The Old Vicarage, up for sale in the village of Taynton, a mile and a half from Burford, caught their attention. Both my cousin and his wife were the children of vicars. It came naturally to them to inhabit a spacious if draughty and old-fashioned house with a large garden and a meadow.

The vicarage in question had been sold off in 1957 by the diocese of Gloucester (into which, confusingly, it just fell, for reasons that go back to the time of Edward IV). Its price then was £3,000. For ten years after that the new owners had run it as a bed-and-breakfast establishment, so the otherwise minimal bathroom arrangements had been modified just a little by the addition of handbasins in two or three of the big first-floor bedrooms. The place was now on sale for £17,500, which the Milners managed to get reduced to £15,950. With the money thus saved they also acquired a lot of what had originally been the vicarage carpets, curtains, beds, wardrobes and china. The year was 1968.

Thirty-nine years later, when the house with its land was finally sold again in 2007, the 'ramshackle old place', of which the diocese of Gloucester had briskly divested itself fifty years before, had been transformed by time and the growth of prosperity into a Valuable Period

Residence, whose antiquated state was in itself a selling point. An article in the property columns of the *Telegraph* breathlessly called it 'probably the last unspoilt and unmodernised house in this sought-after area . . . which is why potential buyers have been stalking it for years. There are seven bedrooms but only two bathrooms (and only one of those upstairs), four reception rooms and two kitchens, one with a stove you have to shovel coal into like Thomas the Tank Engine.'

In the thirty-nine years it had been home to the Milners, the place to which the children variously and periodically returned, and also home, in the early days, to a trickle of elderly and faintly eccentric paying guests who were known collectively (and well out of their hearing) as the Crones. One of these refused to leave her room, and hardly left her bed, for many years, but seemed quite happy in her Lady of Shallot existence. She was cared for till the end and now lies in Taynton churchyard. During some of this time the house was also home to Raphael, a bearer who had followed his employer from Delhi, and who eventually succeeded in bringing his own wife and daughters from India to inhabit a tumbledown and hastily renovated cottage in the vicarage gardens. Raphael, with his archetypal Indian habit of waggling his head sideways to mean both yes and no, and a cloth permanently draped over one shoulder, brought an air of oddly appropriate Raj exoticism to the stone-floored kitchen with its sulphurous, coke-consuming Aga. Born in a village in the south of the subcontinent, he happily redeployed the chicken-rearing, vegetable-growing skills that had not been called for in a diplomatic compound in Delhi.

Granny Milner, too, came to spend her last years there, in a flat organised for her in the warren of rooms between the kitchen and the garden. (That was when the downstairs bathroom was installed.) Later again a Milner son and his own growing family occupied the same flat,

proliferating by and by into much of the house. And over
the years a number of other people including me came
and went to this place, where the front door never seemed
to be locked at any hour of the day, and where you never
knew if you would be sleeping in the attics, where electric wires hung like vines from the beams, or whether
you would have one of the palatial spare rooms with a
big, old, squashy bed and a cat and her kittens in residence in the cupboard.

In an autumn early in the 1990s, when my cousin's previously dynamic life was gradually ebbing away, he spent
most of his time on a divan bed in the smaller sitting
room that was an oasis of warmth from the wood-burning
stove set in the ancient fireplace. One weekend I drove
from London to a meeting in Oxford, and then on to
visit him. From Witney, all along the valley of the
Windrush, the fields to the north of the A40, which was
the old coach road to Cheltenham, were flooded: they
shone silvery under a cold, full moon. Down the hill into
Burford, and at its foot the river was running ominously
high, almost up to the arches of the fourteenth-century
bridge. Beyond it, the waters were even more widely
spread, lapping the edges of the side road to Taynton.
And it seemed to me, as I drove, that I was seeing this
ancient countryside as I would have long, long ago, before
the swamps were dried and the fields hedged and tamed
and drained; and that this night was a kind of summation
of my long relationship with the vicarage and with the
people I loved who lived there.

   That same night, I dozed wakefully in the small, warm
room, alert to the possible needs of my cousin (his wife
was away, getting a brief break) and also to those of the
intimidating Aga. I heard strange noises – of these, more
later. I reflected that the house must have seen a great
many deaths over the centuries, and was unlikely to be
fazed by one more. Centuries? Yes. For though the front

of it looks like any mid-Victorian country vicarage or rectory, complete with two bay windows and a heavy, pointed porch of vaguely ecclesiastical design, a more careful look at the garden side and at parts of the interior will reveal it to be much, much older.

It is in fact possible, though hard to prove with certainty, that the essential bones of this house – some of the walls, maybe even some of the roof timbers – were established on its prime site, just above the road through the village and so safe from the Windrush, before the Reformation ever arrived and the house's official history tentatively begins.

As Hornsey has to be viewed in relation to London, ever present and near, so Taynton cannot be described without reference to its nearness to the town of Burford. Yet Burford itself, in spite of the beautiful and substantial old houses lining the famous steep hill of its high street, its inns, its ancient school, its Priory and its almshouses, is tiny, the size of a village. Its present population is only 1,100 and it never went much above two thousand even at its most populous. It has always counted as a town because, from an early date, its position on a navigable river that joins the Thames, and also just off the main route between Oxford, Gloucester and the Severn estuary, gave it status and significance. It received its charter as a market town, the first in the Cotswolds, from a Norman overlord before 1100: this granted its householders independence from the feudal system. It thus became a centre for the buying and selling of goods, and also their making, in the long period when communications were poor and much agriculture consisted of subsistence farming.

Burford was never home to the great Cotswold wool merchants of the later Middle Ages who created the wealth of the area, but it was where the wool harvests were sampled and auctioned at biannual fairs which attracted buyers from as far away as Italy. Burford citizens also fashioned and dealt in the products and by-products of the wool trade: it was a place of weavers, dyers, tailors, tanners, fullers, leather-workers and the makers of bone buttons and buckles. By fortunate chance its lords of the manor remained remote for centuries, so that the town was run, far earlier than most places, by the commercial and artisan middle classes – first formed into guilds and then into a fully fledged Mayor and Corporation. There was money in Burford: people took a pride in their habitations, and the evidence of all these centuries of prosperous commerce is there to this day, when its old-fashioned and variegated architectural beauty has made it famous the world over.

Taynton, similarly, was little troubled throughout most of its history by any resident lord of the manor. There was and is no Great House in Taynton. Judging by the extensive parish records that have survived, the men who effectively ran the village were a handful of fairly substantial farmers, tenants of the absent lord, often owning additional land in their own right. These were the same men who would have provided Burford, an easy walk or cart-ride away, with some of its sustenance and brought back to the village the things that were not manufactured on the spot, such as cloth, saddles and harness, some metalwork, wax candles, and paper and ink for the keeping of records and accounts. The lane between the two places must have seen a small but steady traffic of people slogging to and fro, and the youngsters of Taynton sought domestic work or apprenticeships in the town close at hand. Today, the string of mellow stone cottages and houses along the road by the church is still what Taynton village is. It has no shop any more, it never had an inn: much of its real life was always out in the fields and woods, or down at the mill by the Windrush – or up at the quarries.

For the other big occupations in Taynton were

quarrying and masonry. Although Burford itself had quarries, including Kit's Quarry that provided high-grade stone for All Souls College and St Paul's, and whose owner is commemorated with a weeping cherub in Burford church, they are not mentioned in records before the fifteenth century. The several quarries of Taynton were producing stone much earlier than this. The coming of the Normans, with their dedicated church-building programme, probably marks the first demands beyond the immediate locality for Taynton Freestone, as the fine-grained whitey-yellow Jurassic limestone is called. It is found in churches all over Oxfordshire and as far as London. In the mid-thirteenth century some was used for Windsor Castle, and more of the same was ordered at intervals over the next six hundred years. It was used in building the oldest part of Merton College in 1310; and when Cardinal Wolsey, two centuries later, was planning his own great Oxford college (Christ Church, completed only after his downfall) he stipulated that Taynton stone must be used. A century on again, when Christopher Wren was rebuilding St Paul's after the Great Fire of London, he not only chose some of the stone from Taynton but also his clerk of the works, mason Thomas Strong.

With the good money he had made in London, Strong built himself a handsome house back in his home village of Taynton, which is there to this day. (He also presented the church with three books including a copy of Foxe's *Book of Martyrs*, an extremely popular seventeenth-century work.) In the following century Strong's son worked with Taynton stone on Blenheim Palace. A little later again a Taynton family called Pittaway, of whom we shall hear more, became the pre-eminent hands-on masons in the village, working on many houses in the district and on repairs and extensions to Oxford colleges. The quarries they used were still being worked in the 1960s by someone who knew all about Windsor Castle requirements, but today, after more than nine hundred years, they are abandoned.

The sheer weight of stone tended, for a long time, to limit its use to places that had ready access to it. Cottages and farmhouses in the Cotswolds were frequently built of stone because it was there to hand, whereas in parts of England without quarries such modest dwellings never were. Only the owners of very great houses would think of paying to have a large quantity of stone brought from a distance, and even then it might only be possible if there was a river (or, much later, a canal) nearby. The fact that the Windrush, running by Taynton and Burford, connects with the Thames and hence with a route to both Oxford and London, was what made Taynton's fortune. Stone far too heavy and bulky to be conveyed on lumbering carts over unmade roads twenty-odd miles to Oxford, let alone seventy-five to the capital, could be put into flat-bottomed boats on the Windrush near Taynton and the two adjacent villages of Great and Little Barrington, and floated down to Burford. There, larger boats conveyed the blocks onwards in stages, till a stone-yard on London's Bankside opposite St Paul's eventually received them.

The classic Church of England vicar or rector with his wife and often numerous family, ministering to villagers but socially at ease with gentry, is an established if now dated figure.[2] However, he is a post-Reformation one. Indeed, he is a post-Civil-War, post-Restoration one, only coming into his own once the land had settled to Anglicanism, and once the gradual rise of the local clergy into a phase of security and financial comfort had begun.

Before the Reformation, the manorial lands in which the parishes lay, and with which they were often contiguous, frequently belonged to distant – sometimes very distant – monasteries or bishoprics, and it would be false to suppose that this made the monks, or the great princes of the Church, into any kind of local presence. In the Middle Ages, wealthy men seeking the ultimate salvation of their souls would make gifts of land to the Church in order to secure divine indulgence and forgiveness of their sins: it was a form of prudent insurance. By the late fourteenth century (when John Wycliffe was just beginning to set in train the first stirrings of Protestant rebellion) it has been estimated that as much as one-third of English land and revenues had come into the hands of the Church. But the actual work of serving the parishes was done by a huge army of quite poor men in plain black gowns who were 'clerks' by virtue of having acquired a little education at the hands of monks. It was they who celebrated masses, married, baptised, listened to the fears of the dying and buried the dead. Chaucer's undernourished 'clerk of Oxenford' on his lean horse was one such. Late-medieval England was full of them. It has been calculated that there was one clerk for every sixty-nine lay men or women and children, and this figure does not include the monks and friars of whom, before the Black Death, there were said to have been about sixteen to seventeen thousand. All these, in a kingdom whose population was only about two and a half million. It works out that almost one in eighteen of all adult males counted as clerical.[3]

It has been pointed out that, given the rule of celibacy of the pre-Reformation clergy, and the lack therefore of the dynastic Church families that are such a feature of the eighteenth and nineteenth centuries, there had to be constant recruitment from peasant stock into these clerical ranks. For a bright boy it was the only way to escape the timeless drudgery of plough and cow-byre and the demands of a possibly oppressive lord. Not that the escape was complete, for the lowly clerk of those days tucked up his gown and tilled his own glebe land alongside his neighbours. But, however poor, he had a certain status. He could deal with the mystery of pen strokes on

Taynton church, and yet another spring beginning to whiten the blackthorn above the old grave stones.

paper as he could with the mystery of God, and he was supposed to extend hospitality to wayfarers and to the needy. By a Norman ruling, a landowner whose holding included the 'avowson' or disposal of a parish, and who was thus termed the 'patron of the benefice', whether he was Church or secular, had to provide for the support of a clerk and also a house for him to live in. It is this last provision, dating from the beginning of the twelfth century, which seems particularly significant to Taynton. The church there, St John the Evangelist, dates from well before the Reformation, and is almost certainly built on the site of an older one. The clerk who attended to the parish must have lived somewhere. Thus the vicarage, or parsonage house, is an older feature of English villages than is commonly realised.[4]

Taynton, alone of all the parishes around Burford, does not appear in the Domesday Book. The reason is that seven years before the Norman conquest Edward the Confessor (who was half Norman and had been brought up in France) had given the manor of Taynton away to the monks of Saint-Denis, outside Paris, along with some more land and a priory near the Severn, in Gloucestershire. This link with Saint-Denis lasted four centuries and was only finally broken during the Wars of the Roses, when Edward IV wrested the holding away from Saint-Denis and eventually gave the whole lot to the monks of Tewkesbury to encourage them to pray for those killed in the Yorkist cause.

Eighty years later the monastery at Tewkesbury was disbanded by Henry VIII, and the manor of Taynton, like many other ecclesiastical spoils was for the time being back in royal hands. Again like many of the lands seized from the Church, it was passed on within a few years to one of Henry's associates, as a reward for services rendered. The fortunate recipient, in the case of Taynton, was Edmund Harman, who was one of Henry's

barber-surgeons and a trusted courtier. He was eventually
a witness to Henry's will. His stiffly capitalised signature
suggests that he was not a fluent reader or writer; but
this was still an era of halting literacy even among the
great, and people remarked with admiration when a
scholar could read swiftly and silently to himself as we
do today.[5]

We know what Harman looked like because he appears
in a large painting of Henry presiding over the Company
of Barber-Surgeons. It was commissioned from Hans
Holbein the Younger in 1540, to commemorate the
merger of the two trades and their grant of a royal charter.
Harman kneels in a prominent position fourth on Henry's
right, wearing the clipped and pointed beard that would
become more fashionable in the reign of Henry's daughter
Elizabeth. His expression is determined. He does not
have a hood: these were reserved for accredited surgeons,
but he wears the puffed, padded and fur-trimmed gown
and lawn sleeves of a gentleman. He would then have
been in his early thirties. He was not, it seems, particularly well-born; his father was a merchant in Ipswich,
possibly of Germanic origin, but in those uncertain and
combative times the son did well. He began to acquire
properties, and became one of the servants of the Privy
Chamber. After a little trouble in the early 1540s, which
could have gone badly for him, even taking him to the
stake, he was rehabilitated and given a lease on the
ex-religious hospital in Burford, along with other
monastic prizes. He was also accorded the right to bear
arms and to call himself Esquire. By that time he was
married to Agnes Silvester, the daughter of a prominent
Burford merchant whose own fine house, Falkland Hall,
stands in Burford to this day.

But the most solid and enduring possession, bestowed
on him by the slowly dying king in 1546, was the manor
of Taynton, along with the rectory and advowson of its
vicarage – that is, the right to the parish property there

and the power to appoint whom he wished to hold church services. I dwell on Harman because I believe that he was not merely the owner of Taynton but, at any rate at certain seasons, the occupant of a house there that was already well established as a Church dwelling. I think it likely that it is some part of this lost house that survives within the Old Vicarage that stands on the site today.

Direct and incontrovertible evidence of this is missing. But the word-of-mouth claim that Harman actually lived in Taynton persisted down the generations in local families almost to the present day. A late-nineteenth-century researcher[6] was assured by a local source that Harman's daughter and son-in-law, who inherited from him, lived in 'the old priory-mansion house' in Taynton in the 1580s. As early as 1240 a 'mansion' is mentioned in Taynton, which would have indicated not a huge house in the post-Renaissance sense but a solid stone edifice. (The 'Manor House' which figures as a name in Taynton today, is simply one of the several buildings belonging to the one-time manor farm. There are some indications that an early medieval house may also have existed, on a field nearer the river, but it is unmentioned in Harman's Will and all trace of it has disappeared.)

My cousin Donald Milner, in the late twentieth century, was also told that Harman had lived in a house on the site of the vicarage. His informant was Phillip Lee, who was the last man to own and work one of the Taynton quarries before their role in the village's history was finally at an end.

In the Will that Harman dictated on his deathbed in Taynton in 1577, he referred to 'my house which is called the parsonage house and glebe land of the parsonage of Tainton'. The 'parson', a term that was to become more general in the seventeenth and eighteenth centuries, was the 'person' who represented the accredited rector of the parish, otherwise known as the 'vicar'; or vicarious occupant of the benefice. The 'parsonage house', therefore, would have been where a succession of clerks had lived before the parish came into Harman's hands, when, for a while after the Reformation, a 'parson' did not have to be in holy orders. It looks as if this was the village's one substantial dwelling, which Harman made over to his own use – the other good houses were to arrive with the following century.

There are other signs, also, of Harman's family in Taynton in the 1550s, '60s, '70s and beyond. For a shadowy figure, divulging, over the four and half centuries that separate him from us, little of his true personality and plans, Edmund Harman has remained oddly present.

Chapter VII

EDMUND HARMAN'S LEGACY AND THE HOUSE HE LIVED IN

In tracking my three houses in the order in which they crossed my own life, I have moved forward in recent time but back in terms of history. With Edmund Harman dying in 1577 we are in a period earlier than we can reach with either Stanhopes in Limpsfield or Stapleton Hall in Stroud Green. It may well be that Thomas Draper, when he had his own initials and his wife's carved into the woodwork of Stapleton Hall in 1609, built his fine house in the footprint of an older one, but this is conjecture. It may also be that the 'two cottages' that seem to have formed the core of Stanhopes in Limpsfield High Street were already standing when Harman witnessed Henry VIII's Will, when the sickly boy-king Edward replaced his father, when he was replaced by Catholic Mary and then her regime was turned on its head by Queen Elizabeth – but this again can only be a logical guess.

Taynton vicarage is different. Not only does its long role as the parson's house give it a continuity that most houses do not enjoy, but the village of Taynton itself remained, till the arrival of wealthy incomers in the late twentieth century, less touched by change than most places in England. The copious surviving records tell this story. Taynton, economically boosted by its masonry business with the wider world and by its proximity to Burford, but protected from physical change by its rural seclusion, seems to have been much the same sort of community for hundreds of years. There was only a distant manorial presence: once the Land Tax begins in the late seventeenth century it is soon clear that several of the largest taxpayers (including 'His Grace the Duke of Marlborough') merely owned land in the area and did not live there. Instead, over several centuries, the prominent citizens were a handful of prosperous farmers, with a cottage-dwelling class below them of agricultural labourers and artisans. It was a world in which everyone knew everybody, at least by sight, and the poorest were helped because they were known neighbours – unlike a fashionable, overgrown village such as Islington, where the poor were both feared and despised and were consigned when possible to a workhouse well out of the way.

And always, at the centre of things in Taynton, there was just one educated man, the vicar, doing more or less what he was paid to do by his patron, present at the Vestry meetings where all local affairs were decided, writing or at any rate signing the reports, the church accounts and the all-important records year on year of who married, who bore children or who was laid in the ground around the church – bones upon bones, over innumerable generations. Eighteenth- and nineteenth-century headstones sprinkle the churchyard, many of them the works of stonemason families honouring their own dead with a carved skull or a sculpted wreath of laurel. Their weather-beaten elegance obscures the fact that men, women and children of Taynton had been disappearing into this ground for centuries before ordinary citizens ever thought of erecting permanent memorials. The present church, which is itself rich in carved heads by and of local men, dates from the mid-fifteenth century, but it is unlikely to have been the first one on the site or even the second. It is probable that the accreted remains of almost a thousand years of Taynton parishioners lie beneath its drifts of late-winter snowdrops: white above and white below.

The registers of this undisturbed place go back a long way, farther than those of most parishes. The earliest book, though battered-looking, has been wonderfully durable, since its pages are of fine vellum (calfskin). This has occasional imperfections and discolours with time, but does not tear nor disintegrate as paper does. With baptisms, marriages and burials all bound up together, the entries begin in 1538, which was the year that Henry VIII's powerful secretary, Thomas Cromwell, ordered that every parish was to keep such a record. Apparently, unlike many parishes, Taynton promptly complied – though it must be significant that both the loyal inscription in the beginning and the first few decades of entries appear to have been re-transcribed at one later time, presumably from a provisional list:

This Boke of Regester agreeth with the Booke of Regester begone the 26 Day of October in the yeare of our Lord god 1538 & in the 30th yare of our late souveraiyne lord of famouse memory Kinge Henry the 8 the onely supreame head under christ of the Church of England & Ireland. Wheareine are Recorded the names of all swich persons that have ben chrissened, Wedded & Buried in the parrish of Teynton in OxonShire. Verbatim as followeth.

That volume lasted till about 1700. A new one was started with the new century, and we owe the survival of both books, and other ones, plus a mass of mouse- and worm-eaten minor scraps of other records, to a much later vicar. For on the facing page of the eighteenth-century

book is written 'I, William Patrick Lennard Hand certify
... that I found these defective registers on my being
inducted into the Vicarage and Church of Taynton
September 1873.'

Mr Hand had evidently decided to delve into the parish
chest, that traditional, capacious and unorganised reposi-
tory of all documents to be kept, often including notes
on ad hoc Poor Law decisions, on objects offered to the
church, on sums given for charity, and sometimes other
Deeds, conveyances or sworn agreements which had
nothing to do with church affairs but were merely desired
to be in a 'safe place'. There, they inevitably tended to
moulder, since an unheated church (and most churches
were not heated till the second half of the nineteenth
century) is damp. After Hand's timely intervention all
the material was sent to the Bodleian Library in Oxford.
It briefly returned to Taynton under the next vicar, who
had a taste for history and had good connections – then
it went back to the Bodleian – then for a spell to the
diocesan archives in the Oxford district of South Hinksey.

Today it has at last come to rest in the Oxfordshire
County Archives in Cowley, in another church building
as it happens. In the 1930s Lord Nuffield, the maker of
Morris cars, thought a new church was needed for his
workers and had one designed and built; but now the
place is surplus to modern religious requirements:
instead, it is populated by brisk researchers into the dead.
So the long line of Taynton vicars, along with the
stonemason Strongs, the Pittaways, the Lees, the Wood-
mans, the Cozens, the Colliers, the Eldridges and the
other village dynasties live again in a new immortality,
if not quite the sort they were promised.

It is among the entries in the earliest register that the
presence of the Harman family in Taynton makes itself
felt. In October 1550, three years after Edmund Harman
had acquired the manor, we find his son, Edward, being

baptised there. The baby's burial in Taynton is recorded two months later. In the sixteenth century wealth and status were no protection against the high rate of infant mortality that afflicted all classes, though in the sheer number of children he lost Harman does appear to have been particularly unlucky. All his boys seem to have died, as he had no male heir. Some were found to say that the monks whose properties he had taken had cursed him.

Then, in 1559, Harman's eldest surviving daughter, called Agnes like her mother, was married in Taynton to Edmund Bray. Harman must have been very satisfied with this match, for the Brays were a prominent Oxfordshire family. We have, by coincidence, already heard of them, for it was the Brays who acquired Brownswood manor around Stroud Green at the Reformation, and a female descendant of theirs who married the eighteenth-century William Stapleton. Before the industrial revolution, when most wealth lay in land, the world of people with power and money was a relatively small one, the same names frequently recurring in different connections.

In fact Edmund Bray the son-in-law was to inherit Taynton. We find Edmund, his own son by Agnes, being married there in October 1580, probably aged about twenty. A Silvester Bray, surely a son also, was married there later the same year. The year before, a much younger brother, John, had been baptised, and the following year, some eleven months after the two weddings, two baby boys who would have been first cousins were baptised – Edward son of Silvester and Giles son of Edmund. That Edmund Bray, grandson to the original Edmund, died in Taynton three years later, but it is evident that the family was flourishing materially. Among the family possessions was the manor of Great Barrington, just a little further up the Windrush valley from Taynton. It is in Great Barrington church that a life-size effigy of an early seventeenth-century

Edmund Bray lies, complete with both armour and ruff. Other grand marble monuments stand to later generations of Brays, who seem to have suffered rather frequent visitations of mortality especially in the guise of smallpox.

By the early eighteenth century a further dearth of male heirs led the remaining Brays to sell the manor off to the Talbot family, and so the church of Great Barrington is also full of eulogies in stone to the Talbots and to their descendants under other names. The close link, between the parishes of Taynton on the edge of Oxfordshire and Great Barrington over the border in Gloucestershire, has led to fragmentation in record-keeping. This has confused some church historians into thinking that Taynton did not have a resident vicar when it did. It has its origins in the Harman daughter's marriage.

To return to Harman himself, a church Visitation in 1574 refers to 'Harman of Teinton' as the local patron of the benefice, which suggests an actual presence. So does the fact that, two years later, in his capacity as lord of the manor, Harman was drawing up 'Ordinances and Orders for the Tennants of the Manor of Taynton'. These were mainly sensible rules for good husbandry: 'none shall tye their horses or mares in ye cornfields untyl harvist is endyd every year . . . That every tennant do sett and plant every yeare three trees, ashes, ellemes or appletrees . . .' Geese were to be ringed for identification purposes and not be allowed to bother people, no manorial tenant was to keep more than one stallion (to avoid two male horses fighting), and sheep were not to be bought in for fattening on the common land and then sold on – which would clearly be an abuse of the other tenants' rights. The rolled parchment document, now worn brownish and friable, is in a clerk or lawyer's Chancery hand, but Harman signed it in the same careful capitals with which he had signed the King's Will.

That same year, 1576, Harman's wife Agnes died – at the end of March which, under the old calendar then in force, was the beginning of the new year. She was buried in Taynton church as 'the wif of Edmonde Harman Esquire and Lord of this Manner', and for a long time the site of her vault was lost, but during church repairs in the early nineteenth century her lead coffin-plate was found under the south side of the nave. It is now in the Tolsey Museum in Burford. I have held it, heavy in my hand, this last physical relic of a vanished person.

In November the same year Harman seems to have married again.[1] It looks, from his subsequent Will, as if he were still hoping for a living male heir, but as he was by then sixty-six or sixty-seven, and in fact within a few months of his own death, this seems to have been rather a forlorn attempt. There is no trace of the marriage in Taynton, or of the presence of the second wife there: she was called Katharine, but her surname we do not even know. He was to die the following March. On the 17th and 18th of the month, feeling that his end was near, he dictated his long and complex Will, making full provision for this second wife and any child she might bear him to inherit Taynton, but she must have died herself after a while without issue since, as we know, everything eventually went to the daughter who had married Edmund Bray and hence to their successors.

Having made his effort, Harman died the next day, on the cusp of the old year and the new. His burial in Taynton church beside Agnes was delayed till 10 April, an unusually long lapse of time for those days. Can the inconvenient presence of the second wife have had something to do with it? Certainly his Will took a while to prove, and two commissioners were appointed to an *Inquisitio post Mortem* to make sure all was being carried out appropriately, but by the time they made their report the mysterious Katharine seems to have been permanently out of the picture.

In his Will, Harman left £210 to provide for the poor of the parish in perpetuity (a handsome bequest that was still producing handouts of bread at the end of the nineteenth century), and also money for the maintenance of Taynton church. Here too was his reference to 'my house called the parsonage house and glebe land'.

It is, however, clear that Harman and his family, like many well-to-do clans at that time, were peripatetic, moving between their various properties according to the seasons and current local fears of pestilence. We know that many of his numerous but fleeting progeny were born and died after he became lord of the manor of Taynton, but only the one son, Edward, appears in the Taynton registers. Maybe his wife Agnes generally preferred life in Burford, where her father's grand house was and where, of course, Harman had property too, including the lease on the old hospital of St John. Death came for him when he was in Burford, but there is no evidence of him having played a role there over the years as a prominent local citizen, as you would expect if the town had been his principal residence.

It looks, however, as if, at one time, Harman did contemplate being buried in Burford rather than in his own parish and manor. For in Burford church, among many other memorials to those, whether esteemed or hated in their time, who contributed to Burford's prosperity and renown, is a pedimented monument resembling an altar but with a commemorative plaque in place of a cross, and a coat of arms above. Below, as on many traditional funeral monuments of the time, are small kneeling figures, in this case sixteen of them – the Harman children, of whom only two daughters are known to have survived. The plaque contains a Latin inscription appearing to commemorate both the Harmans (Agnes is referred to as his 'only and most faithful wife') but written as if from the mouth of Edmund himself. It translates thus:

I was not; then by God's will I was born to be a man; and I shall live again from my own seed. In the Great Day the bodies which we think have perished by decay shall rise again whole at God's word . . . Laugh at the threats of disease, despise the blows of misfortune, care not for the dark grave . . .

But there is no dark grave because, although a vault was originally left beneath it, we know it was never filled, and Taynton church received both Edmund and Agnes. This empty monument has been chiefly remarked on because, on either side of the inscription, are carved the figures of what appear to be two Amerindians from the Amazonian coast of Brazil. What, one may well ask, are they doing in the Cotswolds? It has been suggested that, among his other financial dealings, Harman had trading interests with the New World that was just beginning to open up on the other side of the Atlantic. Or he may simply have liked the cosmopolitan citizen-of-the-world air that these two exotic figures gave him.

If Edmund Harman did indeed live in the ex-parsonage house that formed the core of what is today the Old Vicarage in Taynton, what was it then like?

Today, it is a complex and rambling house, altered and added on to at a number of different dates. Some of the region behind the large kitchen, at the east end of the building, including the back stairs, is generally agreed to be Victorian, and the Georgian kitchen itself seems to have been modified in the later nineteenth century. The official Listing description states that the house is mid-eighteenth century but (as with Stanhopes in Limpsfield) this ignores evidence of earlier construction within it.

An architectural survey made when the Old Vicarage

in Taynton was sold by the Milners in 2007, remarked mournfully on the lack of documentation – 'The Centre for Oxfordshire Studies . . . has no photographs of the house. The Oxfordshire Record Office has no record . . . Nikolaus Pevsner's *The Buildings of England* series has no mention . . . The house has never been featured in *Country Life* magazine . . .' This survey concluded that some of the building probably dates from the mid-seventeenth century, with front façade and windows redone in the eighteenth. This too, however, may turn out to be an over-simplified story, since other details do not fit with it. It has been generally regarded in the village as a seventeenth-century building, but Phillip Lee, the last quarryman, who died towards the end of the twentieth century, was convinced from looking at some of the stonework in the back of the house that it was older.

Another architectural historian, to whom I appealed while researching this book, also thought that the central core of the house, only one room deep but forming a T-shape with a gabled back-projection, suggested a seventeenth-century building, but that one could not exclude the possibility that the remains of a still earlier building had been incorporated into it. The entrance hall and dining room were originally one big room, with a door – probably once the main door – at the back. At this place, near the stairs, there are traces of chimney stacks which do not today serve any fires. On one side of this big central area is the smaller sitting room, clearly a long-ago kitchen with a great fireplace. There may once have been a further one-storey building beyond this that has been obliterated by later construction. There was a well adjacent (now under the floor of the Georgian/Victorian kitchen). On the other side of the hall-space is a large room with a gable end to the west which does not originally seem to have had a fireplace, or many windows, but once had a sizable back entry and may possibly have started its history as a barn. Beneath the whole are extensive cellars (as in Stanhopes) reached by a stone staircase.

My friend also noticed something else which the previous surveyor did not. Observing and measuring one winter afternoon in the third-floor attics above the central section of the house, he established that the entire roof timbering had apparently been raised up at some point, like an upturned boat, and reinstated at a higher level. Gaps had been made good in ad hoc ways, with some beams sawn and refitted, and that was when a staircase tower within a gable, to accommodate a necessarily reconstructed stair, was added at the rear. In other words, what we are looking at is a house that did not originally have the first floor at all in its present form, but rather an upper floor with simple attics. These may have been serviceable as sleeping quarters, but they would hardly have been the bedrooms that later generations knew.

It is therefore possible – though now unprovable – that a big hall as main living-space, with a fire in it, a kitchen on one side of it and a barn on the other, great cellars below and attics above, was the layout of the house that Harman and the Brays knew. Its staircase would probably have been a spiral one above the cellar stairs in the hall corner by the then chimney stack – the usual position for a staircase in those days. Clearly, the 'parsonage house' that Harman prized and that was known as a 'mansion' must have been of at least these dimensions.

We cannot tell what works, if any, the Harmans or the Brays did. There were no plans to turn the old place into a grander dwelling, as Thomas Draper apparently did with an old farmhouse at Stroud Green in 1609, for such a scheme would have left some trace. In any case, there is no evidence of Brays in residence in Taynton after 1584. They owned a number of properties in Oxfordshire–Gloucestershire, and seem to have preferred their neighbouring manor of Great Barrington, where their descendants were to build themselves a Palladian country house a hundred and fifty years later. The parsonage house at Taynton presumably reverted at some point during the reign of Elizabeth, or at any rate by that of James I, to its original use.

Most parsons were not then, or for much of the next hundred years, from particularly grand families. The incumbents of Taynton were not rectors in their own right, who would have received all the tithe income from the parish, but simple vicars on stipend. It seems unlikely that, for the first half of the seventeenth century, anyone in the parsonage house would have had the means or the desire to undertake significant building works on it.

In 1602, the year before James I came to the throne, the vicar appointed by 'Ed. Bray, *armiger*' – esquire – was a John Elkes. He was there till 1615. Married clergy, rather than celibates, were now favoured. He buried a son of his in the churchyard in April 1614, and in the September of the following year both he and his wife joined the boy there. Plagues, not necessarily bubonic but one of an array of often fatal diseases including malarial fevers and smallpox, affected country places then as well as the towns. After Elkes, for fifteen years, the vicar was Francis Alden or Aldernes, apparently also known as 'Francis of Bicester'. He baptised two of his own sons in Taynton in 1619 and 1621. His tenure lapsed for some unspecified reason in 1630, by which time tensions about religious differences were running high. The Civil Wars were looming, and the current Bray patron was now styling himself a knight, or possibly just a fighter (*militem*). Another man took over for two years, then died and was followed by Henry Fletcher, who was an MA and there-fore a man of education.

I suspect that the 'Joane Fletcher, widdow' buried in 1651, with the fact noted in a different, more elaborate hand from that of the other entries, may have been this vicar's relict. It is not clear when Fletcher himself died since, during the Commonwealth, there is a gap in all the church records, as happens very often in parishes. Under the deadening edicts of the Cromwellian regime – no singing in churches, no celebrations even for Christmas Day – the clergy hardly led a comfortable life; indeed, more than a quarter of all incumbents were evicted and lay preachers took over.

A new era began in many ways after the Restoration of Charles II to the throne. In 1661 the Taynton registers began to be kept again, and by 1664 there was a new vicar, Thomas Dudley, another MA. As *caecus* is written against his name in the diocesan registers it is assumed he was blind, or more likely went blind, like Milton, in middle life. I do not know if he was related to the family of Elizabeth I's favourite, Robert Dudley, but he must have had the means to pay a curate to do his paperwork for him, to steer him around and to identify parishioners. And in fact we know something about his financial situation because now Taynton records of those assessed to pay the Poor Rate begin – or rather, a few worn scraps from this era have survived, frayed and mouse-nibbled from their long sojourn in the bottom of the parish chest. Here in 1666 we find Thomas Dudley the vicar and his wife Margaret living with an unspecified number of servants, assessed to pay four shillings per annum.

For comparison, Edward Eldridge, a prosperous farmer who was then a churchwarden, whose family name occurs and recurs over the Taynton generations and who was also living with his wife and servants, was assessed at six shillings, while Stephen Gascoigne, gent, had to pay the far more substantial sum of two pounds, eight shillings. Ann Strong, a widow from the thriving family of masons, was assessed at one shilling. Most inhabitants paid nothing: a number were themselves the poor in receipt of handouts.

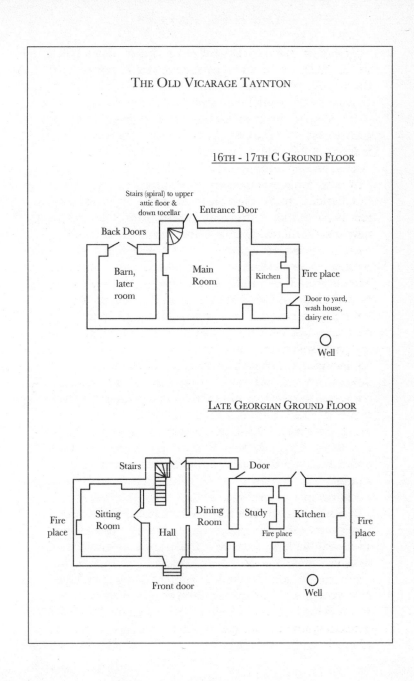

THE OLD VICARAGE TAYNTON

16TH - 17TH C GROUND FLOOR

Stairs (spiral) to upper
attic floor &
down to cellar

Entrance Door

Back Doors

Barn,
later
room

Main
Room

Kitchen

Fire place

Door to yard,
wash house,
dairy etc

Well

LATE GEORGIAN GROUND FLOOR

Stairs

Door

Fire
place

Sitting
Room

Hall

Dining
Room

Study

Fire place

Kitchen

Fire
place

Front door

Well

I think it was during Dudley's near-twenty-year stay in Taynton that the old parsonage house got its first proper makeover. Standards of comfort had risen since the days when gentlefolk and servants had all spent much of their time cheek by jowl in large, draughty halls. It was, perhaps, in the 1660s or '70s that the central hall was partitioned, the barn made into living space and the old, twisting staircase replaced by a gate-legged one with the back gable enlarged to accommodate it. If so, the first modifications must have been made to the roof height then, though I believe that more was done later. The upper floor might have been made more comfortable, perhaps with ceilings to conceal the rafters. No changes were made then to the old kitchen. The days when the kitchens would be in a separate wing of a large house were still far distant, but, most importantly, the front was made grander. The rubble-limestone wall was clad in a coat of superior ashlar stone. More windows were put in, classic Cotswold windows most likely, each with a central timber or stone mullion, but not as large as those that would succeed them in the next century. The doorway in the front of the house was probably constructed at this time.

An entry in the church register reads 'Thomas Dudly, master of Arts, late vic. of ye parish of Taynton deo. Oxford, was buryid on ye fifth day of August 1681 by me Ben. Griffin, vic. of great Barrington in ye Deo. of Gloucester.'

It was from this time that the parishes of Taynton and Great Barrington began to be linked. The Bray family were still the patrons, with the power to appoint vicars, now in the person of a Lady Bray of Barrington. But more significant is that the Griffin family (who had already made some appearance in the Taynton marriage register) seems to have been related to the Talbots, who would acquire the manor and patronage from the Brays in 1735. A number of later vicars similarly had links with the Talbots, who became barons Dynevor in the later eighteenth century, then Rices or Rhys as the inheritance passed through the female line. Finally, in the twentieth century, they became Wingfields, and were somewhat famed for their eccentric neglect of Great Barrington, most of whose houses they owned.[2]

With the Griffins, the era was beginning when vicars were more and more apt to be the sons of landed families, comfortably set up – often a vicar would hold more than one parish at the same time – and entirely able to take their place among the local gentry. Such a one was Edward Loggan (or Loggin) Griffin, whose birth is to be found in the Great Barrington register in 1667. He was the eldest son of the incumbent who buried Dudley. He was newly ordained when he arrived in Taynton, after several short-term vicars had filled the post since Dudley. His appearance in the parish was announced with a certain flourish on the first page of a new register book, though a couple of spelling mistakes have been corrected in a darker ink: 'The Register Book for the Parish of Taynton begun at the Rever'd Mr Edw. Loggin Griffins Enterance upon the Viccariage wch was in the year of our Lord 1703.'

'Entrance upon the vicarage' means taking up the job as vicar rather than a physical entrance into the house above the high road, but I am sure that Loggan Griffin did live in Taynton. Although Great Barrington produced more income for a vicar than Taynton did, there was apparently no house there suitable for a clergyman, which is doubtless why successive incumbents settled in the solid house in Taynton. Loggan Griffin, indeed, seems to have set out to beautify it further. For when my cousin, about 1970, was looking for the ideal sheltered, sunny spot to plant a peach tree, he finally selected a place against the house wall on the south-west corner. He set to work to clear creepers, finally to discover when he reached bare stone that on it was scratched in an elegant, looping hand 'Nectarin 1705'. Someone, more than two hundred and fifty years before, had selected this same place for an identical purpose. A little later another inscription in the same hand, 'Peach 1705', was unearthed beneath some wisteria further up the south (front) wall.

> *The Nectaren, and curious Peach*
> *Into my hands themselves do reach . . .*

Andrew Marvell's famous poem about a garden luxuriant with flowers and fruit was still very much in fashion, with more and more species of plant being developed or brought from far-off places in the expanding world. I have a soft spot for Loggan Griffin, his fruit trees and his fine handwriting, and his numerous younger brothers and sisters both living and dead, up the road in what old-fashioned clerks still referred to as 'Barrington Magna'. But in the event he did not stay to see his trees grown to their full strength. In 1712 he was off, and the parish was taken on by a James Stiles, BA. He was there for thirty-eight years, till he died in 1750, and in many ways seems to have incarnated the mildly autocratic, not particularly hard-working, not particularly fervent eighteenth-century Anglican parson.

Chapter VIII

'The spiritually comatose base of the Church of England'

I do not know where James Stiles came from, but I assume, from the fact that he had a degree from Oxford, that he was of the local gentry, for there were later Stileses in Northleach, in the Gloucestershire Cotswolds. There is no trace in the Taynton registers of a Mrs Stiles, or any young Stileses. The register book of baptisms, marriages and burials that was begun with a ceremonial inscription upon Loggan Griffith's appointment in 1703, continued in use for the next half-century. From about 1716 it is written up for over thirty years all in the same hand, rather rapid and careless but with conventional spelling. This is Stiles himself, for the writing matches his signature. It becomes increasingly untidy and shaky in the 1740s, and disappears in 1749, the year in which he died; actually, in the spring of 1750 by the new calendar. The writing has little in common with the far more laborious and elaborate hands of the parish clerk and churchwardens, who tended to spell by ear – 'plomours' for plumbers, and once 'koarpintours' (carpenters).

However, it was quite an achievement – and one replicated all over England at the time – that long before the era of village schools so many countrymen could nevertheless read and write. This was thanks, no doubt, to the wide dissemination of the Bible and several other popular works, such as *The Pilgrim's Progress* and Foxe's graphically gory *Book of Martyrs*, as bestowed on the Taynton church by Thomas Strong. It was not yet quite true, as Pascal had claimed already in the previous century, that 'a Protestant country is one where everyone can read', but ever since the Reformation there had been encouragement in that direction and this had produced results. In contrast, in Catholic France, even well into the nineteenth century, rural illiteracy was still the norm.

All the years that Stiles kept the register, in the church-wardens' accounts an intermittent entry is made, reading, with minor variations, 'Paid to Mr Stiles for righting of ye Ridguster 1/-' That an incumbent should require a formal payment from church funds just for keeping his own register up to date strikes us today as hardly in the best traditions of Christian service, but a number of things about the Church of that time are now alien to us. Towards the end of his long stay in Taynton Stiles even charged four shillings to the church accounts for 'a book of sermons' – presumably so that he could read one aloud each week rather than writing it himself.

The Reformation, which is traditionally dated to the reign of Henry VIII but which in practice continued to roll in contentious stages through the next hundred and twenty years, through the Civil Wars and the Common-wealth, was not substantially complete till the so-called 'Glorious' Revolution of 1688 with the crowning of William and Mary. Anglicanism had by then become far more than a version of Protestantism. The King (or Queen) was head of the Church, and it was royal as much as heavenly dignity that was exemplified in parish churches throughout the land. The vicar in his pulpit was therefore a local representative not just of God but of the monarch. The Vestry, over which the vicar presided, along with his churchwardens, overseers of the poor and overseers of highways (frequently all the same people) was almost the sole source of local control and organisation. It decided and dispensed such organised welfare (Poor Relief) as was then available. It was also closely intertwined with the system of law and order. The powers of the pre-Reformation church courts had, by the seventeenth century, been given to the Justices of the Peace, some of whom were local gentry but many of whom were also clergymen.

It was perhaps inevitable, in the circumstances, that country rectors and vicars should be men of the world rather than saintly ministers. In a country and an age when a fixed belief in God and in the general tenets of Christianity was more or less taken for granted by all, the decision to become a clergyman rather than, say, to join a regiment or to become a lawyer, could be a straight-forward practical choice more than a matter of strongly felt vocation. A taste for books was desirable, but not essential; a liking for the easy life of a country gentleman, with a general benevolence towards one's fellow men combined with a solid sense of one's own proper place in society, were probably more important. Good contacts within the Church or the aristocracy were the surest way of getting on.

Through the rather chaotic system of tithes and bene-fices some parsons were much better remunerated than others. Serving both Taynton and Great Barrington, James Stiles and his successors got about £300 a year, a sum considered adequate but hardly generous, whereas the Limpsfield incumbents, who were rectors in their own right, received more than twice that. It thus became the habit of many clergymen to make up their income by being vicar of more than one parish. When the parishes were near to one another, and in the gift of the same patron, as in the case of Taynton and Great Barrington, this was logical, but sometimes the extra parishes would be remote from the one where the incumbent lived; even in a different part of the country. Such 'plural' parishes tended to be ill-served, with infrequent offices, by a retired local priest or by a succession of underpaid curates, but even where the vicar was very much a presence not a great deal was expected of him.

Reading aloud in church the Prayer Book form of service (not chanting it: that smacked of popery!), and delivering – or at any rate reading – a sermon just once each Sunday, was the extent of his weekly duty. Communion was given to the dying, but to the parish in general just twice a year, at Christmas and Easter, and then it was usually only taken by a minority of parishioners. Many people remained wary that the consecrated bread and wine as well might be a little too close for comfort to a papist doctrine (transubstantiation). Vestments were kept to a minimum: not all clergy even wore cassocks. However, Dissent was not approved of either. 'Enthusiasm' and 'fervour' were generally felt to be suspect and not in the best Anglican tradition. Rather than baring their individual souls to God, eighteenth-century congregations, and their ministers, felt much more comfortable with prayers for good harvest weather and with thanksgiving services for military victories, or for a sovereign's recovery from illness.

The record of churchwardens' accounts for Taynton begins about ten years after Stiles became the vicar. It is a substantial, calf-bound book inscribed, like the register in huge, elaborate writing on the facing page: 'The church-warden's Book for Taynton, Anno Dom. 1725.' In the accounts for that first year is an item of six shillings for binding the book – the cover of which, after almost three hundred years, is now detaching itself from the spine. There is also a hefty sum of nine shillings and tenpence for the thick cream paper of which it is composed. Paper was not then a commodity to waste, which led to an admirable succinctness in records compared with our own wasteful modern repetitiousness. Over the years, various churchwardens doodled on the tempting endpapers, practising their fancy signatures, such as 'Edmund Maddox his Book March the 30 1768'. There is also a jotted list of churchwardens from 1724 to 1749 (the end of Stiles's watch), in which Taynton names such as Maddox, Newman, Cozens, Lambert, Dalby, Woodman and Eldridge rotate. This creates a feeling of comfortable permanence, although, as the decades pass, the Cozens and Lamberts who are present in the mid-eighteenth century, and beyond, must be a couple of generations removed from those who played much the same roles before Queen Anne ever came to the throne.

'The days of man are but as grass: for he flourisheth as a flower of the field . . . As soon as the wind goeth over it, it is gone: and the place thereof shall know it no more (Psalm 103: 15–16).

It is 'the place' that counts in the story I am telling. We have to allow many of the individual people who cross these pages, however flourishing, to disappear once their allotted span is over. Their family names, however, endure.

Over time, several old village families such as the Strongs and the Colliers had moved on to business interests in Burford, Witney, Oxford or London. The Colliers ran the George Inn, the largest in Burford, for a period in the seventeenth century, and other members of the clan were manufacturing blankets in Witney. One Collier started a brewery in Shoe Lane, Holborn, near the City of London. In the summer of London's Great Plague, 1665, six Colliers in one household in Taynton, including John Collier the head of the family and three of his grandchildren, died between 6 and 28 August, and these deaths are marked as 'plague' in the margin. No one from other households in the village died in that period except one old man, which suggests that a Collier with affairs to see to in London, possibly John himself or his son of the same name, had ridden home with the sickness on him. Sixty years later, in 1726, another John Collier, still based in the parish of St Clement Danes in the same Holborn area of London, left money in his Will in perpetuity to educate the poor of Taynton 'the place of my nativity' – money that was still providing scholarships to Christ's Hospital school in the twentieth century.

The local role of Strongs and Colliers was taken on by the rising Pittaway clan. They proved more firmly attached to the village, often returning from London or other growing cities where their masonry skills had taken them, to find their long home in Taynton churchyard. Among annually recurring items in the eighteenth-century accounts, along with 'Bread and wine for Sacrament' and money for bell-ringers or for singers on special occasions, is payment to John Pittaway. He was for many years parish clerk and therefore official record keeper, though not all the entries are in his hand. He earned a guinea a year (slightly over £1) plus more for 'extra duties'. These seem to have included winding and oiling the church clock, and 'cleaning snow of ye Ledes' (the leads, or church roof). A Betsy Pittaway is paid four shillings every so often for 'washing serplises'; and once 10¾ ells of Holland cloth plus thread are bought for making new ones, to the substantial cost of three pounds, eighteen shillings. A Robert Pittaway also appears frequently, doing general minor repairs. When John Pittaway the clerk died in 1782, his role was taken on by another Pittaway, 'Edward senior'.

No great works were done on the church in the course of the eighteenth century, and I do not believe that under Stiles's long incumbency any changes were made to the vicarage either. He was a single man: even with servants the house would have been plenty big enough for him. However, in 1735 (the year in which the Talbots took over as lords of the manor and hence patrons of the parish), some stonework repairs and whitewashing were carried out in the church, and new glass was put in the windows. A painter, too, was paid four guineas for 'drawing the kings arms and righting the 10 commandements and L'ds prayer and creed and gifts'. The 'gifts' were the sums left in perpetuity for charity. The work was touched up again fifty years later. Churches up and down England had such embellishments then, a replacement for the saints and altars lost at the Reformation and under Cromwell, and an inducement both to patriotism and to literacy. Most have long since been removed, or were painted over in the course of Victorian renovation, but Taynton church still displays the royal lion and unicorn over the door to the porch.[1]

Every so often the church's possessions are listed in the accounts, as if these represented negotiable monetary assets. In the first half of the eighteenth century they include a silver chalice, a pewter flagon, a hearse-cloth, a Bible, the three 'books about martyrs' given by Thomas Strong, and also a 'book against Quakers' which, later in the century, becomes more benignly described as 'a book about Quakers'.

But some of the most constant and significant recurring expenses throughout the eighteenth century concern the hire of horses, or the provision of horseshoes for owned horses, attendant expenses such as hay and corn, and other unspecified 'charges' which probably refer to human sustenance. These expenses are variously for Mr Stiles himself and/or his churchwardens when they had to make trips to Woodstock or Witney for the Bishop's Visitation. Such occasions were supposed to be the opportunity for the Bishop to check that all was going on as it should in his parishes, but it is hard to avoid the conclusion that they were the pretext for a day out, a journey and fun, in the otherwise rather leaden passage of the rural seasons.

* * *

We do have some direct insight into the life led by Stiles and by the large number of other Anglican clergymen who lived isolated in eighteenth-century English villages. Time and chance have left us the diaries of Parson Woodforde of Norfolk, who certainly never intended this mundane record of succulent meals eaten, favourite remedies dispensed, duties performed and neighbours visited, to be published, but who has now become the iconic figure of his time representing all the others.

He is actually a generation later than Stiles, since his journal covers the second half of the century rather than the first, but the two men belonged to the same world. Both had degrees from Oxford, both were bachelors, both long-term tenants of rural parishes of three to four hundred souls that offered few companions of their own social standing. It was, in the words of one present-day chronicler of parochial life 'the spiritually comatose base of the Church of England, still unawakened by Wesley [or] by the sacramentalists of the Oxford Movement'.[2] Meanwhile Woodforde, like Stiles or any gentleman farmer, rode on horseback around his country domain. He loved dogs and always had several; also kept pet cats, hawks and a cow for milk. He took it in turns with a small handful of monied neighbours to host dinners, card parties and ponderous romps featuring wig-snatching. When one prominent family moved to Bath, and a fellow clergyman died, their company was sorely missed and not easily replaced. He had his niece to keep house for him and several servants, male and female, whom he called, in the old style, his 'family'.

He regretted having no one (he meant no other Oxford-educated man) with whom to 'converse', but there are few references to books in his diary, or indeed to ideas. He did not go in for moral speculation. The growing issue of slavery did not disturb his equilibrium, nor did the readiness of the law to apply the death penalty for a mass of petty offences against property. He was quite at ease noting a purchase of brandy from 'Andrews the smuggler'. 'Saucy' was his word of general disapproval for the lower orders who misbehaved, but when a boy-servant ran off and enlisted as a soldier Woodforde paid him his wages and also gave him a tip. When unmarried maids became pregnant he treated this as a practical inconvenience rather than a grievous sin. He disapproved rationally of the Bastardy Act of 1733, under which a man named on oath by a girl as the father of her child had to marry her, or face a fine or imprisonment – 'Very disagreable . . . a cruel thing that any person should be compelled by Law to marry'. Yet a bad dream, or a raven flying over the house, or the thought that perhaps he should not have shaved on the Sabbath, would inspire in him superstitious forebodings that seem to belong to a much earlier era.

Essentially Woodforde was a kindly man, marrying and baptising his parishioners without the charges he could have levied, giving 'poor old people' a dinner of roast beef and 'plumb' pudding at his own house every Christmas Day, and dispensing much minor charity and frequently a reviving glass of Geneva gin as well to those who came begging at the vicarage gate. On one occasion he gave one of his own shirts to 'poor Roberts . . . to put on in the small-pox – His, poor fellow, being so extremely coarse and rough . . . Very painful for him'.

I have no evidence that Stiles reached this level of empathy, but, judging from both the churchwardens' accounts and the Poor Law records that have survived there seems to have been a general culture of giving in Taynton also. It is a theme throughout the eighteenth century, and continues in the Vestry minutes of the nineteenth. Probably every parish in England then had some needy parishioners who required saving from literal starvation or from death from cold, but a preoccupation with what was called Poor Relief can be evidence not just of the prevalence of poverty but of humane and energetic efforts within that society to alleviate it. Taynton, with Harman's Gift and Collier's Gift, and other charitable bequests including a forestry endowment from the Bray family, was better placed than many districts to carry out this duty. Parishes such as Islington and Hornsey had their ancient charities too; but by the eighteenth century, with London expanding next to them, they were already preoccupied with establishing workhouses and getting the destitute confined. By contrast, the existence of any workhouse in the vicinity of Burford is hardly mentioned in Taynton at this time. The jumbled scraps of surviving Poor Law papers from the parish chest provide evidence of coats and gowns bestowed at regular intervals on parishioners, most often the elderly, for their protection, or on the young – to enable them to seek work respectably clad. Later in the century, when the current patron of the parish, Lady Talbot, died, she left a whole two hundred pounds for this purpose. Two established charities, John Collier's (1726) and Edward Bliss's (1739) were specifically to pay for promising youngsters to be educated, and there is early evidence of a young William Maids, Richard Dalby, Thomas Newman and Robert Pittaway receiving ten shillings each.

The churchwardens' accounts note what seem to have been incidental acts of kindness to strangers, initiated either by the vicar himself or by his wardens. 'Gave to several passangers' (passers-through) occurs intermittently; also 'Gave to poor Travellers' – usually sixpence a person. There is also a note at one point that some people 'spent their own Money and because it was for the Pore had nothing' – that is, they claimed nothing back from church funds. The recipients would not have been Travellers with the modern connotation but itinerant haymakers and the like, the precariousness of whose livelihood was well recognised.

But occasionally in these early accounts there surfaces

that preoccupation with charity beginning and staying at home which later tended to dominate Poor Law records everywhere and became an obsession in the larger towns. According to a law enacted in the last years of Queen Elizabeth's reign in an attempt to suppress roving gangs of beggars, the destitute could expect help from their own parish but nowhere else. Determined attempts were therefore made to return anyone who looked like becoming a charge on the rates back to where they came from. That was the reason why, in 1726, sixpence was paid out not to a beggar but to 'Goody Hearn for conducting a Great Belly'd woman back to the town'. The town was presumably Burford, Goody Hearn a formidable local matron, and no one in Taynton wanted the parish landed with the upkeep of a newborn child who had no family connection there.

Disputes as to which parish might be financially responsible for a child, or for a whole family, mark the century, for this was a world before the industrial revolution began transforming great tracts of England and long before its effects were felt in villages remote from these transformations. The 'place of nativity' was still a fixed and verifiable concept. An ongoing dispute in the 1770s between Taynton and Hoo in Kent, regarding a couple called Evans and their several small children, eventually exonerated Taynton. But in 1780 Mary Westwood, a 'Rogue and Vagabond' found wandering and begging at Hemel Hempstead in Hertfordshire with three children of eight, four, and nine months, was thought to be married to a Taynton man and was therefore despatched there by the Hertfordshire Justices. More usually, since children tended to be conceived between people who lived within walking distance of one another, the dispute would be between Taynton and one of the neighbouring parishes. In 1770 Ann Lambert, of the established Taynton family, swore before the Justices that the child she was carrying was the work of William Baker of Asthall, and ten years later Elizabeth Maids of Windrush made the same affirmation in respect of Edward Clark of Taynton. Four years later again a Rebecca Maids of Taynton was carrying the child of a stonemason of Great Barrington, but the baby girl baptised on 18 December was buried on the 21st. The amount of grief, guilt, resentment and shamed relief bound up in such commonplace stories reaches out to us across two hundred years.

The Clark family, like the Maids, seem to have been prone to such misadventures, since, in 1789, John Clark was ordered to pay the parish forty shillings (i.e. two pounds, a substantial sum) towards the lying-in expenses of one Mary Hearn – perhaps a descendant of Goody Hearn – plus twenty pence a week to the parish for the child's support and tenpence a week for Mary. These last two amounts add up to two and a half shillings, or 'half a crown' a week. No agricultural labourer could have spared such a sum out of his few shillings a week pay. The Clarks must have been a relatively comfortably off family, and John Clark must have been perceived as having seduced and then let down a respectable girl. Quite often one is aware of some such probable logic, which does not become explicit in the sparse contemporary record of human weakness. However, on one occasion it is noted that a Hannah Hibble should be allowed to give birth to her baby at her mother's house in Taynton, since the churchwardens of Great Rissington, where she lived, sent a message to their opposite numbers in Taynton: 'we will hold you harmless'. In other words, we recognise that the child will have no claim on Taynton parish.

Sometimes complaints became more acrimonious. In 1769 the wife of a Stephen Pittaway stated that 'she is very poor and not able to provide for and maintain herself and 4 small children, her husband being committed to Goal [spelt thus]'. The Taynton overseers allowed her three shillings and sixpence a week, but she subsequently swore to the local Justices, one of whom was the vicar of Burford, that this was not enough. She eventually obtained five shillings. It is not evident why her husband was in gaol, though the charge is most likely to have been poaching. Countrymen used to getting what they could from the land, and gamekeepers paid to 'protect the landowners' interests', were traditional sworn enemies, and the conflict was sharpened in the late eighteenth century by the Enclosures.

Evidence of local sympathy for poachers appears after the end of the century, when a John Hall of Taynton was convicted by the Justices of having 'snares to kill and destroy game' and fined £5 – half of which was to go to the keeper in the employ of the Duke of Marlborough who informed on him. A warrant was issued enabling the Taynton constable (by that time villages had constables, not the policemen of later date but just one of the familiar local names) to enter Hall's home and collect goods – 'distress' – to the value of the fine. Pinned to this is a note written by the constable himself, who was one of the long-standing Dalby family: 'Sirs, I do here by certify to you that no sufficient distress cannot be found in the property of the said John Hall.' How did these papers come to be preserved in the parish chest? Presumably because village feeling on the matter was running high in Hall's favour.

Fifteen years later again a Pittaway, Henry, aged twenty-five, was to be executed under the jurisdiction of Oxford Assizes, along with an older man, William James, for the murder of a keeper in the Forest of Wychwood. This was a then still-large wooded area to the north-west of Taynton, and poaching there was endemic. Bordering the Forest were some separated-off Taynton manorial and parish lands, including a big farm called Paines or Paynes, and there are indications elsewhere in the registers that both Henry Pittaway and members of the James family lived and worked there. The hanged men were buried in Taynton in the same grave, with the brief facts of their death noted in the burial register. Many years after, someone quite other is said to have confessed on his deathbed that he had really been the person responsible for the killing – though the identity of this other person now appears to have been lost.[3]

We have moved on now well beyond the mid-eighteenth century, at which point Stiles died and was buried in his own churchyard. His place was taken by James Pitt, who seems to have been a rather different personality and certainly had much more elegant handwriting. I have not traced any link between him and the Pitt family (a branch of the Stanhopes) that was to produce two Prime Ministers. However, he was related to the ancient and armigerous Gloucester family of Pembruge, of which his wife (Elizabeth, but to her husband 'Betty' even in formal records) was also a member. He was twenty-five when he was inducted as the vicar of Taynton and Great Barrington in 1750, and was presumably newly married. Near the end of the early register of marriages, baptisms and burials one finds 'William son of James Pitt Vicar and Betty his wife was baptised Jan 7th 1752. Born November 28th 1751'. When a new register book had to be started two years later William Pitt's birth and baptism were re-inscribed on the flyleaf by the proud father, no doubt to keep the record all in one volume. Another Pitt son, Edmund, was baptised in June 1755, but the burial register reveals that he died the following March. A third boy, James like his father, was born and baptised in August 1759. This son was eventually to become an Oxfordshire vicar in his turn. He married a Pitt cousin whose father was a local MP. Such was the tensile web of connections that bound the county families together.

I have not found any more Pitt children's baptisms in Taynton, but if there were others maybe they were born and therefore baptised at the family home in Gloucester. In 1787, by which time James the father was in fact dead and his children would have been grown up, a Benjamin Pitt appears – perhaps the youngest son? He was there in Taynton transcribing, in an easy, educated hand, the Last Will and Testament of an elderly farm labourer, for whom he also acted as chief witness. The old man held the manorial tenancy of a cottage and garden at Payne's Farm, and was bequeathing this to his daughter and her husband. These were members of the James family, for whom fate was to take such a dark turn a generation later, when William James was convicted of murder.

James Pitt is very much a presence in Taynton through the 1750s and '60s, though rather less so in the '70s. He often signs the register himself; and among the crumpled and yellowed papers from the parish chest are regular receipts for money from church sources given to the churchwardens for sundry purposes, each one signed for by them and counter-signed by Pitt – not something Stiles had bothered with. On one occasion in mid-February 1756 there was a bill of over £11 for church repairs owed to a John Collier, who was descended from the successful Taynton family and was in the carpentry business in Burford.[4] He was paid in full, but a note was appended to the bill, written out in Pitt's hand, witnessed by him but signed by John Collier: 'I was allowed my bill as above, of Eleven pounds, one Shilling and Sixpence halfpenny by the Minister and Churchwardens of Taynton. I acknowledge myself indebted to the Poor of Taynton in the sum of £5.11/9½ which I promise to pay on or before the fourteenth day of May next –'

It is clear that James Pitt and his churchwardens (currently a Phillip Woodman and a John Lambert) had used spare cash in hand from the Poor Relief account to cover some of the bill for the repairs, but why over five-and-a-half pounds of this should be owed to the poor by Collier rather than by Pitt and his wardens is not apparent.

I think that it was under the tenancy of Pitt, with his background and his growing family, that the vicarage, in the 1750s or '60s, assumed something more like the aspect it has today. As in houses all over England, including Stanhopes in Limpsfield and, a little later, Stapleton Hall, the fenestration was reconfigured to present a classic façade of regular, twelve-paned Georgian windows, eight in all, with a central door under a small porch or canopy. This pattern did not necessarily provide the best arrangements of light for the irregular rooms inside, but evidently that was not felt to be as important as the house's upgraded appearance. The heavy church-style porch would not be added for another hundred years, and nor would the front bay window. The ashlar cladding of the front would have had to be redone round the new windows, though not so comprehensively as to obliterate the 'Peach' and 'Nectarin' labels inscribed half a century before. Some back windows also received attention, but there was no pretension to classical regularity at the back. Instead, the seventeenth-century staircase was remade and extended upwards and, it would seem, the entire roof timbering was raised to create more elegant bedrooms on the first floor and large attics with dormer windows above.

No large kitchen or ancillary rooms as yet, and no back stair. No water piped into the house (a tap in the kitchen was still a luxury of town-dwelling at that time) and certainly no water closet. At this period Woodforde recorded in his diary that he had been 'Busy in painting some boarding in my Wall Garden which was put up to prevent people in the kitchen seeing those who had occasion to go to Jericho'. Since the walled town of Jericho was famous for being out in the desert and also 'a place of humiliation',[5] it became a standard euphemism for a garden privy: hence the later 'jerry' for a chamber pot. Woodforde had recently had some lady guests staying, and a degree of refinement was in any case setting in. The seventeenth-century practice, found even among the well-to-do, of relieving oneself casually in any corner and even in the fireplace, was now definitely a thing of the quaint and distant past.

It is possible, since James Pitt came from a comfortably off family, that he footed the bill himself for the alterations. Clergy were, of course, tenants rather than house-owners, but so were very many people at that time. A vicar could usually stay in one parish all his life, if he so chose, and it was quite common for a long-term tenant to spend his own money making over a house to his taste. Alternatively, it may be that some or all of the cost in Taynton was met by the Talbot family, who were, in 1780, to be created barons Dynevor, and perhaps wished to keep their socially satisfactory vicar happy.

James Pitt remained thirty-four years vicar of Taynton and Great Barrington, almost as long as his predecessor. He died in office in 1784, aged only fifty-nine. His wife, who was seven years older than him, followed him less than three months later. They are buried, not in Taynton, but under the chancel in the church in Maisemore, just outside Gloucester where both their families were established. The sense of him being less present in his own parish in his last years may be down to failing health, but it seems to have set a bad precedent for after his death Taynton suffered a period of neglect.

This was all too common in that relaxed era before the nineteenth-century pressures of either low church evangelism or the high church Oxford Movement. There is a gap in the record for seven years, then three different curates follow between 1791 and 1810, standing in for a non-resident vicar called John Delabere of a mildly grand family. I do not know who lived in the parsonage house then, for it was certainly too big for one underpaid

Watercolour of the back of Taynton old vicarage in the 1980s. The oldest sections are to the right and centre: the doorway just off-centre below the back gable is the original entrance to the house. The back projections to the left are Victorian additions, the greenhouse twentieth century.

curate on his own. It seems clear that Delabere hardly had a firm hand on what was happening in Taynton because, in 1808, after a Visitation, the Bishop of Oxford wrote to the churchwardens of Taynton a reproachful letter indicating that he did not think the sum left for education by Edward Bliss seventy years before was being used appropriately. The letter was forwarded to Cheltenham, thirty miles off, which was where Delabere lived.

Yet something within the Anglican Church was gradually beginning to stir. For the first time, in 1785, there is an item in the accounts for 'mending the bassoon', and in 1801 a new bassoon was purchased, partly financed by the church. Evidently music was back in the services, supplied by a troupe of local singers, fiddlers and blowers such as figure in Thomas Hardy's *Under the Greenwood Tree*, written towards 1870 but, like almost all Hardy's novels, set back much earlier in the century. The village depicted in this book, or the one in the more sombre *The Woodlanders*, represents very well the Taynton of the time, with the difference that whereas Hardy's rural, pre-lapsarian world is perpetually vulnerable to destruction by modern inventions, many Cotswold villages were to remain notably untouched by the huge changes the nineteenth century brought.

In 1791, when the French Revolution was becoming a bloodbath and news of this was filtering through England thanks to good coach routes and a wide dissemination of news-sheets, the plight of French Catholic priests was noted in Taynton and prayers were said for them. This would never have happened thirty years earlier, when the Catholic faith was still, in theory, proscribed. By the end of the century the costs of confirmations were appearing regularly in the accounts. And in 1809, for the first time, is an item '1 Pound of candels', those previously abhorred signs of suspect ritual. The same year a 'communion cope' was purchased. The year before (the year also in which a special collection was made for the relief of British soldiers languishing as prisoners of war in France) there is an odd item of one shilling for 'carriage of books'. Several years later, when one of the routine inventories of church goods is being made, the famous books about martyrs and Quakers have disappeared, but there is now a reading desk (lectern), a communion cloth, a pulpit cushion and even a small stove. We would begin to recognise the place as the church of our own childhood.

By this time William Meyrick has appeared, so getting rid of the books, with their glorification of sectarian violence, was probably his idea. He was Delabere's third curate, appointed in 1806. The following year, for the first time, a proper record of Vestry meetings began to be kept, which must have been at Meyrick's instigation also. Yet another Pittaway, Edward, possibly the son of the previous one, was appointed parish clerk. The rate for the job had now risen to £3 10 shillings per annum. In 1809 it was resolved in a meeting that the church 'shall be forthwith placed in a respectable state of repair, suitable to the purpose of the public worship of Almighty God'. Delabere himself was present on that occasion, but he can hardly have been the chief promoter of the idea or he would have raised the matter before. He died the following year and Meyrick was appointed vicar in his place, the role for which he seems to have been angling. One is tempted to think of him as Hardy's Mr Maybold in *Under the Greenwood Tree*:

> '"The first thing he did when he came here was to be hot and strong about church business" . . . "The next thing he do do is think about altering the church, until he found 'twould be a matter o'cost and what not and then not to think no more about it . . . And the next thing was to tell the young chaps that they were not on no account to put their hats in the christening font during service . . ."'

The absent and now deceased Delabere may be seen as Hardy's Mr Grinham, the late vicar, whose hands-off approach suited the village quite well: 'Why, he never troubled us with a visit from year's end to year's end. You might go anywhere, do anything: you'd be sure never to see him . . . There's virtue in a man's not putting a parish to spiritual trouble.' 'And there's this here man never letting us have a bit o' peace . . .'

Meyrick must have achieved some repairs to Taynton church, since it was during his incumbency that Agnes Harman's lead coffin plate was disinterred. But his time for not leaving his parishioners in peace was unnaturally short. For as early as March 1811 he was petitioning the Bishop, the same who had called Delabere to order over the charity accounts, for leave of absence from the parish for two years 'on account of the unfitness of the parsonage house'.

Several possibilities suggest themselves. One is that the vicarage really was in a bad state, in spite of the smartening up it had received some fifty years before. Maybe lowly tenants had occupied it during Delabere's prolonged absence and maltreated it, or maybe it had even been left shut up and was therefore deteriorating. Another possibility is that Meyrick was hoping for some church funding ('Queen Anne's Bounty') to do further works on the vicarage. It has also been suggested to me that Meyrick may have held at least one other parish elsewhere in addition to Great Barrington. Such 'pluralism' was beginning to be disapproved of: might he have been looking for a good excuse for simplifying his duties for a while? Especially since, in the year of Delabere's death, a clergyman brother of Lord Dynevor conveniently came to live in Great Barrington. But no other parishes appear for Meyrick on the not very reliable Church of England database, and his active career in the Church seems to have been brief. Instead of returning to Taynton at the end of the two years' leave the Bishop granted him, he resigned, presumably forfeiting an agreed indemnity. Did his faith waver? Or was he simply too intelligent and entrepreneurial for the bucolic life of a country parson?

Another young man was appointed: Frederick Raymond Barker. He appears to have been the 'foster son' (possibly therefore the illegitimate son) of John Raymond, a gentleman of London. Rather surprisingly, his sparse record seems to indicate a marriage in 1806 when he was only twenty. He subsequently took a BA in 1810 and an MA in 1813, and was established in Taynton the following year. In the period of Meyrick's absence no doubt the neglected vicarage had been put back in order as intended, with any roof leaks, warped doors, rising damp or rat infestation attended to. This is also probably the time when the first large, stone-floored kitchen was added to the house's eastern end, with a bedroom or bedrooms above and a pitched roof at right angles to the main roof. The well immediately outside was still not yet built over, but a pump may have been put on it now to supply a kitchen sink.

At all events, Barker seems to have lived in the house: he was very much present for the next few years at marriages and baptisms. But the Vestry minute-keeping was, for the time being, abandoned, and there is no very evident record in the accounts of the significant work on the church that Meyrick had called for, except for some gravel-path making. Then, in July 1819, Frederick Barker died at only thirty-three. Plague and ague-fevers were things of the past and vaccination against smallpox was becoming general among educated people, but tuberculosis was a significant problem of the period. The Katherine Gresham of Limpsfield who married a Leveson-Gower died of tuberculosis in 1808, after only four years of marriage, leaving three very young children. The poet John Keats died of it in 1821, and the entire Brontë family was to succumb to it over the next generation. One can only speculate on probabilities, but poor Barker was buried in his own churchyard by an otherwise unknown Richard Wilbraham Ford, as officiating minister – perhaps a clerical friend?

It was then that the joint parishes were taken on by Thomas Lewes, twenty-seven years old and recently ordained. He was a protégé of the Dynevors since he hailed, like them, from an ancient Carnarvonshire family. Like Stiles in the previous century, he never married. He was to remain in Taynton for fifty-five years, dying at the age of eighty-two. His resolute character was to set its stamp on the village and on the vicarage for much of the Victorian era.

Chapter IX

BACK TO SURREY, WITH JANE AUSTEN

On the face of it, around 1800 Limpsfield in Surrey, the future location of the girls' school, would have appeared to be a classic English village, not unlike Taynton but bigger, and a little more animated. Whereas Taynton had the significant town of Burford less than two miles away, Limpsfield's nearest neighbours were two other large villages, Godstone and Westerham, respectively half a dozen miles in one direction and a little more in the other. Oxted, which today is flourishing commuterland, only a mile from Limpsfield and with no open country in between, did not exist in 1800 or for most of that century, since it was a creation of the railway and a fairly late one at that (see Chapter X). There was just an isolated hamlet called Oxted, further west along the main road, with its own church. This meandering road, connecting Limpsfield with Westerham and Godstone, ran, as the M25 motorway does today, under the lee of the North Downs, that steep natural barrier with London traditionally distant on the far side.

Limpsfield therefore had always had to be more self-sufficient than Taynton: already, by 1800, there was not just a baker's there but a butcher's and a chandler's or 'candle-maker's', (in practice by that period a general store). Because Limpsfield village had a road through it

there were also at least three inns, the Bull next to Stanhopes, the White Hart and the Bell, whereas Taynton
never achieved an inn actually in the village, just a few
housewives who brewed ale. The population of Limpsfield parish at this time was 727, about twice that of
Taynton, but this included some outlying settlements on
the edge of Limpsfield's still-extensive common lands.
There were, as in Taynton, a few substantial tenant
farmers, and the rather fine old timbered houses lining
the one street indicate that, as in the Cotswolds, there
had been money to be made in the district for generations. Although the general parish records do not go
back as far as those of Taynton, one finds a similar pattern
of family names running down the decades. Millses,
Sandilands, Stears, Dunns, Jarretts, Outtrams or Outtrins,
and especially an extensive dynasty of Lovelands, occur
and recur.

In addition, just to complete the image of a storybook
village, Limpsfield had the Gresham family, whom we
have encountered already in the Stanhope Deeds. At the
beginning of the nineteenth century the name was about
to change, through marriage, to Leveson-Gower
(pronounced Looson-Gore), but it was still the same
enduring family line. They had been almost continuously
in residence in their house on the downs at Titsey since
they had bought it, and by and by many other Surrey
manors, in the sixteenth century, when the upheaval of
the Reformation brought much land on to the market.
They rebuilt it later that century in more splendid style
– it was to be revamped again twice more – and also
owned a house known as Hookwood on land in Limpsfield adjoining the land that was to become part of Stanhopes.

For most of the time since Tudor days the Greshams
had been very visible lords of the manor. They presided,
sometimes with a jury of local men, over regular manor
courts to adjudicate on issues such as defaulting tenants,

drunkenness, blocked watercourses, straying cattle and – perennially – encroachment on common manorial lands, 'the lord's waste'. In the early days punishments were even meted out, but later these became small fines or simply admonitions. The records of these courts had always been kept in Latin. During the Commonwealth they went (by order of Parliament) into English, and after the Restoration many manors retained this modernisation, but Limpsfield returned to the Latin form. The Greshams were Royalists; in fact their house at Titsey had been confiscated under the Commonwealth, but was given back in 1660, along with the baronetcy. One can see why, once restored to their own, they reverted to the old ways, and they would have had well-paid lawyers and clerks to keep up the Latin tradition. In 1709 the steward of the court was one Henry Streatfield or Streatfeild (both spellings remained in use) of the family which, we know, was to provide a wife for Clement Samuel Strong of Stanhopes late in the century, and was eventually to intermarry with the Leveson-Gowers.

English did not replace Latin entirely in the court records till 1733, but English sentences began to creep in earlier, presumably because it dawned on the current Gresham (Sir Marmaduke) that it was somewhat useless laying down the law for manorial tenants in a language no one but lawyers and doctors used any longer, especially now that many of the tenants could read quite well in their own tongue. In 1728, and again the following year, we find: 'That the several tenants of this manor have the right and liberty to dig, cull and carry away for their own private uses (but not to sell) any chalk, stones and gravel, sand, loam, brakes, bushes, broom, Goss [gorse] and Scrubs being upon the Lord's waste.' In other words, manorial landholders might, but no one else. One has the impression that the Greshams and those who came after them had a great sense of their own responsibility and position, even when, in the middle decades of the eighteenth century, a series of temporary 'lords' succeeded one another rapidly. They all tried to be fair, one generation after another, but after three centuries a certain asperity creeps in, when it is felt that excessive advantage is being taken of the copyholders' privileges. In 1885 one case of illicit stone-digging went far beyond the manor court and ended up in the Queen's Bench, with the current Leveson-Gower lord declaring: 'Of late great liberty and licence have been taken by cottagers exercising fancied rights . . . Inhabitants as such, whether poor or rich, have absolutely no common rights.' It was spelt out that no manorial tenant could delegate his rights to others, and that henceforth 'no one further can plead ignorance'.

It must be said that, after one major piece of enclosure to make themselves a deer park in the early seventeenth century, the lords of the manor of Limpsfield seem to have been less guilty of appropriating common land to themselves than many other lords, and the amount of common land still in existence today in upland areas of the parish bears witness to this. At one point in the nineteenth century the Leveson-Gowers firmly repudiated a scheme put forward by a landowner in another large local house which, had it been implemented, would certainly have resulted in the loss of most of the commons. The long existence of the manor courts was finally extinguished in 1922, when surviving, vestigial manorial rights to gravel, bushes, beekeeping etc. were ended by Act of Parliament and very modest sums were paid out in compensation to the remaining tenants, including a Streatfeild. This last entry of all in the long record is the only one to be typewritten.

Let us return more than a hundred years back to 1804, when the late Sir John Gresham's only daughter, Katherine Maria, married William Leveson-Gower, who was the son of an admiral, the grandson of a peer and cousin to the future Duke of Sutherland. How traditional, even feudal, that sounds. But sixty years earlier, when Marmaduke the Younger had died at only forty-two, and the trustees for the under-aged heir had felt obliged to sell off the lordship of the manor and some of the land, including the house and grounds at nearby Hookwood, things had been very different.[1] And it was then, in the mid-eighteenth century, that Limpsfield, in spite of its classic village air, in reality acquired a different character and a slightly different kind of local gentry.

Distances over bad roads, and the obstacle of the North Downs, which had always kept Limpsfield relatively untouched by London influences, were giving way to new perspectives. For Limpsfield was only twenty-one miles from London, and this, by the mid-decades of the eighteenth century, was a relatively easy journey on horseback, by post-chaise or on one of the regular coaches that were beginning to run, if not yet very fast, on a network of better roads then spreading across the Home Counties. By the later part of the century there was a turnpike (a road built or 'improved' and maintained by tolls) from Croydon to Redhill, to the west of Limpsfield; and in 1813 the turnpike treatment was given to the old track from Warlingham over the Downs, into Limpsfield and then on to Edenbridge.

Samuel Savage, the businessman of Hanover Square to whom the actual construction of the house that became Stanhopes is improbably attributed, knew what he was doing when he acquired the 99-year lease in 1735. The district was becoming accessible, and therefore desirable, to people who wished to live in the style of landed gentry but whose true source of income lay in the City or in its wharfs and docks. Of course there had always been a degree of upward social mobility out of trade and into land. In the sixteenth century, the Greshams themselves had exported cloth from England and imported spices from the East, before attaining a higher state. But it is only in the mid- to late eighteenth century that a pseudo-rural gentry begins to appear. The Strongs, who were to begin their long rental of Stanhopes near the end of the century, came 'from Middlesex'.[2] The Streatfeilds, who had acquired actual land in Limpsfield by then, came apparently from Wandsworth, a village ancillary to London comparable with Hornsey. Eugenia Stanhope herself, arriving with her two boys and her clandestine past, was a cosmopolitan stranger to the English countryside.

In 1742, on Marmaduke Gresham's early death, the lordship of the manor was sold as a commodity, along with a lot of land, to a businessman called John Godfrey, described as 'gentleman, formerly a linen-draper of Newgate Street, London'. The nouveau riche of the eighteenth and nineteenth centuries were regularly said to be 'linen-drapers' with the social implication of servile shop-attendance. The man who built or rebuilt Harringay House in Hornsey *c.* 1800 was so described, though the accumulated wealth such a house represented must already have carried him far from a shop counter, and the same would have been true of John Godfrey. By the nineteenth century there was even a phrase 'linen-draper's port', used to refer sneeringly to a provision of wine not up to the standard expected from a true gentleman's cellar. Clearly, in an era when social mobility was actually very great, it was important for those who had safely achieved some social status to keep other aspirants in their place.

John Godfrey also acquired Hookwood House, another Gresham property, and apparently lived there. He took his new status as lord of the manor seriously: he held a manor court in the very year of his purchase. But less than ten years later it had become 'the Court of Bourchier Cleeve Esqr, Lord of the said manor'. At the same time the memorable name Elisha Biscoe Esq. appears as court steward. By 1760 Cleeve had died, and for much of the next decade his widow figures in the record as lady of the manor in her own right. She seems to have married again in 1769, and the manor was then looked after by Elisha Biscoe and another as trustees, with someone else as steward. By 1771 a Charles Goring was lord of the manor, and courts were being held at the Bull Inn. In 1778 the commodity changed hands yet again, in favour of a lord called John Scawen. Sir John Gresham finally managed to buy the whole package back again in 1792, fifty years after it had been sold while he was a minor. Nine years remained to him in which to enjoy his achievement.

Hookwood House itself, with its surrounding land, was left by Godfrey to his cousin Marmaduke Hilton or Hylton, another Londoner in lucrative trade – Marmadukes clearly had an affinity with Limpsfield – who died in 1768 and is buried in Limpsfield church. He in turn left the property in a lifetime trust to his three unmarried sisters with, as ultimate heir, his business partner Vincent Biscoe, presumably a son or nephew of the useful Elisha. Vincent Biscoe had the luck or the astuteness to marry Mary Seymour, a descendant of that ancient family which had produced Henry VIII's one fragile male heir, and also the Lord Protector, Duke of Somerset. Mary died very young, possibly in childbirth as her ancestor Jane Seymour had done. Through his mother's family, the baby became a viscount, and so the social transformation of the Biscoes was complete.

This Viscount Vincent Hilton Biscoe continued to live in Hookwood, which he rebuilt as an imposing Georgian residence, till his wife died in 1840. Then he leased the property back to the Leveson-Gowers and retreated to Cheltenham. There are memorials to the Biscoes in and around Limpsfield church, including one to a baby who lies in the church in a grimly spacious vault next to that occupied by Eugenia Stanhope.

* * *

It is easy to envisage all these people, living in their newly and elegantly stuccoed houses, driving round in the light carriages that could now run on the more smoothly surfaced roads: men in tight breeches and cutaways, women in high-waisted dresses, as characters in a Jane Austen novel. Easy, and also instructive. Let us take, as most relevant, *Emma*, written in 1814–15. *Emma* is set in the (fictional) 'large and populous' village of Highbury, said to be sixteen miles from London and clearly somewhere to the south of it. The real-life large and populous Limpsfield was only a little further from London. Emma's father, an archetypal fusser, is always anxious at the prospect of his other daughter and her young family making the great journey from the capital, but that is because he is living in the past; other people undertake the journey with ease. Highbury has one unequivocally upper-class resident, Mr Knightley, who lives in Donwell Abbey – no doubt his ancestors acquired it at the Reformation. He apparently owns most of the land round about, some of which he rents to the substantial if not yet quite gentlemanly farming family, the Martins. Mr Knightley is, as you might expect, a local Justice of the Peace, and we occasionally glimpse him heading off to talk to other men on 'parish matters'. (This being an Austen novel, we never hear what these matters might be, or what the impact on Highbury might be of any event beyond its confines.)

Mr Knightley's younger brother, who is a lawyer in London, has already married Emma Woodhouse's elder sister. Knightley is, if you will, a Gresham/Leveson-Gower figure. The Woodhouses, living in a large house called Hartfield, sequestered by 'lawns and shrubberies' but actually part of Highbury, are the 'first in consequence' in that place, and have 'no social equals' – except of course Mr Knightley, living a mile or two away in unimpeachable rural seclusion. But are they themselves really quite Mr Knightley's equals? We hear that they 'had been settled for several generations at Hartfield . . . the younger branch of a very ancient family', and that Mr Woodhouse owns very little land but has £30,000 from 'other sources', which Emma will eventually inherit. In other words, this huge sum derives from City investment, probably including profits from trade with the East or West Indies. The Woodhouses are, on a Highbury scale, the Biscoes. And there is no one else. Or rather, there are a number of other people, besides all the scarcely mentioned villagers, but they are each tellingly categorised. There is Mr Weston, a 'native of Highbury, born of a respectable family which for the last two or three generations had been rising in gentility and prosperity'. He has been 'engaged in trade' in London with his brothers before going into the army (more acceptable), and thus has earned enough to buy 'a little estate . . . which he had always longed for'. He has made the subtle error of marrying, in the past, an upper-class girl, now dead, whose relations patronise him. He subsequently marries Emma's governess-companion, which clearly, though the fact is never stated, everyone thinks more suitable.

We are told that the only other people the Woodhouses mix with socially are Mrs Bates, the widow of a former vicar, who lives with her daughter 'in a very small way'; and Mrs Goddard who runs a tiny, genteel girls' boarding school and harbours a mysterious parlour-boarder whom Emma fantasises is the illegitimate offspring of some nobleman. Disappointingly, she turns out to be 'the daughter of a tradesman'. Mr Elton, the socially pretentious vicar and his gushing wife also come from 'trade', but the Church confers a certain status on them (see Mrs Bates). Otherwise, there are some unnamed 'half-gentlemen', probably churchwardens, who attend the whist club at the Crown Inn. And there are the Coles.

'The Coles had been settled some years in Highbury

and were a very good sort of people, friendly, liberal and unpretending; but, on the other hand, they were of low origin, in trade, and only modestly genteel.' They have recently got richer, enlarged their house, engaged more servants and begun giving dinner-dances.

Thus, the prototype of edgy, rural society in villages all round the London orbit in the early years of the nineteenth century. Real-life correlates of all these people are to be found in the short lists of those in Limpsfield sufficiently well-off to pay the Land Tax and/or significant Church Rates. Godfrey, Leveson-Gower, Biscoe, Strong, Mrs Scawen the widow of a former lord of the manor, Miss Streatfeild, the Reverend Mayne and, for a while, a mysterious Moses Boorer – the same few names crop up every season, with the lord of the manor and the rector liable for much the largest amounts. Evidently successive rectors in the parish, who held a lot of glebe land in their own right and whose living alone was worth almost £700 a year, were a more distinguished lot than Jane Austen's Mr Elton. The late-eighteenth-century ones, however, seem to have been as relaxed, not to say negligent, in their duties as the Cheltenham-dwelling John Delabere, vicar of Taynton. The Reverend Legh Hoskins Masters, who was the Limpsfield rector for the last twenty years of the century, was a member of the family who owned the manor of Oxted. He lived very comfortably there, employed a curate to do the work in Limpsfield, but did not hesitate to pocket money for his Land Tax and Window Tax which was actually taken from the Poor Rate.

Not till 1807 did the parish get a rector more on the new, earnest model that signalled the age to come. This was Robert Mayne, who had been brought up by his grandmother in a large house in Kent, one of four orphaned sons of an MP and failed banker. The Rev. Mayne and his large family were very much present in Limpsfield for the next thirty-three years. A tomb-sized tablet listing him, his wife and eight of their nine progeny was finally erected in the church by the last surviving son (a barrister) whose own name was added when he died aged seventy-seven, sixty years after his father had arrived in the parish. They had clearly taken root there.

For a different perspective on this kind of rural society, one may turn to Cobbett, who was making his survey and condemning the state of England at just the same time that Austen was writing her novels, but from a very different vantage point. For one thing, he had a keen awareness of how London was spreading, particularly in the post-1815 building boom:

> In quitting the great Wen, we go through Surrey . . . towards Croydon between rows of houses, nearly half the way and the whole way is nine miles. There are erected within these four years, two entire miles of stock jobbery houses on this one road, and the work goes on with accelerated force . . .
>
> The war and paper-system [the introduction of banknotes, which Cobbett deeply distrusted] has brought in nabobs, negro-drivers, generals, admirals, governors, commissaries, contractors, pensioners, sine-curists, commissioners, loan-jobbers; not to mention the long and *black list* in gowns and three-tailed wigs. [lawyers] You can see but few good houses not in possession of one or other of these. These, with the parsons, are now the magistrates . . .

He contrasts these with the old-time 'native' gentry – 'attached to the soil, known to every farmer and labourer from childhood, frequently mixing with them . . . practising hospitality.'[3] However, Cobbett's apparently hard-nosed view has its own sentimentality, for most of the native gentry he mourns had once, like the Greshams, acquired their lands through activities elsewhere, and some of the newcomers with professions were in fact the younger sons of these same old established families.

In 1819 Limpsfield church expenses included new bell ropes, clock repairs and a new bible. In 1822–23 the church underwent some rebuilding (bricks laid by a Loveland) and for the first time a proper vestry-room was constructed, with a stove, for meetings. A fund was also started for an organ to replace the amateur musicians in the gallery. (One wonders if, like Hardy's village musicians in *Under the Greenwood Tree*, the local music-makers were annoyed by this.) Among those contributing to the organ fund were the usual names. Two Biscoes, older and younger, produced respectively £10 and one guinea; Rev. Mayne came up with £10, plus another sum of between two and three pounds collected 'through some friends'; various Leveson-Gowers gave £7, the Strongs £10, and a clergyman son of the Strongs, who was living in Limpsfield in his own house, gave two guineas. Miss Streatfeild, who was Mrs Strong's sister, gave £5.

There was also Henry Cox, who gave £4 initially but later a great deal more. He had made his appearance in the district in 1817, having bought a large, isolated old house called Trevereux that had previously been occupied by the Sandilands, a long-standing farming family. Cox rechristened it Trevereux Park. In time he became a churchwarden, overseer of the highways and pillar of the community for many years (he lived till the age of ninety), but in the early days he was not accorded in the parish records the gentleman's dignity of being called Esquire. Evidently, in Austen terms, he was a Mr Cole. Aided by his brother, who was a lawyer in London, he researched records and claimed the lordship of a small local manor that had not held a court for nearly forty years. He seems to have made himself unpopular in an abortive attempt to extract obsolete quit-rents from the tenants. Throughout his life he involved himself in disputes over paths and waterways with neighbouring tenant farmers; and there was a long-running battle, punctuated by lawyers' letters, with the Leveson-Gowers about his right to dig gravel out of the commons.

However, it would seem that face to face he was a genial fellow, and in the end most disputes with neighbours were resolved in the interests of maintaining 'our cordial relations'. He made and kept voluminous notes about previous rights and practices, as recounted to him by aged labourers. He and his wife (who was more than twenty years younger than him) harboured for years an embarrassing relative called Solomon Penury Cox, who was said to be paralysed and who left a diary behind him cataloguing the alcoholic habits that eventually finished him off in 1850. A final piece of Cox family bounty, after both Henry and his wife were dead in the 1880s, was 'a patent warming apparatus' given to the church by their son-in-law in their memory. The long centuries of sitting in greatcoats in cold churches were finally drawing to an end.

We shall meet someone I believe to have been a member of the same Cox family in Stroud Green, Hornsey.

In the 1830s, ten years after the works on the church and the organ purchase, the next plan was the acquisition of two rooms to convert into a school. No one familiar with the huge desire to Improve the working classes, that swept through the upper middle classes from the beginning of the Victorian era, will be surprised to hear that a bazaar was held for the sale of Fancy Articles to support this cause, or that this was run by Mrs Biscoe, her relative the Hon. Mrs Adams, the Misses Leveson-Gower and the Misses Mayne. The sum realised seems extraordinarily large – over £221, at a time when an agricultural labourer earned much less than a pound a week and £300 per annum was considered just about enough for a man with a small family to support a genteel lifestyle. Can the sale of beaded purses, fringed writing-table covers and Berlin woolwork, the handiwork of one set of ladies sold to the same set of ladies, really have raised all that?

There was certainly money in Limpsfield. That is obvious when one looks at the churchwardens' accounts, as kept by the parish clerk, in comparison with those of Taynton. Between 1814 and 1837 the clerk of Limpsfield was John Dunn, of an old village family. He seems to have been baptised in 1763, so he was just over fifty when he took on the job, replacing a Harding of another old family. The expenses Dunn listed, much of which consisted of money paid to himself, involved mainly work on 'the Church and Ornaments and the Yard', with much purchasing of new mops and brooms, and things for 'dressing and draping the church' at Whitsun and Christmas. 'To oyl for the clock', at three and a half shillings a time, was a regular item. It is to be hoped that the entry 'John Dunn a Bill for Wine and liquors £2.4s.10d' refers to communion wine, though in a later year there is another entry 'Wine for the Sacrament and other purposes'; and also 'a Taylors bill'. Dunn was well placed to supply wine, since the rates for the early 1820s reveal that he was the landlord in the Bull Inn, conveniently situated near the church – and, as it happened, near Stanhopes also.

John Dunn was, in his way, assiduous. He also listed fees he received as clerk for weddings and funerals, especially the last – items which hardly seem to figure in the Taynton accounts, presumably because much was traditionally done there for free. Dunn himself commonly received a present at the funerals of the richer families. One example from 1814, the first of many, was when Richard Sanderland (sic) the farmer from Trevereux, was buried in a vault. The clerk's fee was a guinea plus the gift of 'a silk hat band'. In 1820, when a sixteen-year-old son of the Rev. Mayne was 'buried in a brick grave' the fee was ten shillings. Six years later, when the boy's mother died, there was no fee but another silk hatband. In contrast, when a 'traveller' (gipsy in this case, one of many who frequented the Limpsfield commons) died in the parish workhouse and was buried, the fee was only four shillings, and the burial of a dead baby one shilling. Four shillings too was the fee at the burial of a Limpsfield man who 'Dyd in London thought to have taken Something to shorten his days from appearance of his corps much destroyed'.

The wealthy citizens of the parish favoured vaults, sometimes as much as 12 feet deep (presumably to leave room for relatives), and these attracted a higher fee. In 1817 two guineas were received rather belatedly from 'Mrs Stanhope for a vault in the church', which had been constructed the year before. This cannot of course have been Eugenia, more than thirty years dead by then, but one of her daughters-in-law. As she bought it in her own name I think it was probably Elizabeth, the widow of Eugenia's younger son Philip, rather than Charles's wife. At all events, the purchase was prescient, for four years later the lady was occupying the vault and her brother-in-law Charles Stanhope was paying the clerk's fee of one guinea to erect a monument on it. He clearly continued to feel an attachment to Limpsfield, where the house that bore the family name was now his sole responsibility. Dunn regularly reported receiving two shillings from Mr Charles Stanhope 'for shewing visitors the church'.

Add to all this, sundry small sums for proclamations at the church gate – 'crying a sheep-fair', 'crying a lost horse', or 'a lost watch' – plus larger ones for informing farmers of manorial land who lived beyond the parish that their tithes were due – and one can see that Dunn's was a comfortable post. When he was appointed in 1814 his annual fee for general duties around the church was fixed at £10 per annum. (Edward Pittaway, the Taynton clerk, was getting less than half as much at the same period.) However, almost at once Dunn seems to have extended his duties to justify awarding himself £5 a quarter, double the agreed amount. Matters caught up with him on 20 June 1822, when one can read this indignant entry in the book:

> The Oficers of the Vestory held that Day at the Church redused my pay to 10 guineas a Year to do all the Work of the Church find Brooms Wash Communion Linnen & Surplises not to hav any thing to do with the Church Yard & paths in Cleaning them . . . This Reduction took place back to Christmas 1821.

He continued, however, as clerk, until his death in his mid-seventies, many years later. Every Christmas he received generous tips from Mr Mayne and the handful of other well-to-do persons, all of which he faithfully recorded.

Today, it is easy to treat someone like John Dunn, with his eye to the main chance, his expeditious spelling and lack of punctuation, as a faintly comic minor figure, just one of those 'endless altered people' walking through the centuries up the church path as in Philip Larkin's poem, 'An Arundel Tomb'. But he was a real person, as three dimensional and complex as we are today – or as was Margaret Harding, she who used empty spaces in an old Limpsfield register to write bleakly humorous little verses almost a century before.[4] Dunn was intelligent, and in spite of his evident lack of formal education he had cultivated a fine hand. Alongside his main occupation of running the pub he had secured valuable extra part-time work as the clerk. He seems to have taken a pride in this post: he inscribed in his record that he had been 'chosen', and he enjoyed meeting people. He was interested in everything; moreover, he bothered to go through the register of baptisms for the previous century and copy out, on the back of his clerk's record, all those concerning his own family and another local family that was presumably his mother's. What would he have made, today, of the opportunities provided by the internet?

In his lifetime he saw some social change in Limpsfield and the country round but nothing spectacular or destructive. He died just before dramatic changes began sweeping over the face of those parts of Britain not obviously touched by the industrial revolution. On one of the last pages in his book, the year before he disappeared, well into his seventies, he noted: 'Gent gave me 2/6 [two and a half shillings] for putting a paper on Church Door about a Rale Road'.

As it turned out, it was to be almost fifty years before the railway came near to the doors of Limpsfield, and, as everywhere in the country, the arrival or non-arrival of this transformative behemoth was to determine what the place became.

*　　*　　*

During the nineteenth century the population of Limps-field grew modestly but steadily. From 727 in 1801, it increased to 746 in 1811, and 918 in 1821. By 1831 it had reached 1,042, with large numbers of people in farming and agricultural labouring, in retail, manufacturing or artisan occupations, plus '8 Wholesale Capitalists Clergy and other Educated men', nineteen male servants of age twenty and over, eleven under twenty and fifty-two female servants. Thirty-five years later, when another two ephemeral railway plans had come and gone, the population would still only be about 1,300. The 'stock-jobbers houses', that would one day swell Oxted into a suburban town and line the road from it to Limpsfield, still lay safely in the future.

Chapter X

LIMPSFIELD CHANGES,
SLOWLY BUT INEVITABLY

By the first proper Census of 1841 both the old Strongs were tucked away in their last home, the brick vault in the churchyard. The house they had lived in so long was described in the rates as 'Mansion buildings, Land Etc. in Village, owned by Charles Stanhope Esq.' The rate was currently being paid by Miss Streatfeild. One may assume, from Miss Streatfeild's earlier presence in the parish, making Christmas donations and so forth, that the two elderly sisters had joined forces in the house following Mr Strong's death in 1827. In the days long before radio or television, and well before the coming of gas or electric light would make evening reading easy, the importance of suitable company in the home, especially in winter, was well understood by all classes. The sisters were fortunate to live in a congenial, intricately linked circle. One of the Strong sons, the Rev. Clement, was married to a Biscoe daughter, and in 1840 a Leveson-Gower daughter was born who would later marry a William Streatfeild. One of their sons was to become Bishop of Lewes and the father of Noel Streatfeild, the celebrated children's writer of the mid-twentieth century.[1]

Understandably, Miss Streatfeild does not seem to have

Watercoloured drawing of 'Stanhope' dated 1821, showing the still-unmade
high road in front and the revamp of the original house that had by then taken place.

remained consistently in the big house once her sister was dead. She was not in residence when the census was taken in 1841, although she was still assessed there for the Poor Rate in 1843. In fact she died in the March of that year, aged eighty-four. I was frustrated for some time because I could not find out who lived in Stanhopes next. From the 1840s onwards proper listings of whole populations were made every ten years, so it is often possible to trace the life of a house, as well as the evolution of families, from one decade to another. However, an incidental absence on census night, or the simple fact of a tenant's stay falling between the ten-year dates, means that that source of information is no use. So it proved to be with Stanhopes.

In 1848 the entire property, along with other extensive parcels of land that the Stanhope family had evidently acquired over the years, was put up for sale by his heirs after Charles Stanhope's death. From the Bill of Sale we shall find out just what the house was like then. But who had been living there for much of the 1840s?

In 1845 the church was subjected to another round of Improvements (always written thus with a capital letter). The eighteenth-century galleries were removed, as were the old box pews that had allowed comfortably off families to snooze in peace, use chamber pots or let the small children play on the floor, seen by no one but possibly the rector in his pulpit. Among the list of people giving donations for the work I found the names of such of the usual suspects as were still alive, plus a sprinkling of newer ones. A Mr Bayley was now a churchwarden, along with Henry Cox, and these two had given the most substantial amounts. A handsome sum of £10 was also donated by a Mr E.P. Sells. His wife had given £5 as had Mrs Cox – it seems that the ladies had got together.

Sells, apart from being a rather unusual name, will mean nothing to most people reading this page, but for me it leapt to the eye. For, in researching and writing a previous book entirely unconnected with Limpsfield[2] the name had become very familiar to me. The Sells family, who were obscure Thames ferrymen in the early eighteenth century, had, by the 1750s, become riverside dealers in shipments of coal, that black gold on which the industrial revolution would run. From father to son they prospered, built up the business, and a hundred years later the firm was amalgamating with others, eventually to become part of the Charringtons' coal empire. For almost exactly a century the Sells had lived on Bankside – very near, as it happened, to the stone yard where the stone sent down the waterways from Taynton and Burford was shaped for the rebuilding of St Paul's, which stood directly opposite. They carried on the coal business there, variously occupying one or another old house or several, as sons or nephews of the family came and went. I knew that by the middle of the nineteenth century they were moving off to a more gentlemanly lifestyle in greener places, in a way entirely typical of the period, but I had not discovered just where, at that point, they had gone.

E.P. stood for Edward Perronet (the Sells family had Huguenot connections). There were to be four generations of E.P.s succeeding one another through the nineteenth and twentieth centuries, but the most likely candidate for Limpsfield is Edward Perronet I, born in 1788. His son, Edward Perronet II, would only have been thirty in 1845, and there is documentary evidence that he remained active in business and in London: he continued to serve on the parish Vestry for Bankside till 1849. Edward Perronet I, redoubtable father of ten children all of whom survived to adulthood, had also been an assiduous vestryman, Poor Law overseer and so forth, but although he still owned the properties on Bankside in the 1840s his name disappears from the Vestry records there. He continued to be treasurer of the parish schools, but when a testimonial to his long voluntary services there was presented to him in 1852 it was stated that 'his residence in the country has obliged the Treasurer to resign the office', which may suggest a residence by that time well established with only occasional journeys to town.

I was delighted to have found the dynamic E.P. Sells again. But readers may imagine my further satisfaction when I came across him in the Limpsfield Poor Rates for October 1843 as occupying a 'house and land in village'. The same house is listed in subsequent entries as 'late Strong': the rateable value is substantial.[3] What is telling is that the extent of the property is marked: 4 acres, 3 rods. That is the exact dimensions of the property put up for sale by Stanhope's heirs and executors five years later. There was no other property of that size 'in the village'. I am therefore almost certain that the occupant of the house for some years in the 1840s was none other than my old friend from Bankside, once a hands-on waterman, now setting up as a country gentleman.

Following on Miss Streatfeild, in 1843 a Minton Sells unknown to me (a cousin of Edward Perronet?) was in Stanhopes, and he was still there in January 1844. By 1845 Edward Perronet Sells had taken over. We know that within months he was making a generous donation to the church building fund, and by 1847 he had replaced Mr Cox as one of the churchwardens. He was still in post the following year, when he turned sixty: apparently the transformation of himself and Mrs Sells into local gentry was working well. Yet then he disappears for good. By the end of 1848 the house is marked 'Empty' on the rating list and once again 'late Strong', as if the memory of the Sellses' relatively brief reign there soon faded. It was the following year that the place was put up for sale.

Perhaps E.P. Sells realised then that he could never afford to buy it and was unlikely to acquire any security of tenure at a reasonable rent. The South-Eastern Railway Company, an offshoot of the London and Dover

Railway, had planned a line from Croydon through the North Downs and had bought a ribbon of land for this very near Limpsfield village, described in the Land Tax listing as '193 rods long' (1,067.5 yards). Although in the end that was one of several railway initiatives that came to nothing (see Chapter XII), the expectation in the mid-1840s, at the height of the first major railway boom, must have been that land values in the district would rise. At the same time anxieties would have been raised in some minds as to whether the area would remain truly rural and 'genteel'.

But perhaps E.P. Sells, after a lifetime in the coal trade, favoured the railway? He may have hoped to benefit from the proposed line, and have been disappointed when it eventually became clear that Limpsfield was not, after all, going to enjoy a direct connection to town by train in the near future. Maybe, indeed, he had been a shareholder in the scheme and had lost money by it. At all events he left Limpsfield. I think he went to Bristol, where an unmarried sister was already living and where he seems to have had connections through the burgeoning Welsh coal trade. He lived to be eighty-five, in a world transformed both materially and socially from the one he had known as an eager and rather handsome young man on the banks of London's Thames.

The branch of the Stanhopes concerned with the Limpsfield house was not destined to flourish and multiply. Eugenia left the house to her younger son, Philip, who married an Elizabeth Daniel. Two daughters were born to them, of whom one survived to adulthood, christened Eugenia after her grandmother. Philip died while Eugenia was a child, and Elizabeth, she who apparently bought a vault in Limpsfield as if she had planned to establish herself there, did not live to be old. Eugenia II was newly orphaned when, in 1818, she married a John Keir Esq., described in her marriage settlement as being 'of the island of Madeira'. One may suppose that he was in the profitable international trade of either sugar or Madeira wine. However, in spite of Madeira's allegedly healthful airs, neither Eugenia nor her husband survived long; no children were born to them, and Eugenia's large settlement went to her uncle Charles, who thus became the sole heir to all the Limpsfield property.

Charles Stanhope had married, but had no children either. Once retired from Lincoln's Inn, he lived in then-select Clapham. His Will (a copy of which, along with Eugenia's settlement, has ended up alongside all the Deeds of the Limpsfield house) was made in 1840 when he must have been eighty years old. It details, with what seems old-bachelor care, books, pictures, miniatures, and bequests of humbler things to faithful servants – 'all my sheets, table linen and the cloathes and linen belonging to my deceased wife and all the six smaller Mahogany Chairs and Kitchen clock and two parlour carpets now in the garret . . .' He left numerous legacies to old friends, or to their sons and grandchildren, and £20 to the Rev. Clement Strong 'to be distributed by him at his discretion amongst the poor of the parish of Limpsfield'. The house there that bore his family name, and all the land purchased there over the years, he left to an Edward Morton Daniel, a solicitor of Melksham, in Wiltshire, and his wife Penelope.

Morton Daniel turns out to have been a nephew of Elizabeth Daniel, Charles's long-dead sister-in-law. The connection seems tenuous for such a substantial legacy, but Charles was also godfather to one of Morton Daniel's own nephews and he left money for this child's education. It appears that the Daniels had become his substitute family.

Five or six years after making his Will Charles was dead. The Morton Daniels, I discovered by chance, were then making plans to leave England for Adelaide in South Australia,[4] which was a recently established and rather idealistic free colony: it appealed to well-educated settlers since it had no convict past. (A couple of Sells sons emigrated there at the same period.) It is hard to imagine that the burgeoning Australian gold rush was an additional motive for the Morton Daniels, who had inherited so much in England. At all events, the house in Limpsfield, its grounds and three other significant landholdings in the parish, amounting to 23 acres in all, were put up for sale. The Bill of Sale 'by Auction, at Garroway's Coffee House, Cornhill, London, at 12 o'clock on Tuesday 29 August 1848' gives us the first accurate description of what the house was then like and what sort of person was expected to buy it:

> A substantial dwelling house . . . The village of Limpsfield is remarkable for its beauty and the healthiness of its situation. The neighbourhood is select and highly respectable; the roads are very good, and the property is most desirable as a retirement for a merchant or professional man. It is distant 10 miles from Croydon and 5 miles from the Godstone station on the South-Eastern Railway [actually the London & Brighton, whose newly built line had scuppered the proposed South-Eastern scheme] . . . Coaches pass Botley Hill (only 2 miles from the house) twice a day to and from the Croydon railway Station.
>
> The Homestead is well sheltered and adorned with an abundance of stately Timber and luxuriance of Shrubbery. The water is of excellent quality.
>
> There are a pew and a seat in the Church within a few minutes walk, which have always been occupied by the proprietors of this property.
>
> The House is placed above the road and possesses a pleasing and extensive prospect. It contains on the Ground Floor, a Dining Room, Breakfast Room, Gentleman's Room, Library and Water Closet; with

capital Cellars in the Basement; Butler's Pantry, Housekeeper's Room, Kitchen, Knife and Shoe House, Pantry, Brewhouse, Washhouse, Dairy, Coal-house and ample other conveniences, and 3 sleeping rooms over the offices for men servants.

On the First Floor, 6 Bedrooms, beside Store Closets.

On the Second Floor 3 sleeping rooms and Store Room . . .

There follow details of a cottage-turned-greenhouse, a mangle room, yet another manservant's room, a double coach house, various stables and a wood-house, as well as 'A Kitchen Garden, a Flower Garden Walled on 2 sides, and a Paddock of rich land (4 acres, 3 rods)'. Also 'a piece of Pasture Ground and ornamental plantation adjoining the Paddock' which was then let, on a 99-year lease with thirty-eight years left to run, to the Leveson-Gowers. This was towards Hookwood House, now vacated by the Biscoes, which the Leveson-Gowers were soon to let to Mountstuart Elphinstone, a former Governor of both Madras and Bombay.[5] There he wrote a two-volume history of India which is still valued. When he died in 1859 he left instructions that the chief mourner following his coffin was to be his Chinese cook, which duly happened but scandalised the village. It is hard to convey, today, just how exotic a Chinese would then have looked in an English country churchyard. Mountstuart Elphinstone never married, and, secure in his culture and intellect, had never cared what anyone thought of him.

One is glad to see that a water closet had now been introduced into Stanhopes, even if only on the ground floor. It is also clear that an extensive kitchen and other 'offices' had been constructed behind the old house, with the three sleeping rooms above for menservants. The female servants, of course, were to sleep well segregated from them, in the three top rooms within the house itself. The whole description suggests a rather male-orientated house, with a Library and a Gentleman's Room indicated rather than a drawing room. It seems designed to invite a wealthy buyer with grown sons who would keep horses, hunt and shoot in best country style, and need menservants to attend them. Mr Jenner, of the Bull Inn next door (the successor to John Dunn), would 'be prepared to appoint a person to shew the property'.

The first detailed Ordnance Survey map of the area, dating from twenty years later, does indeed show a back extension in place and one recognisable to me. This was later to be the school kitchens and domestic staff regions. Something, however, in the Bill of Sale bothered me: the nicely coloured little estate map that accompanies it shows the house without this back extension. Instead, the old barn that formed part of the property when Marmaduke Mills reconstructed it about 1740 appears on the map, sideways on to the house at a quite different angle. The Tithe map (1831) shows the same configuration.

For a while, I tried to convince myself that the extensive kitchens and servants' quarters mentioned in the Bill of Sale must somehow have been accommodated within the ex-barn, and that the purpose-built kitchen regions had only appeared later, in time for the Ordnance Survey. But eventually an architectural historian pointed out to me that the chief purpose of the Bill of Sale map (and the Tithe map) was to indicate the dimensions and shapes of the land-holdings, not the exact footprint of the buildings on them.[6] One may conclude that the solicitors involved in conveyancing the whole Stanhope property (possibly Edward Morton Daniel himself, in his professional role) had simply not felt it important to update the plan in that respect. The essential value was perceived as lying in the land itself, not in whatever bricks and mortar happened to be sitting on it.

In any case, as later became apparent to me, much confusion has been generated about the back-extension of Stanhopes alias the Manor House, which at one time in the late twentieth century was assumed to have been an old, separate institutional building in its own right. It is true that the two high, beamed-ceiling main rooms of the kitchen area, with the attic rooms above and a traditional tiled, pitched roof, are reminiscent of a building of the seventeenth century or even earlier. In addition, there are some genuinely old roof timbers visible in the attics along with many later ones. The conclusion reached by a knowledgeable person who examined the buildings in the mid-twentieth century, and whose notes now seem to have disappeared, was that the kitchens were indeed nineteenth century but that some of the timbers were much older and must have come from a dismantled building.[7] I think that building was the old barn.

No other trace of it remains today, though if one were to excavate a part of the lawns to the side of the Manor House one might find something . . . I do recall, in the 1950s, an odd, high corner-end of flint walling with the remains of a buttress, extending for a few feet along the side of the forbidden lawns, by the vegetable gardens where shivering big girls used to stand in the early mornings chivvying smaller girls into running. That wall too is now cut down to an unobtrusive garden height.

The conclusion has to be that the house was transformed and greatly extended during the Strong family's long tenancy, possibly in the 1820s or '30s. Odd though it may seem to us today, obsessed as we are with home-ownership and with the capital value of a house, it was then not at all uncommon for leasehold tenants to do substantial works simply to make their home more comfortable. We have seen that this may have happened already to Taynton vicarage in the eighteenth century, and it would again in the nineteenth.

The same was done in Limpsfield rectory. In 1841, when Robert Mayne had died and a Thomas Walpole took over, it was noted in the church register that the rectory was 'enlarged and improved' with a loan from Queen Anne's Bounty 'to which the rector the Rev. Thomas Walpole added a considerable sum of his own money'. Walpole, however, only remained in Limpsfield to enjoy his improved house for five years. He was obviously wealthy since he also built, largely at his own expense, a separate boys' school in addition to the mixed one set up ten years before. A later rector, Samuel Charlesworth, noted in the register that Walpole had kept for himself a trust fund set up by Mayne for the benefit of subsequent incumbents. This was a remarkable accusation to make in such a public way, and not necessarily true, since elsewhere he claimed that it was the trust fund set up by Walpole for the school that he, Walpole, had retained.

Charlesworth seems to have been given to grievances. He objected when an 'unsuitable' monument was put on the outside of the church, in his absence, above the grave of the two Elphinstones (see note 5). Still, in a time when the poor were no longer the concern of the parish, he did dispense twenty shillings a month (£1) of his own money to 'aged Widows and old men deserving of such relief, and two shillings to every labouring man's wife who bore a child', plus 'the sum which I expend in meat, wine, tea etc. for the sick and aged'.

But who, meanwhile, had bought Stanhopes?

The answer is that, in spite of the enticing Bill of Sale about the desirability and gentlemanly nature of the Homestead, with its abundance of stately timber, luxuriance of shrubbery and a pew in the church, no one came forward for it. By the time of the auction in the coffeehouse it had already been agreed by the Morton Daniels that the other parcels of land included in the Bill should

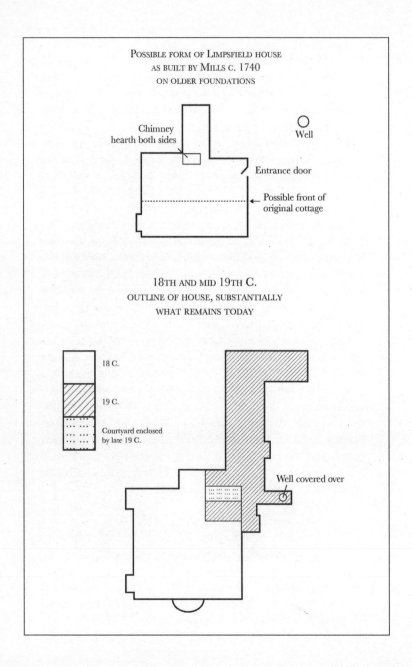

POSSIBLE FORM OF LIMPSFIELD HOUSE
AS BUILT BY MILLS C. 1740
ON OLDER FOUNDATIONS

○ Well

Chimney hearth both sides

Entrance door

← Possible front of original cottage

18TH AND MID 19TH C.
OUTLINE OF HOUSE, SUBSTANTIALLY
WHAT REMAINS TODAY

18 C.

19 C.

Courtyard enclosed by late 19 C.

Well covered over

The eighteenth- and nineteenth-century parts of Stanhopes – alias – the Manor House, seen from the lawns in the mid-twentieth century. Note the belfry on top and the shadow, far right, cast by the huge ilex tree out of shot.

be sold to the Leveson-Gowers, who already owned much property adjoining them. Evidently the Leveson-Gower project, to reacquire as much as possible of the manorial lands that had been lost by their feckless Gresham ancestor, was doing well. And, though the conveyance is missing, they must have decided to buy the house called Stanhopes and its grounds too. Otherwise these papers, and all the older Deeds relating to the house, would not have ended up in the Leveson-Gower collection in the local archive as part of their manorial holdings.

The Leveson-Gowers seem to have rented the house out to a number of different tenants during the 1850s. In the census of 1861 it was noted as being 'To Let' and was occupied only by two ageing Lovelands as caretakers: John Loveland, 'gardener and domestic servant', and his wife. And now, for the first time, it was called the Manor House. As we know, it had no entitlement to the name. Hookwood House, often occupied by Leveson-Gower relations, would have been a slightly more suitable candidate, though the true seat of the lord of the manor was Titsey Park, halfway up the Downs. But someone with a taste for grandeur (who?) had re-baptised the house in the village, and from now on, to avoid confusion with the housing estate called Stanhopes that would not appear till the late twentieth century, I shall refer to it as the Manor House.

By the 1870s in Limpsfield, as in many parishes all over England, another strenuous round of church Improvement had set in, much of it over-zealous and destructive of ancient fabric. (The vicar of Burford was a particular offender. It was, famously, after a public argument in the church between him and William Morris, that Morris founded the Society for the Protection of Ancient Monuments.) A photograph taken in Limpsfield church *c.* 1870 shows the chancel effectively reduced to a roofless ruin for rebuilding. Much of this was paid for, like so much else, by the Leveson-Gowers.

1870, too, is the start of the great era of documentation, and not one but two Directories (Kelly's and the Post Office one) give us a picture of what was generally agreed to be the 'large village' of Limpsfield. The population was not yet twice what it had been in 1800, for the nearest railway stations were still five and ten miles off as they had been twenty-one years before, but Limpsfield was probably the more thriving and self-sufficient for that. There were ten farmers in the parish, one of whom was also a brick-maker – a small but significant sign of greater urbanisation to come. There was a wheelwright, a baker, three carpenters, two grocers, two butchers (which meant, in those days, that they slaughtered their own meat), two blacksmiths, three shoe- and bootmakers, a builder (a Loveland, of course), an owner of a threshing machine, a cattle salesman, a plumber and glazier, a miller, a 'general shop keeper', another grocer combining his trade with drapery, and a 'draper, grocer, clothier, baker and dealer in new and second hand furniture'. There were two pubs, a post office, an insurance agent and a twice-weekly carrier's cart service to and from London. There were various National (i.e. Church of England) elementary and infant schools for both sexes, built on land donated by the Leveson-Gowers and funded by the inevitable church bazaars.

One feels that most of the inhabitants would rarely if ever have needed to go beyond a village which met so many needs so fully. Today, in Limpsfield's picturesque High Street, as in villages up and down England, there is only a handful of specialist shops (a bookshop, an interior decorator, a jeweller). The one remaining village-store-cum-post-office survives with volunteer labour.

Both 1870s Directories list, under 'private residents' (as distinct from carpenters, cowmen and schoolteachers) two gentlemen in the Manor House, Thomas Dent and John Wilkinson, who may have been there for some years already. I don't know just who Wilkinson was, but

Wilkinson was Thomas Dent's own second name, so presumably they were related. Thomas Dent was father of a large family, who were surely already in residence with him, for the census of the following year lists them all. Thomas, aged forty, was a 'barrister not in practice'; his wife was twenty-six. She must have had her first child at eighteen and not stopped since, for there were sons of eight, seven, six, four and one, a daughter of two, and another as yet unnamed baby girl of one month. (And there were more to come.) The centuries when parents of all classes had to resign themselves to the likelihood of losing several children in infancy were at last at an end. Stillbirths and infant deaths were still common among the villagers; in all classes there was the occasional child death from measles, diphtheria or scarlet fever, but smallpox, typhoid fever, cholera and tuberculosis were no longer much dreaded in clean, well ordered households. None of the Dent progeny figure in the burial records for the 1870s. Also in the Manor House when the census was taken was a monthly nurse (childbed nurse) of fifty-seven, and a children's nurse of twenty-two with a nurserymaid of sixteen to help her with all those little boys. There were, too, a parlour maid and a cook, both in their twenties. Since parlour maids did not scrub floors, one would assume that further help with cleaning and doing the washing came in daily from the village.

The Dent family were originally small farmers from Westmorland, but they had made a lot of money early in the nineteenth century in India and in China – probably, in those days, in the opium trade.[8] Were Thomas and his wife planning to settle permanently in this large house and grounds, living the idyll of country life which we recognise from previous incomers to Limpsfield, and which is still very familiar today in the villages of southern England? If so, they changed their minds, for they moved to Hertfordshire and eventually back to their native Westmorland where Thomas set up as squire. They sound a little like the Wilcoxes in E.M. Forster's *Howards End*, who stage a grand wedding in one of their temporary country seats and then move on again, 'leaving a little dust and a little money behind'. By 1881 the occupant of the Manor House was someone quite other, though just as typical, in his way, of the evolution of English society.

His name was Alex Mounterie Bell. He was then thirty-five, born in Scotland, with a wife one year younger, and they had a baby son. They had a middle-aged nurse for the baby, a cook, a housemaid, a scullery maid, and also a manservant of forty. What is distinctive is the unusually lengthy description entered under the householder's profession: 'MA Balliol College, Private tutor preparing young men for universities and army.' Lodging with them when the census was taken were six boys, or rather young men, aged seventeen to nineteen. No wonder this relatively young couple needed a big house and so many staff.

The existence of their cramming establishment (and many others to be found in the London suburbs and the Home Counties at the same period) was a sign of the times. After the shock of the Indian Mutiny, which followed on the near-disaster of the Crimean War, when the army was officered by incompetent aristocrats still mentally fighting the battle of Waterloo, it was decided that reforms were necessary. Gradually, in the teeth of opposition from diehard generals and ministers, these were brought in, mainly under Edward Cardwell, Gladstone's Secretary of State for War around 1870. There was to be a larger, nationally run army, better trained and less brutally treated. The sale of commissions was abolished. To be a gentleman and a good shot was no longer enough, for promotion was now by merit and officers received training at military schools such as Sandhurst and Woolwich. Military academies, preparing teenage boys for entry to these, mushroomed. At the same period a measure of high-Victorian seriousness had overtaken the Oxford and Cambridge colleges too; they were beginning to demand less drinking and more real scholarship. It was the role of men like Alex Bell to take on the large, not necessarily very bright sons of gentlemen, often with East India connections, who had not distinguished themselves at Public School unless by misbehaviour, and coach them into adequate shape to apply for military college or the universities.

It was during this period that a bell in a miniature belfry, engraved with the letters J. B., (B., of course, for Alex Bell, but why J., I wonder?) was put on top of the pitched roof of the back-addition. Part of this building was now probably the boys' dining room, and the sound of the summoning bell would have been audible all over the grounds and into the pasture of Hookwood. Some further sculleries, storerooms or servants' rooms seem to have increased the bulk of the back-extension at this time; and it was probably then that the well – obsolete with the arrival of piped water in Limpsfield – was built over. In the kitchen a fine iron cooking range, bigger than an ordinary domestic one, was fitted and surrounded with blue and white tiles. It is there today, newly revealed, after many decades covered over.

So the Manor House's transformation into a school had begun, with a significant loss of social status. Now that many roads were decently surfaced, well-to-do families tended to prefer houses in secluded spots outside villages: Victorian brick edifices with more modern conveniences. And the status of Limpsfield was beginning to change also. In 1886 a large Church Missionary Society home for children was opened there, in a brand new building of blood-curdlingly Gothic character. A later generation referred to it as 'the cannibals' larder' or made jokes about St Trinian's.[9] Assorted convalescent homes soon followed. The district, in fact, was beginning to be suburbanised, and would soon be more so. A railway line from London to Oxted was finally opened in 1884. Modern Oxted began to be constructed in a convincing 'Tudor' style, complete with carving on the beams, that owed much to William Morris's enthusiasm for all things traditional. It was a distinguished forerunner of the mass of more degraded and formulaic 'Tudorbethan' housing that was soon to line the arterial roads of south-east England. Ten years after the railway opened, the population of Limpsfield was 1,600 and said to be steadily increasing.

And yet, in 1891, Mr Bell was not there. The house, seemingly, had reverted to genteel occupation. Or had it? An Ambrose Boyson was there with his wife, and with sons aged twenty and seventeen and daughters of nineteen, twelve and nine, waited upon by a cook, a parlour maid, a lady's maid and a kitchen maid, none of them local. The parents and all the children had been born in Wandsworth. The father was a 'timber merchant's agent' (a Thameside occupation like that of the Sells). He had clearly made money, as he presented a drinking fountain to his old London district, the classic gesture of the Victorian philanthropist.[10] He evidently wished to train his sons to work rather than to enjoy gentlemanly leisure, as they were listed in the census as 'merchant's clerks'. The male members of the family must, I think, have been commuting to London on the new railway line, then an entirely new way of life.

The older Mrs Leveson-Gower, who was then in Hookwood House and lived to the age of eighty-eight, might still expect the village young to bow or bob to her carriage as it went past, but she was of a bygone era.

The Boysons did not stay long either. In fact the Bells, even if they had given up their school, must have remained the principal leaseholders of the house, for they reappear in reminiscences gathered in the mid-twentieth century from someone born in the parish in 1882.[11] She recalled that in the Manor House, when she was growing up, had lived 'Mr and Mrs Bell and their daughter Mary'. It seems likely, in view of the size of the place, that they were once again taking on boarders for coaching. At all events, when a long lease on the Manor House was acquired by the Misses Lyon in 1897, its fate to be a school was sealed.

For a period in the early twentieth century the more rural parts of Limpsfield became a fashionable retreat, especially for the Fabian circle. David Garnett grew up there, Laurence Olivier's father had a house there, G.B. Shaw visited and so did D.H. Lawrence. But none of this can have impinged on the old house in the village that was by and by to lose its distinction, its contours and even its identity in a monstrous outcrop of further buildings.

Chapter XI

Taynton Vicarage grows,
but Burford does not

So, throughout the busy nineteenth century, when industrial growth, railways and the effects of the ever-expanding British Empire were transforming life more decisively than in any previous era – how, in all this, was Taynton faring?

The answer is that Taynton, in its corner of Oxfordshire, remained remarkably unchanged. Between 1800 and 1900 Limpsfield's population more than doubled, and was soon to increase a great deal more as the commuterland of Oxted grew up barely a mile away. In the same hundred years Stroud Green turned from countryside into unrecognisable London streets, already socially on their way down in 'the full declension from meadowland to slum', as one urban historian has put it.[1] In this, Stroud Green and Limpsfield were representative each in its own way of very many other places up and down England. But none of the changes that variously affected them affected Taynton. This, in itself, tells its own story about the divergence between town and country that tends to open up in rapidly developing societies (it is observable in Asia and Africa today). The house and grounds in Limpsfield that had been a 'principal seat' in the village were, by 1900, descending into institutional use; the house at Stroud Green that had been given 'a handsome stuccoed front' as it stood among its ancient barns in the 1820s would, in 1900, be right on the edge of a road lined with terraced houses. But the house in Taynton was still in 1900 what it had been in 1800, and indeed in 1700 and 1600 and possibly long before. It was, as ever, the parsonage house.

Of course Taynton had, for a long time, been smaller and more deeply rural than Limpsfield. But England's remarkable nineteenth-century population growth – from about 8.3 million in 1800 to over thirty million by the end of the century – affected different places very unevenly. In that hundred years London's population grew from about one million to 6.7 million, and that of the big new manufacturing centres of Manchester, Birmingham, Leeds and Sheffield grew even more dramatically, particularly in the first half of the century. Rural, agricultural England was left right out of this increase though its population did not, at least till near the end of the century, actually decline. Farming remained labour-intensive with plenty of ill-paid and somewhat seasonal work for manual labourers, and for the supporting artisans of a self-contained community.

It is true that the coming of Enclosure and of a capitalist approach to land-owning led to fewer small farmers and tenants, and many of these felt deprived of their ancient rights and were left to seek jobs in the growing towns. But the popular-history view of a dispossessed and starving peasantry being driven into urban slums is somewhat contradicted by the fact that, during the same late-eighteenth/early-nineteenth-century period, in country as in town, the birth rate went up, more people survived into adulthood and length of life generally increased. The bigger landowners were busy Improving their land with new ideas of fertilisation and crop rotation: apart from the notorious suffering occasioned in some years by the Corn Laws, more food was more

cheaply available. Agriculture did not diminish in importance: it simply became, as the century went on, a smaller
part of the national economy. So the populations of
innumerable places such as Taynton, well away from the
burgeoning towns, remained more or less what they
always had been.

To scroll through the nineteenth-century census
forms of many other districts, decade by decade, is to
see the world in which these apparently countless, but
actually enumerated, people lived evolving and changing
before your eyes, as in a speeded-up film. Stockmen,
dairymaids, coach drivers and gardeners are replaced by
clerks, engravers, pianoforte tuners and engine drivers,
alehouse keepers by grocers and then by gas fitters.
Numbers continually increase – but in Taynton there
was no such transformation. As well as farming, the area
had its traditional industries – the quarries, and a paper-
making mill at the Barringtons using wood pulp from
the forests around. Apart from the addition, as the
decades went by, of one or two schoolteachers and eventually a postmaster (a Thomas Pittaway in 1871, who
doubled as a carpenter) the occupations remained as they
always had been. The current parish clerk was once again
a Pittaway too. And while big villages such as Limpsfield
had plenty of shops by then, Taynton had just one
combined shop, bakery and beer-seller's, run by two
unmarried sisters.

In 1811 Taynton's parish numbered 343 souls, including
some who lived in the farming hamlet on the extra-parish
land by the forest of Wychwood. Thirty years later the
total had only increased a little, and after another thirty
years it was back at 341. By 1881 it had dropped to 232.
Further consolidation of the smaller farms into only three
big ones must have played a part, and also the establishment of such labour-saving machines as threshers and
reapers-and-binders which reduced slightly the numbers
of farm labourers needed. The agricultural depression of

those years, due in large part to increasing foreign imports, probably had its effect too, though the Cotswold stone-providing districts suffered less than wholly agricultural parts of England. There is also the fact that by then universal education, even in small villages, was for the first time equipping almost anyone to seek a job in the nearest town if they felt inclined. Or, indeed, to look much further afield. There was some emigration from the area in the 1880s and '90s: a Pittaway clan thrive today in the United States.

It is from this last quarter of the century, and not before, that the phrase 'flight from the land' begins to appear, and it was to become a mournful mantra in the early decades of the twentieth century. Today, the parish of Taynton has a little more than one hundred people, many of them part-time residents.

The Vestry Book of Taynton that was begun by the temporarily enthusiastic Mr Meyrick in 1807 continues, with some substantial gaps, right up to 1923. By that time almost all the old Vestry duties had been ceded to local or national government, and it was reduced to a Parish Council. The phrase 'a Vestry holden this day' had long since given way to 'a meeting held on such-and-such a date'; spelling was now conventional, vicars kept the record, and the meetings were no longer in any case held in the church vestry but in the Reading Room (inaugurated by a high-minded late-Victorian parson) or in the village school. Arguments over the Poor Rate had long been superseded by discussions about the need for gravel paths in the churchyard, or for a coal shed, or to upgrade the insurance on the church, or – increasingly as the twentieth century unreeled – about the creeping deficit in church funds. But still all decisions taken were written down in the same stiff, parchment-bound, foolscap-sized book that had sufficed for over two hundred years. I like to think that the latter-day churchwardens sometimes looked back through the pages and reflected on how time, the ever-rolling stream of the hymn, in the end bears everything away – or at least, everything debatable. Parchment, like stone, is more enduring.

By 1819, when Thomas Lewes took up his fifty-five-year incumbency, the main preoccupation of the Vestry was Poor Relief, the need to raise more money for it, and the conflicting need not to impose so much on those prosperous enough to pay the Poor Rate that they objected. Small windfall sums came in handy, especially 'fines for robbing orchards' – presumably extracted from young men who were themselves fairly poor – but often in these years the few wealthy citizens had to make up the Poor fund out of their own pockets. This was the case then in parishes up and down the land, and various reasons are commonly listed: bad harvests or the artificially maintained price of bread, soldiers returning to unemployment from the Napoleonic wars. But one may also surmise, looking back at earlier records, that people's needs were not much more pressing in the early nineteenth century than they had always been. It was rather that general sensibilities were a little more developed than in the past.

The village stocks and whipping post were, like plague and scrofula, things of a bygone day. In the world beyond Taynton laws had been enacted to forbid slavery in the British Empire and to prevent the employment of young children in factories or women in mines. Efforts were under way to abolish child chimney sweeps, and there were moves to put a limit on working hours for all. The kind of absolute deprivation and want that would have been commonly apparent in earlier times, and regarded stoically as fate or God's Will, were no longer generally tolerated.

In Taynton and Great Barrington there is much evidence, at this period, of comprehensive efforts to provide linen or calico for needy families, and in February

1823 the Lady Dynevor of the time lent out a large quantity of blankets as it was a particularly cold winter. The following year a whole pound from the Taynton Poor Rates was allowed to one woman to clothe herself and her children, and another pound went to an unmarried Mary Pittaway towards her lying-in (confinement at childbirth). Another woman received the much smaller sum of five shillings towards the same expense. In April and on through the next three months, Henry Pittaway is regularly awarded sums of money – five shillings, ten shillings, eight shillings – as is William James. Both men are referred to as being 'of Swinbrook', a neighbouring village, but this is simply because they belonged to Payne's Farm which was over in that direction.[2] They counted as Taynton parishioners, as did both their wives. Although the Vestry Book does not say so, these were the same Henry Pittaway and William James who were to be hanged at Oxford for killing a gamekeeper in the forest of Wychwood. At a meeting on 2 August 1824, the very day on which the execution had taken place early in the morning, a sum of twelve shillings apiece was voted to 'Henry Pittaway's widow and likewise to William James's widow'.

It is clear where parish sympathies, including the vicar's, lay. He had married the younger couple himself five years before, one of the first weddings at which he had officiated. In September Jane, Henry's widow, gave birth to twin girls.

The following year a Pittaway family's doctor's bill was paid, something unheard of in the previous century. In 1832 various men were given handouts because they, or their wives, were ill. An entry in 1834 stating that 'it was resolved that Byshop's wife be allowed a little port wine' introduces a momentary sense of levity. Were the church funds being expended, at a junketing for a Bishop's Visitation, on the Bishop's wife? Then one realises that there was a family in Taynton called Bishop, and port wine was considered a restorative tonic. We have seen, from the Limpsfield church accounts and a rector's note, that the same benign view was held there.

Under the Poor Law Act of 1834 the whole business of direct relief began to be taken out of the hands of the Vestries. New Poor Law Commissioners were appointed; new collectivised Union workhouses were built. Taynton was now part of the Witney Union, some ten miles off. By and by all parish responsibilities, including the diffi-cult decisions about who had rights of settlement where, were extinguished. Whether the poor were better off under the new system is highly debatable. Except where the Taynton charities such as Harman's or Collier's were concerned, they disappear from the village records.

With Thomas Lewes we come upon a figure who seems symbolic of mid-Victorian stability, though his origins lay well before the Victorian era. Born in 1792,[3] he took his BA at Oxford in 1815 and his MA two years later, and arrived in Taynton and Great Barrington at rising twenty-eight. He was to remain there till he was eighty-two. I do not know just what his religious leanings were (though there is some indication – see below – that they were not high church), but one may surmise that his unchanging presence must have sheltered his parish from the waves of controversy that raged through the Church of England in the 1830s and '40s.

On the one hand, the high church Oxford Movement (also known as the Tractarians), peopled by figures such as Newman, Manning, Keble and Pusey, felt that the Church should recognise its pre-Reformation roots and that Anglicanism and Roman Catholicism were really two tributaries of the same spiritual stream. Turning away from the utilitarian, government-orientated Church of the previous century, the Oxford Movement favoured sacramental ritual. This meant the increasing use of vest-ments, candles and bowing to the altar, and intoning the

Creed and the responses rather than speaking them – 'Popish affectations' which infuriated their opponents. These opponents were low church Protestants much closer to the proliferating Nonconformist churches; they favoured evangelising – actively spreading word of the Gospel through missionary work at home and overseas. At best, they were exemplified by such social reformers as Wilberforce, the anti-slavery campaigner. At worst, they became bullies, intimidating their congregations with threats of eternal damnation for commonplace human failings. When Newman and Manning eventually did 'go over to Rome' the controversy became still fiercer. In Burford, successive vicars pulled in different directions in this dispute till, near the end of the century, a particularly honourable and diplomatic vicar (William Emeris, who till that point had been presiding peacefully in Taynton for several years) was drafted in by the Bishop to try to unite the various factions.

By this time, though no one close to the matter seems quite to have realised it, the heat was going out of the contest in a way that turned out to be definitive. After the general popularity and social importance of the Church of England in the nineteenth century, and the building of hundreds of additional churches up and down England in locations as different as Limpsfield and Hornsey, the twentieth century was to bring a long, slow but inexorable retreat from formulated religious belief and from the whole idea of worship. The story of the vicarages and rectories in the twentieth century is essentially the story of this decline.

From his arrival in Taynton and for many years, Lewes was an active presence, officiating at marriages, baptisms and funerals, and at the very frequent Vestry meetings. For fifteen years, no doubt following his wish, this became a 'Select Vestry', that is, a self-perpetuating, self-electing body rather than one open to all parishioners. The accounts were better kept now, itemised by the month and in ruled columns. Edward Pittaway had died, aged seventy-three, the year of Lewes's accession, and John Maides became parish clerk. Visitation expenses were curtailed, and more seems to have been spent on cleaning the church. Lewes's approach appears to have been rather unimaginatively practical. Three times in one year (1826) sums of money were paid out to 'Boys destroying sparrows', and this remained an item in several subsequent years. Presumably the sparrows were nesting in the church eaves and causing damage and dirt, but, as a symbolic act, killing them hardly seems in the best traditions of Christianity. (*Are not two sparrows sold for a farthing? And one of them shall not fall on the ground without your Father* – Matthew 10:29)

Like almost all ancient parish churches in England, Taynton church was much restored in the nineteenth century. Meyrick, before he lost interest, had already declared that this was desirable in 1809. Finally, almost forty years later, there was a special Vestry meeting 'for the purpose of taking into consideration the dilapidated state of the nave of the church; it was resolved that immediate steps be taken for its repair and that a rate be levied for that purpose.' This was written and signed by Lewes. An estimate for the replacement of the roof timbers was pasted in, and the receipt (for £110. 4s. 3d.) added a few months later. There was a further round of much more expensive works in the 1860s. This was the peak period for church 'restorations' that were really more like rebuilding exercises and often ill-judged. It was true of Limpsfield, and also of Burford where, notoriously, gravestones of ancient worthies who had been buried within the church were broken up as hard core for a new tiled floor.

In Taynton, the chancel stones were numbered and put back carefully in place afterwards, and the windows were reconstructed as before. A medieval staircase, once leading to the rood loft, was discovered within a wall, but 'Mr Lewes had it enclosed, and the doorway was only opened in 1884 when the Organ Chamber was built'.[4] Fortunately, the fifteenth-century carved faces on the top of the pillars, the legacy of the local masons who originally worked on it, were allowed to remain, as were the Royal Arms from the previous century. But another relic of the past that came to light was condemned. When the porch was being rebuilt a small, headless male statue was found, in two pieces. It must have been a victim either of the altar-stripping of the Reformation or of the mass destruction of statues, angels and stained glass that was ordered in the following century under the Common-wealth. In either case, some Woodman, Cozens or Collier of the period apparently gave it a decent burial within the precinct of the church, perhaps hoping to resurrect it when times became easier again. The workmen who found it in 1861 realised that it fitted an empty shrine-recess in the north aisle and put it up there. However, 'old Mr Lewes he didn't care nothing for such things and he said "Take him away". So they took him away and brake him up. It was only freestone' – i.e. Taynton stone.[5]

It is Mr Lewes's behaviour over the statue (which one must assume he regarded as 'an idol') that inclines me to think that he was not a sympathiser with the Oxford Movement and its reverence for the Church's long history.

Lewes was by then old. He seems to have been absent, probably ill, in 1857–58, when six out of eight funerals were taken by a curate, and again in 1865. From 1867 till his death in 1873, nearly all services as well as funerals were taken by one of two curates, though Lewes did take one last funeral on Midsummer's Day in 1871, that of an old woman whom he had presumably known for many years. Less than two years later he was buried there himself, in a rather grand box-tomb.

Like James Stiles the century before, who clocked up
thirty-seven years in Taynton, and like Parson Woodforde
of Norfolk, Thomas Lewes did not marry. Unlike Woodforde, he did not apparently summon a female relative
to keep house for him. There were one or two socially
compatible people 'of independent means' living in the
parish, descendants of families such as the Strongs who
had done well in previous generations; there were the
Dynevor descendants established in a handsome house
in Great Barrington where Lewes was vicar also, but one
feels his life must have been essentially solitary. Possibly
he was wary, on his relatively modest income, of encum-
bering himself with what might have turned out to be a
very large family – and some of the vicarage families
produced in the bucolic comfort and peace of the high-
Victorian era were enormous. But he owned a parcel of
land in Taynton as well as his glebe land; he never lived
particularly frugally, and as his life went by he seems to
have acquired rather more wealth since he was able, in
old age, to employ curates. Not, I think, that he would
have expressed it quite like that to himself, since, once
proper censuses began to be taken, he habitually though
not always consistently understated his age. Perhaps he
wished to maintain an appearance of vigour, and considered his years no one's business but his own.

At the census of 1841 he lived in the vicarage with
two female servants in their twenties and a fifteen-year-
old 'man-servant'. He had the same establishment ten
years later, though the names had changed and the boy
was now a 'groom'. In 1861 he told the enumerator (who
was the young village schoolmaster) he was sixty-eight,
though he must have been almost seventy. He had living
with him by then a brother, 'barrister-no-longer-in-prac-
tice', which probably indicates that the two old bachelors
had pooled their resources. They employed a housekeeper, a housemaid and a footman, none born locally.
Lewes's curate, George Bode, also lived in the village,

with a wife, a son of five, two even smaller daughters and two maids. He was apparently a more sanguine personality than his employer.

By 1871, when Lewes was soon to be eighty but only admitted to seventy-five, his brother was gone, presumably dead – though he had not apparently died in Taynton. There were still a housekeeper, a maid and a footman, again different individuals from the previous decade and again strangers to Taynton. Thomas Lewes does not seem to have been a man who inspired lasting affection and fidelity in his servants. He does seem to have been a conscientious pastor and fundamentally a decent person. As a young vicar, only three or four years in the job, he buried Henry Pittaway and William James, the two men hanged for murder, in Taynton's consecrated churchyard, which he could well have refused to do. His action was charitable and honourable, as his support for them and their families in Vestry meetings had been. But he is remembered today, if at all, as the destroyer of the medieval statue.

At some point – or possibly more than one – in the course of Victoria's reign the vicarage in Taynton was transformed, from a conventionally shaped house with a Georgian appearance concealing ancient stones and timbers, into a Victorian-looking building so warren-like and complex that even visitors who knew it well found it hard to hold a coherent plan of it in their heads.

Who was responsible for this? Was it Thomas Lewes's initiative, or that of his successor William Patrick Leonard Hand? Neither the Oxford County archives, nor the Gloucester archives where some papers have ended up, nor the central archive of Lambeth Palace Library, have anything relevant to reveal. The nicely drawn and colour-washed architect's plans I hoped to find, dated, with exquisite hand-lettering and perhaps fancifully Gothic titles, are evidently long since used to line shelves or to light kitchen fires. Or perhaps, if the building works were done by local labour, Pittaways or other, supervised by the vicar in person, formal plans never existed at all.

It is tempting to believe it was all done at once during Thomas Lewes's time, perhaps when the church too was undergoing substantial works in the 1860s – that the Lewes brothers came into family money and decided to use it this way, as Thomas Walpole of Limpsfield used his own money on the rectory. But Lewes was by then too old to have much expectation of benefiting for long from such an outlay. Might he have had the work done when he was still a relatively young man? Possibly the extra rooms – but the makeover of the front façade, with the addition of the heavy enclosed porch and the bow windows to one side necessitating the removal of some of the Georgian windows, cannot date from Lewes's youth or even his prime: they are mid- to-late-Victorian work.

I am fairly sure it was Lewes who enlarged the Georgian kitchen by extending its gable further out in the front, since this extension dates from the 1830s or '40s. This absorbed into the house the area where the well stood, which was covered over but presumably continued to have water for the household pumped out of it. Later, after mains water came to the village, it was entirely forgotten, hidden as it was under the pantry floor, and not till the house was receiving another round of alterations and modernisations *c.* 2008 was it rediscovered.

But at some point, probably rather later, there was the much more substantial addition of two further rooms on the ground floor behind the kitchen, along with a passageway from the side door near the kitchen to the centre of the house, and also a back stairs. Above these, on the first floor, an extra corridor was constructed branching off the main one, which already went round an awkward corner to the rooms built earlier over the kitchen. The extra passageway led to two more bedrooms over the new back-extension, a landing with a water closet off it, and an odd central wedge of apparently solid wall that no one has ever satisfactorily explained. These large additions effectively transformed a spacious but compact house into an eccentrically rambling one capable of accommodating a big family with several live-in servants – now more segregated by having their own back stairs in the approved Victorian manner.

Maybe this *was* Lewes's doing, but one has to ask oneself why, as a middle-aged bachelor, he should have wanted so big a house, however aloof he wished to be from his servants? He already had outbuildings, including a stable and loft, a carriage house, a dairy with a room above, and another stable, two cowsheds and pigsties down in the orchard. The other possibility is that the whole enlargement was done by the vicar who took over in the early 1870s, and that the revamping of the façade with the pointed porch and bow windows took place at the same time.

W.P. Leonard Hand (so he usually signed himself) was vicar of Taynton from 1873 to 1896, so had time to enjoy his enlarged vicarage. He employed curates to help him from the outset so he must have had private means, but he was not idle. It was he who thought to excavate the composted contents of the parish chest, thereby saving many scraps from oblivion, and also rescued from damp and dissolution the earliest registers. He was only twenty-four when, with a BA, ordained, and apparently newly married, he settled into the vicarage. When the next census was taken eight years later he was absent that night, but his wife Amy was there with daughters of six, five and three, so the young couple had not wasted any time. Amy ('clergyman's wife') was then twenty-eight, four years younger than her husband, so she was twenty-two when she had her first child. To help her, and to populate the extensive kitchen regions, she had a nurse, a cook and a teenage housemaid. One or both of the Hands must have come into family money when they took on the vicarage, if indeed (as I think) that was when the extra back wing and the fashionably Victorianised façade were constructed. They may also have hoped – or accepted with Christian equanimity – that they might be destined to produce one of those huge nineteenth-century broods of children all in dauntingly robust health, like the Rev. and Mrs Quiverful in Trollope's *Barchester Towers*.

But ten years on the census of 1891 shows only one further daughter at home, then aged eight. Her sisters were now teenage, and the family were keeping just one young living-in maid, which rather suggests a decline in fortunes. Of course they may, like the various occupants of the Limpsfield house with its equally capacious kitchens, have had other employees coming in daily from the village. The daughters were not entered on the census form as 'scholars', which the village children who all attended the school now were, so one must suppose they were being taught at home.

It looks as if the Hands, who moved away during the 1890s to another parish, in Gloucestershire, were on the way to fulfilling a rather different stereotype from Trollope's Quiverfuls – though nowhere near that epitomised by Trollope's desperate Rev. Crawley and family in *The Last Chronicles of Barset*, attempting to live and keep up appearances on only £130 a year. The country vicar with a stipend and land-holdings both declining in value, and too many unmarried daughters, living a quiet, old-style life in a world that was relentlessly changing, was to become a feature of both real life and novels in the early twentieth century.

There is in fact a novel that depicts exactly that situation and in the same district, set not in Taynton but in the Old Vicarage in Burford. The writer Compton Mackenzie

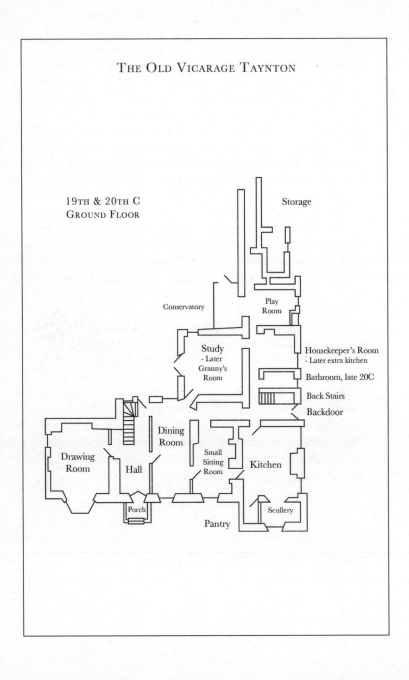

THE OLD VICARAGE TAYNTON

19TH & 20TH C
GROUND FLOOR

Storage

Conservatory

Play
Room

Study
- Later
Granny's
Room

Housekeeper's Room
- Later extra kitchen

Bathroom, late 20C

Back Stairs

Backdoor

Dining
Room

Drawing
Room

Hall

Small
Sitting
Room

Kitchen

Porch

Scullery

Pantry

Views of various parts of the house, including the front elevation that was redone, probably in the 1870s. Painted in the late twentieth century.

and his friend Christopher Stone lived in two cottages down by the river bridge in Burford as young men in the early 1900s, and the result some years later was *Guy and Pauline*. The setting, near to the vicarage and its big garden – then in real life occupied by William Emeris, the vicar who was moved from Taynton to make peace among the warring church factions of Burford – is exactly portrayed in the novel. So is the then-derelict 'Priory' nearby, built on the foundations of the monks' hospital once owned by Edmund Harman. But Mackenzie populated his fictional vicarage with a stock charmingly unworldly old incumbent, his sympathetic wife, and three occupationless daughters who are clearly intended to be attractive figures also but do not evoke much empathy in a present-day reader.

The central male character of the book had already appeared as a subsidiary one in Mackenzie's very successful *Sinister Street* – which we shall come across in Hornsey – and the author had conceived the idea of a series of novels, each self-contained, but linked by a shared cast of people. However, the coming of the Great War, cutting, as it realistically would have to, a swathe across the lives of all his young male characters, made him abandon the scheme. Indeed, by the time *Guy and Pauline* was published in the autumn of 1915 the book was already out of date: the tranquillity, sensibility and idleness it depicts, while only of a year or two earlier, had vanished. By then a real-life Guy would have volunteered for the army and be in France, if not already dead for his country. Marooned in a pre-twentieth-century world, the infantile Pauline and her sisters, the vicar's daughters, read a great deal of Jane Austen, and their secluded life seems to resemble that of Austen's young women rather than that of the rapidly developing new century. But this tells one something about Burford itself at that date (Wychford in the novel), and it is for a portrayal of this that the book still holds some interest:

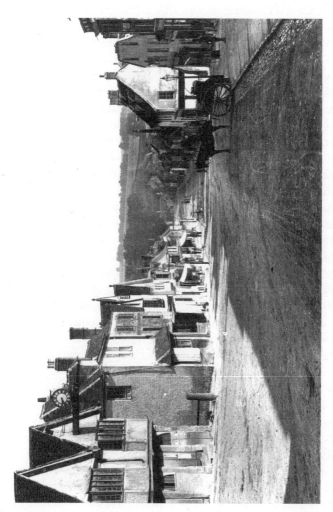

The slope of Burford High Street running down toward the river. Photo taken c.1895. Almost all the buildings, including the old Tolsey market building on the left with the clock, are readily recognisable today, but the quietness of Burford then has long been transformed by the coming of cars.

'Wychford is mortal dead in winter,' says the station porter at Shipcot (Witney). 'Time walks very lame there, as they say.'

There is no station at Wychford, only a twice-daily horse-bus to make the connection to Shipcot, and in this fact we have the history of Burford – or rather, the stagnation of its history, and thus of the villages around – over the preceding two generations. Guy loves his riverside location and presently discovers that 'a richness of pastoral life lay behind the slumber of a forgotten town', but forgotten is what Wychford–Burford then was, by all but a few antiquarians and would-be poets.

Burford had escaped the full ravages of the seventeenth-century Civil Wars (except for one famous incident when mutinous Leveller soldiers were imprisoned in the church) and after the Restoration the place became positively fashionable. There were regular race meetings there which were announced in London news-sheets and visited by Londoners, including Charles II and his entourage. By 1685 there was a postmaster in the town to receive and despatch letters. Inns were rebuilt and, by and by, some of the timbered structures in the High Street were given a contemporary elegance with new stone frontages and bigger windows. The town now had a small but significant population of gentry unconnected with local trade or manufacture, and the road traffic, which was later to constitute one of Burford's major businesses, had begun.

During the eighteenth century coach routes gradually multiplied to and from London, Oxford, Gloucester, Cheltenham, South Wales and Hereford, and the town buzzed with the attendant activity. At the peak of this trade thirty-nine coaches passed through and stopped at Burford day and night, including eighteen long-distance 'flyers' and many shorter-haul ones – and right through the town was where they went. Not till 1812 did the owner of the Priory manage to get the main route diverted from the streets around his property, taking it up on to the ridge where today the A40 runs from Oxford via Witney to Cheltenham. An even faster coach came in after the Napoleonic wars, leaving Burford at six every morning to arrive in London at four in the afternoon. It must all have seemed exciting and modern to the generations reared in the villages around.

But the railway age, which was to energise and enlarge so many other towns elsewhere, was to be Burford's undoing. In the mid-1840s, when the first phase of general railway-building was reaching its peak, there was a scheme for a line that would branch off the London to Birmingham line north-west of London and pass through High Wycombe and Oxford to Burford and Cheltenham before continuing on to Ledbury and Hereford. The boom collapsed and the plan came to nothing. Three years later another line was authorised, from Oxford to Gloucester, which again would have passed by Burford, but the hilly route was hardly ideal for a railway and that came to nothing either. Then, in 1852, the Oxford to Worcester section of the Great Western Railway opened, putting an end to Burford's hopes of a station. It ran, as it runs today, half a dozen miles further north and on the far side of a hill. Meanwhile, with other main lines now cutting across England, the coaching business was rapidly dying. Inns were going out of business, their stables emptying of ostlers and grooms. Trade routes were shifting.

Ten years later there was one more effort to bring a line right past Burford, with a station on the ridge road at 'Burford barns' where, today, a twice-daily long-distance bus from Oxford sets down passengers near the roundabout and there are two or three hotels. A 'Cheltenham and Oxford Direct Union Railway' was proposed: in the *Oxford Journal* in 1862 there were advertisements for 'future shareholders' and a list of supporters. For some years the project seemed hopeful but it, too, died in the 1870s. Burford settled into the 'slumber of a forgotten town'. Its population in the mid-nineteenth century just before the collapse of the coach trade was almost 1,600; by the end of the century it was down to 1,146. Some venerable houses were left untenanted.

Taking a long view, we can say this turned out to be an enormous blessing for the town, with its main street curving steeply down to the river and its wealth of varied and beautiful buildings dating from the Middle Ages to the end of the eighteenth century. A railway line and station near to hand would probably have brought new prosperity and, with it, new industry, warehouses, and a suburb of red brick villas. It would have favoured the piecemeal destruction of Burford's architectural heritage for replacement by respectably Victorian blocks not necessarily even constructed of stone. If a line had run through the Windrush valley (a more logical route for a train than the ridge at the top of the town) then the villages on that side – Asthall, Swinbrook, Fulbrook and Taynton – might, as the years went by, have been swallowed up in an expanding Burford and have lost their rural character, as Limpsfield village has now been subsumed into the suburban expansion of Oxted.

The disapointment of Burford's citizens in the 1850s was to be compensated many times over by future generations' delight in the ancient town's extraordinary state of preservation and in the visually unspoilt villages around – but in the nineteenth century they could not know that. The coming of the railways wrought more changes upon the face of England than any other development, even those of our own time, but in some places the non-arrival of a railway was an event just as significant and with repercussions just as long-lasting.

Chapter XII

THE DYNAMIC RAILWAY AGE. AND ITS DARK HEART

The year in which both Taynton and Limpsfield had their hopes raised for the coming of a railway line, 1845, was the peak year for speculative schemes in Britain's major decade of railway-building. Under the heading 'The Battle of the Railways' *Punch* wrote in the spring:

> The railway mania is committing the most frightful ravages on the senses of the people, and the most deadly feuds are springing up between the various supporters of the different projected lines.
>
> Every man who has got a 10-pound-note is rushing into the market to purchase an interest in some thing or other which he don't understand, but he is satisfied with the fact that an advertisement has appeared calling the concern a railway.

Punch had already had fun with bursting engines and collapsing bridges and with cartoons of the sheep-pen design of the third-class carriages, which were open to the rainy sky. It had also commented on attempts to ban the third class from Sunday trains – 'as if it were a sin to travel on Sundays only for the working classes'. Later in the year, which was also the year in which Newman, the High Church Anglican, finally threw in his lot with the Roman Catholic Church, to the dismay of many of his own Tractarian supporters, *Punch* gleefully announced the coming of 'A railway from Oxford to Rome. We understand that a prospectus of this scheme (provisionally registered) will appear in a few days. The Pope, averse to railways in general, has given his heartiest concurrence to the project. The route has already been marked out by some well known tracts of late travellers.'

I like to think that some casual *Punch* readers were so innocent, and so preoccupied with the magic of railway shares, that they believed in the possibility of an Oxford to Rome line as readily as they did in the proposed Oxford to Cheltenham one, though, as we know, that didn't get built either.

By the autumn it was dawning on some people that the sheer number and variety of lines being proposed was self-defeating. Beside a map of England entirely criss-crossed with tracks, *Punch* ponderously declared, 'though England will never be in chains, she will pretty soon be in irons . . . We can only say that we ought to be going on very smoothly, considering that our country is being regularly ironed from one end of it to the other.'

From such ironing, Limpsfield had a lucky escape. The ribbon of land in the parish '193 rods long', that the newly formed South Eastern Railway Company acquired at that time from the Leveson-Gowers, was planned to be part of a grand scheme. The line was to come down from London to Croydon, then through the North Downs to Caterham and thence to the vicinity of Oxted. There, one branch was to continue south to Brighton, while another was to run eastwards to Dover. As a local inhabitant of today has written: 'Had this proposal materialised, Oxted and Limpsfield, at the juncture of two important lines, would almost certainly have become one sprawling railway town complete with locomotive works, wagon shops, engine sheds, endless vistas of sidings, and all the grimy paraphernalia of Victorian industry.'[1]

However, the government gave preference to the London & Brighton Railway, which had plans already well advanced for its own main line south to the coast from Croydon, running a little further to the west, so the Limpsfield idea was judged redundant. In any case, that bout of railway mania had now collapsed. By early 1846 *Punch* was proposing 'a Cemetery on a large scale' – new cemeteries were also assiduously being laid out at the time – 'for the interment of the late much-lamented railways . . . [which] would be visited by many sincere mourners, in the shape of attorneys, engineers, scripholders, and provisional committee-men'. There was also a full-page cartoon under the heading 'The Momentous Question', showing a couple recognisable as Queen Victoria and her Consort (he in chains, head bent), she asking tremulously: 'Tell me, oh tell me, dearest Albert, have *you* any Railway Shares?'

Twenty years later, in the mid-1860s, there was another railway boom, largely concerned this time with branch lines between previously established routes – the intricate network of country lines for which Britain was to become famous. As an offshoot of what was now the London, Brighton & South Coast Railway, the Surrey & Sussex Junction Company was formed. The aim was to link Croydon to Tunbridge Wells, which already had one line to London, with a new line to pass via Oxted and Groombridge. Work had hardly started when, in 1866, the Overend Gurney bank failed spectacularly, largely due to over-investment in shaky railway schemes worldwide. This brought bankruptcy and ruin to many of its customers and landed Britain in a financial crisis.

In spite of this, work continued, and a tunnel through the Downs over 2,000 yards long was completed just north of Oxted. Belgian navvies were employed to speed things up, to the fury of the British navvies, who rioted. Then what appeared to be cholera broke out in the navvy camp: this was the year of the last significant cholera epidemic in London, and also in Paris and Brussels. Panic followed in Limpsfield parish, for the camp was in part of its woodlands. One local lady, Harriet Kenwood, nursed the sick devotedly till she caught the disease herself and died, joining the Stanhopes, the Strongs, the Maynes, the Leveson-Gowers, the Dunns, the Millses, the Lovelands and all the others in the churchyard.

Meanwhile the Surrey & Sussex Junction Company was in liquidation. The parent company took over the project, but in 1869 decided to cut its very substantial losses and terminate the construction. For a dozen years the earthworks languished like ruins left by giants, leading nowhere, and, in the words of a local guidebook, 'Kind nature in a short time covered the embankments with verdure and closed the entrances of an important tunnel with shrubs and vegetation.'² Children found the site great fun to play in. Not till the end of the 1870s was a new plan made by the joint enterprise of the two old rivals, the South Eastern and the London, Brighton & South Coast. This time, the line from London was to run via Oxted to Lingfield and East Grinstead – as it runs today – and originally on to Tunbridge Wells. It was at last triumphantly opened in 1884. It is from then that the modern development of Oxted dates and, with it, the gradual but inexorable alteration of Limpsfield from a rural settlement surrounded by fields into a preserved oasis in London's outer commuterland.

There seems a certain significance in the fact that the Leveson-Gower who was very much still the Squire of Limpsfield in the first half of the twentieth century married a member of the Brassey family, who had made a substantial fortune in late-nineteenth-century railways.

* * *

And how, in all this enthusiasm for railways, did Stroud Green fare? And Hornsey parish in general? Here, indeed, we are at the dark heart of the dynamic railway age and the satanic transformations it could effect.

We left early-nineteenth-century Stapleton Hall when it consisted of a group of several buildings, a farmyard and a large barn. Surrounding it were eighty-odd acres of pasture, some of this adjacent to the long strip of common that was Stroud Green which now had up its length 'a well-made road with quickset hedges on both sides'. Within a few years of the road being laid down, the main house, which is to say the main part of the Jacobean house with its big old fireplaces and heavy timbering, was done up by William Lucas, the current owner of the property. It now had 'a handsome stucco front' with new, regular Georgian windows to give it 'quite a modern appearance'. It is likely that, at the same time, new, smaller fireplaces were inserted into the old, wide flues, but there is no evidence, then or later, of any further building-out at the back as happened in Limpsfield and Taynton. A watercolour said to be of the 1820s, which is now lost but survives in a photographic reproduction and in a much later oil painting signed 'R. Fenson', apparently made by copying this photograph, shows the house with a rather pretty lightweight open porch with a fluted canopy. In front there is a garden with small trees, its fencing and gate made of simple, country-style palings.

The contemporary description states that the site now contained two distinct houses. Indeed, the drawing and its painted copy also show, adjoining this main house, immediately to the east, a more rustic-looking house with a lower roof-line, assorted gabled additions and some weatherboarding. This is the farmhouse, seemingly consisting of one segment of the original Jacobean house plus extensions. Part of another weatherboarded building across a yard is visible at the edge of the picture. This farm side of the property was also sketched in 1821, from another viewpoint, by the watercolour artist Thomas Hosmer Shepherd. A rather amateurish unsigned oil painting, probably dating from much later in the century, shows the same view in closer focus.[3] Considering the various pictures together, it becomes clear how the two conjoined houses related to one another, the one facing south-west and the other, at right angles to it, south-east. Several maps from later in the century, including the 1870 Ordnance Survey and also a detailed plan done when road development was being considered, show this configuration of buildings.

The OS map also shows that the front garden of the main house, which would be seen as one approached up a track from the corner where Stroud Green Road becomes Crouch Hill, was nicely laid out with a semi-circular pathway between the trees, and that there was a larger ornamental garden at the back. What we have here is only a semi-rural setting, though one still with all the fabled charm of a country farm. It was *rus in urbe*, just what the comfortably off middle classes were increasingly wanting to find on the edge of London, now easily accessible by the gravelled road up Stroud Green. Since 1834, Hem Lane, at the southern end of Stroud Green, had been extended as Seven Sisters Road, linking Holloway at one end with the distant fields of Tottenham at the other. Properties like Stapleton Hall and much grander – Middleton's 'elegant villas' that were supposed to beautify London's northern hills – were now in evidence higher up the slopes of Crouch Hill, on Mount-pleasant, and down into Crouch End. These dreams of country life continued to be built as late as the 1880s, after which the tide of smaller terraced houses that had by then submerged Stroud Green became too obtrusive to be ignored.

For much of the century, farming continued at

Stapleton Hall: indeed it was eventually to be the last working farm in the district. The census of 1841 makes the distinction between the house proper and its adjoining farmhouse clear.[4] William Lucas had been succeeded by John Lucas II, who would himself die ten years later, passing the increasingly valuable land-holding on to yet another generation; but by the 1840s the third Lucas, Joshua, had ceased actually to live at Stroud Green and had acquired a grander home south of London – which he named Stapleton House.[5]

So, in the first census of '41 we find Stapleton Hall, clearly marked as such, occupied not by a Lucas but by a middle-aged wine merchant called Richard Williams, his wife, a son in his twenties in the same business, another son who was a solicitor, and a teenage daughter. Trading in alcohol has always, for some reason, been considered more gentlemanly than trading in linen or soap, and I note that Richard Williams's occupation coincides with that of Thomas Draper, 'merchant and brewer of London', who had built the house more than two hundred years before. Richard Williams, like Draper, was considered a prominent local citizen; he was a Vestryman, and some years later was one of a small committee set up to enquire into the gathering crisis in footpaths. He employed three living-in servants, one male and two female, the younger of whom was a Sarah Turner. Evidently the Williamses lived in some style in their nice stucco-fronted residence, and probably had a carriage to take them to and from town. For the previous twenty years there had been short-stage coaches going and returning between Hornsey and the City several times a day. Towards 1840 these began to be replaced by the new horse omnibuses, but both coaches and buses would have passed at a little distance from secluded Stapleton Hall.

Next door in Stapleton Hall Farm, also clearly indicated on the census return, was a middle-aged tenant

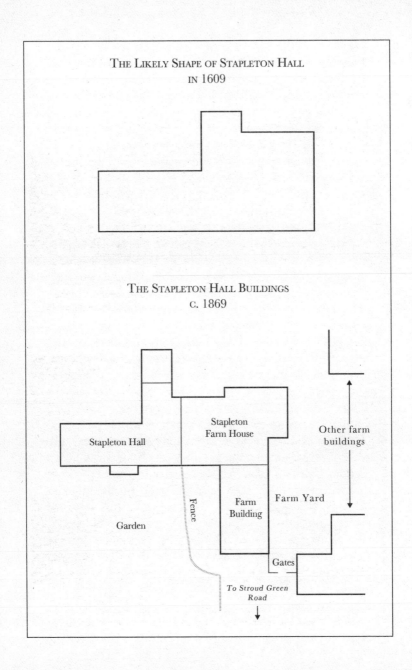

THE LIKELY SHAPE OF STAPLETON HALL
IN 1609

THE STAPLETON HALL BUILDINGS
C. 1869

Stapleton Hall

Stapleton
Farm House

Other farm
buildings

Garden

Fence

Farm
Building

Farm Yard

Gates

To Stroud Green
Road

The Stapleton Hall complex in the 1820s, from a lost original. The house, done up with a stucco front and a porch by the Lucas family, is on the left. The farmhouse and extra farm buildings are on the right, facing away.

A slightly later view of the farm, taken from a different angle so that we can see into the yard. From the configuration of the roofs, and especially the gable and lean-to on the left of the picture, it is clearly the same building.

farmer called John Wells, his wife, a daughter in her twenties down as a 'serving maid' (possibly she waited at table on the Williamses next door?) and two sons of about twenty.[6] One of these, Henry, was a yard assistant, presumably working with his father, while George is described as an 'artist'. I wonder if he was eventually responsible for the anonymous oil painting of the farm-house and another companion painting of the stockyard, both of which have a slightly sentimental, valedictory air? The Wellses kept just one girl-servant, as would have been usual in a hands-on farming family, but they had five farm labourers living on the premises. Three of these were a father and his two sons, and all were apparently lodged in one of the farm buildings, probably in lofts above a barn or cow-shed. Their employer, who supplied the enumerator with information, did not venture any guesses as to their ages.

The census of ten years later designates the exact buildings less clearly, simply marking a whole cluster of households as living at 'Stroud Green'; but, as a focal point, John Wells and his wife appear again with son Henry, who is now down as a 'professor of languages'. Evidently both the sons had forsaken cow-tending for more cultured occupations. Also there, at any rate on census night, was a small granddaughter. Next door to them now, in what must therefore have been Stapleton Hall itself, was William Prowse, a musical instrument maker, his wife, a small son and daughter, and three servants. This, I have established, was the William Prowse (1801–86) who formed a partnership with another instrument maker and composer, Robert Keith, which became Keith Prowse the famous musical publishing firm and eventual ticket agency.

Another moderately genteel family was also accommodated in part of Stapleton Hall, a jeweller called Jonathan Hazel with a wife, Martha, and two sons. Staying on census night was also a Hazel niece and the niece's own little boy. No separate servant is listed with them, but I base my assessment of their social status and where they lodged on the fact that, two years later, Martha was writing to the ten-year-old son who was then away at boarding school. The letter came to light, tightly folded and tucked behind a beam, in the late 1980s when Stapleton Hall was undergoing substantial building works. Presumably the child, when home for the holidays, used the space behind the beam as a private storage place. The contents of the letter apparently suggested that the family sometimes lent a hand on the farm, in best classless country style. However, although presented to the local archives at the time of its discovery, the letter is for the moment lost – slumbering, it is to be hoped, in some neglected box, only awaiting a further resurrection.

The 1840s–'50s may also have been the period when the large, eighteenth-century barn on the opposite side of the main house from the farm was converted into living quarters, with plaster and metallic-painted wallpaper. For also listed as living here at 'Stroud Green' were more ordinary families: a gardener with a wife and young son; a farmhand, with a wife and three children. There was also a cow-keeper with a wife, a daughter who was an 'apprentice dress-maker' and four younger children. The gardener may have worked for the Prowses, among others, and the farmhand was presumably employed by Wells; but the cow-keeper would have been a man with a few cows of his own to supply the area's need for milk, since an employee in charge of a whole diary herd would have been called a 'cowman'. Independent cow-keepers were common in expanding cities till late in the nineteenth century, since, until the coming of refrigeration, getting milk to the customer before it went sour was a constant preoccupation. It may be that the cow-keeper, Jackson, had rented from Wells some of the other farm buildings, to house both his cows and his family. The absence of more farmhands on the site makes me think that perhaps at this time the farm was mainly producing hay, a much less labour-intensive business than dairy farming. The Wellses were by then getting old, and clearly neither the artist son nor the one who went in for foreign languages was going to take on the business.

Jackson was still there ten years later, father by then of three grown daughters and four young sons. All the boys went to school and he had two living-in male servants (cow hands?) so clearly the milk business was flourishing. On the opposite side of the Stroud Green Road at this point stands a building ornamented with engraved and tinted scenes of cows, milk delivery and butter-making, known as the Old Dairy, one of the few distinctive buildings in the area. It would be nice to think this was a trace of Jackson's enterprise a hundred and fifty years ago, but it seems, rather, to have been an outlet for the Friern Manor Dairy Company, constructed *c*. 1890, with conscious nostalgia for the vanishing past.

In 1861 the Prowse family too were still there, in the principal house. On census night two daughters were at home and a visiting sister-in-law, Mrs Mayer, and her own daughter; also two young female servants. In some part of the same property marked in the margin as being 'the Lodge', were a young coachman in his twenties called George Stield, with a wife who also acted as a servant, a baby daughter, and a niece of nine who was staying that night. Robert Keith, William Prowse's partner, was now dead, but as the Prowses had become 'carriage people', clearly the business continued to flourish.

Also still present, somewhere in the collection of Stapleton Hall buildings, were the jeweller, his wife and his wife's sister. They are now listed as if they were living in part of the farmhouse, but so too is a carter, so it may simply be that the enumerator that year or his informant was once again not particular about the exact living arrangements on the complicated site. Also accommodated thereabouts were three male servants and one female, a proportion suggestive of outdoor work with horses or cows. Mr and Mrs Wells, who would by then have been in their seventies, were no longer in evidence.

Now the chief inhabitant of the farmhouse was Charles Turner, who proudly announced himself as 'farmer 226 acres [employer of] 8 men and one boy'. The Turners were a long-established family in the area; Charles had been born at another farm off Hornsey Lane and both his parents lay in the parish churchyard. I do not know if the Sarah Turner who had been employed as a maid in Stapleton Hall twenty years before was related to him, but it seems likely. Now Charles Turner was a vestryman and a surveyor of the highways. The land he farmed was not his, for the Lucas family were the ground landlords: in 1856 they had succeeded in converting their copyhold tenancy of the land in the old Brownswood manor into freehold. Later, they were to sell some of it on to Charles Turner, but already by 1861 he had done well for himself. He had acquired a lot more land by renting part of Hornsey Wood, the small section of old forest not far from Stroud Green, and clearing it.

With him in Stapleton Hall Farm were his wife, Dinah, a teenage daughter, two female indoor servants and – rather surprisingly – two unmarried male boarders. One was a member of the Stock Exchange and the other a 'Russia broker', who presumably represented Britain's expanding trade relations with that vast land. The Turners would hardly have been in serious need of the money these paying guests brought, but possibly, in a down-to-earth way, they saw no reason not to make something out of unused rooms, or perhaps simply enjoyed company of an educated sort. 'Boarders' as distinct from lodgers would normally take their evening meal with the family.

There must in any case have been a demand for

accommodation which increased exponentially with London's ever-growing labour market. Houses were now, in the 1860s, beginning to line the Hornsey Road and two new roads off it laid out across the Tollington estate, but Stroud Green Road itself was still a country lane with hedgerows. The cluster of buildings round Stapleton Hall must still have looked very much as it had done in the 1820s. I think that the stockjobber and the broker probably felt themselves fortunate to have found such a rustic retreat within easy reach of the City, even if the smells of the farmyard and dairy were rather pervasive in hot weather. There was even a long-standing tea garden, the Japan House, nearby at the foot of Crouch Hill.

But the writing was on the wall not just for Stroud Green but for the whole of Hornsey parish. Let us backtrack twenty years to see why.

Early-Victorian Hornsey, with its spread-out hamlets and its dream villas standing in their own grounds, was a place which had for generations been affected by the arrival of outsiders with business interests in town, but which still continued to function as a country parish. It prided itself on its separation from noisy, increasingly dirty London, and was genuinely shocked and upset when external forces dragged it into the world of metropolitan progress. Ironically, Hornsey village, which had always been rather inaccessible from town, was to find itself by the mid-century at the heart of the transport revolution.

Many citizens of such villages adjacent to London were to see the landscapes of their youth utterly transformed by the time they reached middle age. When Dickens's Scrooge is magically transported by the Spirit of Christmas Past from the sordid streets of London to a clean country scene under a fresh fall of snow, he exclaims: 'Good Heaven! I was bred in this place. I was a boy here!'[7] The shift back that carries such an emotional charge is to a world of lost innocence, which is why it resonated so much with the Victorian reader and resonates today. But Scrooge was transported in place as well as in time, whereas many people in the nineteenth century yearned nostalgically for a similar journey back to the past within their own much-altered district.

One man in particular in Hornsey was in a position to monitor the change of habitat step by step and yet find himself essentially impotent before it. Like Thomas Lewes in Taynton, the Rev. Richard Harvey remained a fixture for over fifty years, but unlike Lewes he saw his familiar world altered out of all recognition. He was appointed vicar of the parish in 1829, when the population of Hornsey was double what it had been at the beginning of the century but still not above five thousand. By 1851 it was ten thousand, and by 1871 twenty thousand. Thirty years later it would be over seventy thousand.

Harvey arrived just as a new church was scheduled to replace the dilapidated medieval one. Dilapidated churches, as we know, were a feature of the period, though most parishes fortunately baulked at a total replacement. Possibly their churches were less ruinous than Hornsey's well-known old one, which had always been on an unstable site and was now apparently on the point of collapse. At all events, its demolition and its rebuilding in Gothic revival style began in 1829. A new Vestry Book was started in 1834, by which time the church was completed all but the tower, the only bit where much of the old structure was preserved. The work had, as is usual in such cases, gone over budget – nearly £15,000 over, a very substantial sum for that time. There was much discussion in the Vestry as to whether they could get the parish's many wealthy inhabitants (the dwellers in elegant villas and in a few older mansions) to offer 'subscriptions', but it was feared that some of them would now be attending the other new church that had recently been built at the Highgate end of the parish.

Over the next several decades a number of other churches would be built in Hornsey's scattered districts, including Stroud Green, to serve the supposed religious fervour of the ever-increasing population. The new churches, resplendent in vaguely Byzantine brick or carefully rugged Gothic ragstone, may have seemed to Richard Harvey a cause for celebration – he encouraged their building – but in practice they can only have diminished the significance of the original parish Vestry, whose power was in any case eroded as the years passed by the inevitable rise of secular district authorities.

Harvey, by then a canon of the Church, finally announced his retirement in 1880, after fifty-one years of conscientious and apparently much-appreciated service. It was probably no coincidence that this was the year it was decided that the 1830s rebuilt church that had cost so much was no longer adequate to Hornsey's needs. In another bad decision a larger church was erected alongside it, a squat, ill-proportioned pile. Fifteen years later, after Hornsey had narrowly escaped being subsumed entirely into the London metropolitan area, the last vestiges of parochial power were ceded to a new Urban District Council.[8]

In the early years of Harvey's ministry all this lay in the unimaginable future. Cows, we know, grazed the fields round Stroud Green, and the New River still curled picturesquely, open to the sky, through water meadows on the other side of the parish. A kind man, Harvey would offer, in the best Christian tradition, to carry the heavy baskets of wet linen for washerwomen making their way back from the stream. Old folk ceremonies, such as the yearly 'perambulation' of the parish boundaries by boys and men (and a dinner afterwards in a tavern at parish expense) were much honoured. Ominously accelerating change only began to be signalled in January 1845, and was not immediately recognised as such. On the 9th a special Vestry meeting was called (at ten in the morning, the customary gentlemanly hour) to consider 'a notice received by the overseers of this parish from the projectors of the London and York Railway of their intention of carrying the proposed line through property belonging to this parish'.

The parish, as represented by the Vestry, did not think anything of this proposal, and decided to oppose it, evidently under the impression that such a stand was possible. It was resolved that railway lines 'while they cannot in any degree benefit the parishioners are calculated to produce serious injury to the values of property in this parish and to destroy the retirement of its locality and neighbourhood'. The later statement was all too true, but the issue of property values was more complicated, as many a watchful builder could have told the gentlemen in their retired, garden-girt houses. Parishioners were to be earnestly recommended 'to write in the most strenuous opposition to the projected undertaking' and a deputation to the Bishop was planned – as if the Bishop would have power over the railways. There were further remarks about 'private speculation' being put above 'public advantage'.

Certainly this was the beginning of the year of Railway Mania and the rush for railway shares, so one sees the point the vicar and Vestry were trying to make. But unfortunately for them the London to York line was not one of those over-optimistic, short-lived schemes such as the line through Burford or the one through Limpsfield. This would be only the second northbound route out of London to be built, after the London & Birmingham which had recently opened its terminus at Euston Square. The new route all the way to York was planned to start from a terminus at the inconspicuous crossroads called King's Cross, till then a place of rubbish tips, and to travel up the eastern side of England. It would be a key part of the country's developing railway infrastructure, and would inevitably pass through Hornsey parish on the first stage of its journey.

While many other schemes were abandoned as the manic year drew to its close, the Great Northern Railway Company (as it was now hubristically called) proceeded with its grand plan. In spite of active opposition from other main railway companies, including the London & Birmingham, its enabling Act of Parliament was passed, and received the royal assent in June 1846. Four years later the line was opened. King's Cross station was still being built, so the first train steamed triumphantly out from a temporary station up Maiden Lane, which is today's York Way – the ancient route to the same destination as the train.

The Great Northern, running in tunnels, deep cuttings or on high embankments according to the lie of the land, did not directly affect the Stapleton Hall end of Stroud Green. It crossed only the southern end, just before the point where Stroud Green Lane met the fairly new Seven Sisters Road, and it disturbed only a dairy/tea garden. But thereafter it swept straight up towards the eastern side of the parish, cutting a wide swathe across the edge of the village of Hornsey not far from the church, demolishing cottages, and incidentally ploughing through the moated site where, from the sixteenth to the eighteenth century, had stood a Tudor Great House. On the far side of this newly constructed barrier, and a little to the south, lay meadows where the New River still curled. Also here stood Harringay House and its grounds, then occupied by Edward Henry Chapman of the Bank of England with fourteen servants to attend on him. Members of Parliament, many of whom must have known him socially, allocated him the huge sum of £6,200, payable by the railway Company for 'residential damage', to which the Company tried unsuccessfully to object. Most of the owners of swept-away cottages, being only tenants, would have received nothing.

It is evident from the minutes of meetings that the Vestry's initial illusions about their power to stand in the way of the trains soon had to be discarded. Instead, from 1850 on, angry rumblings appear about rights of way. The railway plan that had been produced for the approval of Parliament showed the old footpaths that the line would encounter, but not how they were to be dealt with.[9] Towards the end of the year there were complaints in the Vestry that a path had been stopped up by the railway embankment 'near Harringay House'; and also another path a little further south, coming all the way from Highgate, passing near Stroud Green and then crossing Hornsey Wood – before which it now met a cutting. A public meeting was held, and a small committee of local notables was formed, including Richard Williams the Stapleton Hall wine merchant.

By and by, the cutting was provided with a footbridge (one wide enough for cows), but regarding the path near Harringay House that led to the New River, it was reported: 'Your Committee observed, with astonishment, that not only has the Great Northern Railway Company presumed to attempt the diversion of this ancient footpath without obtaining or asking authority from anyone so to do, but that a station, or other large brick building, is actually in course of erection by that Company right over and across that footpath.' It was indeed Hornsey's first station that was being built, as the unhappy committee were no doubt well aware but preferred not to accept. It was, for a while, to be the first stop out of London, 'among the cornfields' as a jubilant and not very observant journalist remarked in the *Illustrated London News*.

It was also noted by the committee that boundary stones put down by the parish in previous years had been 'removed, or buried in heaps of earth', and it was strongly suggested that Mr Chapman (no doubt sweetened by the £6,200) had connived at the closure of the footpath. By the end of the year the committee was in correspondence with the railway company and also with Mr Chapman's solicitors, and counsel's opinion was being taken. The matter went on and on, with Chapman offering to buy the field through which the footpath ran – 'being desirous to stop the litigation . . . between the parish and the Great Northern Railway by a fair and liberal compromise' – though how his ownership of the field might help preserve the right of way to the river was far from clear. In any case the issue was soon further complicated by an Act of Parliament, instigated by the railway interest, to straighten out the New River and enclose part of it in pipes, thus 'affecting the rights and interests of the parish of Hornsey', as the Vestry angrily expressed it. Alas for the washerwomen, the fishers for sticklebacks and the naked bathers.

The Vestry, led by the vicar, continued to fight this battle too for some time, maintaining that the New River Company had no right to 'stay that fresh stream of running water which has now existed for two hundred and fifty years'. Eventually they were warned that the River Company itself had no power against Parliament.

The Vestry did succeed, in 1852, in making the railway Company restore a number of footpaths, mainly through dank pedestrian archways in embankments, but the juggernaut of Progress could not of course be stopped. Five years later, in February 1857, another special Vestry meeting was called. It had a twofold agenda of foreboding. It was 'To consider whether any and what steps should be taken [a note of desperation is here apparent] in reference to a Railway which is intended to pass through this parish, to be called the Tottenham and Willesden Junction railway, and also with reference to the formation of a Park, to be called Finsbury Park, which is proposed to be situated principally in this parish.'

The Vestry's apprehensions were well founded. It was to be the coming of the local line (shortly to be renamed the Tottenham and Hampstead Junction Railway), and the creation of an urban park where there had previously been pastures and the remains of Hornsey Wood, that together were to bring about the transformation of a rural parish into a densely built suburb.

Chapter XIII

Cow pastures become Finsbury Park

The story of the actual Finsbury Park is one of frustration and increasing desperation. It was originally meant to have been created further south. Through a chapter of false starts and delays, it made an alien incursion into Hornsey parish; then, by the chance siting of a railway station, its name was eventually applied to a large part of the district, reconfiguring old geography and old perceptions.

With the insidious growth of London even before Victoria came to the throne, and then the Reform Act of 1832, a new metropolitan parlimentary borough of Finsbury had been created out of parts of the old, large parishes of Clerkenwell and Islington. Nine years later the radical Member for Finsbury, a flamboyant Thomas Duncombe, was of the opinion that his crowded and largely working-class borough needed a place of recreation. There had been cholera epidemics in the 1830s, mistakenly believed to be due to 'foetid miasmas', and public health was a newly fashionable issue. The air and greenery of public parks were considered highly beneficial to those who dwelt in 'sunless courts' (as narrow old streets were routinely described) and parks were, you might say, in the air. Victoria Park in the East End and Battersea Park near Lambeth were both planned and laid out in the 1840s.

The first initiatives for a park in Finsbury failed, but in 1850 the scheme was revived. This time it was hoped it would be under royal patronage, and it was to be called Albert Park, after the Prince Consort. An elegant plan was drawn up with the park occupying land in Highbury, south of the Seven Sisters Road. This was in the borough of Stoke Newington, but mostly still within the parliamentary constituency of Finsbury. Haste was urged by the promoters, because the price of unbuilt land bordering London was steadily going up. A deputation composed of several Members of Parliament, local worthies, magistrates and the like, visited the Home Secretary Sir George Grey, nephew of the more famous Earl Grey, Prime Minister and tea connoisseur.[1] Grey was a Whig and a reformer; however, his particular obsession was not green spaces but the establishment of public wash houses and baths. It was enquired of him if anything could be done to prevent builders making 'undue claims' on land within the proposed park. Disappointingly, Grey replied, in Tory laissez-faire style, 'If that were done we should interfere with the private rights of the proprietors of the land. It certainly seems a very pretty ground, and I believe the New River runs through it?' 'It does, Sir; but in the course of a few years thousands of houses will be placed upon the ground. They are already asking £1,000 per acre . . .' 'That makes the matter more difficult,' replied Grey. 'We cannot bring parks to every man's door, nor can we pull down rows of houses.' He also remarked that, as soon as word of a planned park got round 'landowners would double their prices'.

A scheme that had already been used in the case of Battersea Park was mooted: one third of the land purchased should be put into building lots to finance parkland for the rest. However, the money required was not raised and once again the scheme was dropped. Then, in 1855 the Metropolitan Board of Works was set up. This was an appointed but genuinely public-spirited body: it was to become the means by which the governance of London was rationalised and centralised, and it eventually evolved into the London County Council. The board revived the Finsbury Park scheme. However, such had been the activities of builders around Highbury that yet another site had to be found further north, and this new site was entirely in Hornsey. Although Hornsey was not counted as one of the London boroughs 'within the Bills of Mortality' (and never, in the end, became part of the LCC area), it was decided that it should fall with the Metropolitan Board of Work's remit. This decision already gives a clue as to Hornsey's equivocal nature in the mid-nineteenth century. And arguably the case for Finsbury needing an open space – albeit at some distance away – was more pressing than ever. Parliament, in a new spirit of Gladstonian Liberalism, promised £50,000 towards it. The estimated total cost was now £200,000.

The long-term leaseholder of much of the newly designated land, which was now north of the Seven Sisters Road, adjacent to Hornsey Wood, had recently died. After some trading of bits and pieces of land, his executors had leased 189 acres to the Turner family of Stapleton Hall Farm and to the publican who ran the Hornsey Wood Tavern. This had become less of a 'retired' spot for assignations, duels and pigeon-shooting and more a place of popular resort, especially since the omnibuses had begun to ply from the City, Finsbury and Islington. Hornsey village residents regarded the rebuilt Tavern as rather vulgar.

By that time, the Great Northern Line had already been open for several years. It ran northward in a deep cutting west of Hornsey Wood, and, as we know, a bridge had been built over the line to provide a right of way for the cows (which now included Mr Turner's) that went to graze in the meadows north of the Wood. The bridge had, however, been made as wide as a carriageway,[2] which raised suspicions in a number of minds that a builder or builders had future plans for that land and had been talking quietly to the railway Company. It began to seem likely that even this scheme to create a park so far from Finsbury borough, if it were not soon implemented, might be inexorably overtaken by what George Cruikshank had already, in a famous cartoon of 1829, called *The March of bricks and mortar*.

The Finsbury Park Act was passed by Parliament in 1857, in the teeth of objections from various bodies in Hornsey, in Islington, in Finsbury, in Parliament itself, from ratepayers in unrelated boroughs who feared they might have to contribute, and from the New River Company who thought the park would interfere with their access – the river ran through part of the proposed site, as it did through the original one. The Act gave the Metropolitan Board the right compulsorily to purchase 250 acres, twenty of which were to be laid aside for building plots to help finance the whole. But six more years elapsed in delays, disputes, and in the illusion (continually resurrected by hopeful property developers and ratepayers) that somehow building villas right round the edge of the park would enhance it rather than merely making it smaller and more closed off from the main access roads. Various parties tried not to pay the monies that they had undertaken to, and meanwhile the price of land in the area continued to rise. At one point our old acquaintance, Joshua Lucas weighed in, with the alternative offer to sell 200 acres of the meadowland he now owned freehold round Stroud Green. If this proposal – which was only narrowly defeated – had gone through, the park would have ended up west rather than east of the Great Northern Railway line. In that case it would have included Stapleton Hall, whose destiny might then have been to become a park keepers' headquarters, a Civic Centre or, today, some battered Education Unit.

* * *

Meanwhile a new station between King's Cross, Holloway and Hornsey village had been opened in the summer of 1861, at the point where the bottom end of Stroud Green Lane was crossed by the Seven Sisters Road. It was at first called Seven Sisters station (not to be confused with the modern tube station of that name in South Tottenham). Local opinion was that it hardly deserved the term 'station' since it consisted of two wooden platforms up on the viaduct 'for the accommodation of a few local residents'. Few they were, for the viaduct stood among fields, but to anyone watching current trends it must have been obvious that the land near to it was now going to be 'ripe' for conversion from hayfields to building plots.

Stroud Green Lane was still too liable to flooding to attract immediate attention, but some rather grand houses began to go up on the south side of Seven Sisters Road. Clearly, if the designated parkland on the other side was to be protected, the Metropolitan Board had to move with decision. All the more so, as the threatened Tottenham & Hampstead Junction Railway was authorised by Parliament the following year. It was to sweep across Holloway and into Hornsey not far from Stapleton Hall, then diagonally across the fields to pass under the Great Northern line a little to the north of Hornsey Wood. I was entertained to find, coming across the handwritten record book of the Company's meetings in Bruce Castle archive, that one of the shareholders and promoters was a Thomas Biscoe, and that a William Biscoe was also involved.

Clearly the extended Biscoe family, however grandly rural the family seat at Limpsfield, did not hesitate to profit by commercial ventures. The Leveson-Gower family, too, had sold land for a railway (which was never actually made) and the head of the family was later to become chairman of the Oxted Gas Company. However, this was arguably a more benign venture than the

Tottenham & Hampstead Junction Railway, which compromised the environment of others and was unashamedly exploitative. When it expropriated pieces of common land on the Hornsey–Tottenham border the only compensation for loss of parishioners' rights was paid to the Tottenham Burial Board, whose job it was to lay the bodies of the poor in the earth.

'*Man comes and tills the field and lies beneath . . .*' But the fields were going fast. There was no more land on which the poor could put their chickens and donkeys, and apparently even land for the dead was problematic. There was trouble about Hornsey parish churchyard, which had become too restricted for the numbers now needing to lie there and was anyway waterlogged: a dense, undrained mass of heavy clay and decomposed remains. The Hornsey Local Board, which in the 1860s took over many of the rights and duties of the old Vestry, tried to get use of one of the arches of the Great Northern Railway to accommodate the dead – which the Railway Company, to their credit, refused.

The Metropolitan Board took their final decision about the park in 1863, in the teeth of futile opposition from a number of Vestries within London, who all feared (the traditional Vestry preoccupation) that their wealthier citizens would be forced to contribute to a public amenity they might not use. The land available was now reduced to 120 acres where the park lies today, on a wedge-shaped site contained between the Great Northern line and the Seven Sisters Road. When it was bought – after a final skirmish as the Great Northern tried to get Parliament to approve a branch line right through the park, to join the half-completed Tottenham & Hampstead Junction Railway – Hornsey Wood stood at the heart of the parkland.

In 1866 Hornsey Wood House, with its popular beer and tea garden, was pulled down, and nearly all the Wood uprooted. A contemporary inhabitant wrote: 'the last

remnant of forest is therebye obliterated, and the great
pigeon preserve is destroyed. The wild wood of Hornsey
will be transformed into the pretty park of Finsbury, but
those who can remember this last vestige of the forest
land will sometimes sigh, as they promenade in the park,
for the lost rusticity of the wood . . .'[3]

By 1868, in spite of an ongoing wrangle about whether
houses were to be built round the edges, a landscape
gardener's plans for the 'pretty park' were approved. The
bit of New River that curved through it was to become
an ornamental pond. A bandstand, and a refreshment
room forbidden to sell beer, wine or spirits, would replace
the Tavern.[4] The same year, the Tottenham & Hampstead
Junction Railway was opened, a true suburban line, with
a station just above the foot of Crouch Hill, not far from
Stapleton Hall. Another suburban line, the disputed
Great Northern branch line, now named the Edgware,
Highgate & London, had already opened some months
before. It ran on an embankment across the fields of
Stapleton Hall Farm. Stapleton Hall itself, though still
a rural spot, now had two railways running in different
directions, the one crossing the other, within a couple
of hundred yards, in addition to the main line a mile
down the road.

The Edgware, Highgate & London had managed, in
the end, to sneak a small piece of track over a corner of
the parkland to bring its line down to the Seven Sisters
station, which thus became a junction. Future development all the way up Stroud Green was now inevitable,
the more so because a new, big drain had been incorporated into the embankment of the Edgware, Highgate
& London line. Spongy Stroud Green, where cows had
once got stuck in bogs, was now properly drained for
the first time, though complaints about the quality of
the drain were to surface at intervals for years.

In early August 1869 the new Finsbury Park at last
had its opening ceremony, consisting of an ad hoc

procession of worthies, a military band, maroons let off, and 'some confusion' as the park was open at any hour anyway. Eight days before that, the Great Northern had cannily renamed its Seven Sisters station 'Finsbury Park'. Greater Hornsey was not only losing its rusticity: it was now fated to lose its very identity.

On the Ordance Survey map surveyed during that decade and published in 1869–70, the outlines of the park are not properly delineated and Hornsey Wood and its Tavern still appear. Map-makers of a rapidly evolving terrain have a difficult time of it. However, across a whole area considerably larger than the park itself is written as general designation 'Finsbury Park'. And when, ten years on, the district was so populous that it could support a local newspaper, that paper was at first christened the *Seven Sisters and Finsbury Park Journal*. It was to become the *Hornsey & Finsbury Park Journal* two years later.

Transformations, however swift and unstoppable, do not happen overnight, or all over a district at the same time. On Stanford's Library Map of 1863 the Holloway Road is ribbon-developed but much of the backland both to the south and north of it is still fields, and the same is the case with the Seven Sisters Road leading off from it at right angles. There has been some building on the Tollington estate near Hornsey Road, and more is laid out in neat building plots that appear, on the map, as the ghosts of roads to come. However, Stroud Green itself is almost untouched along its length, as is the slope of Crouch Hill, and the Stapleton Hall group of buildings is very much as it was in 1820, and indeed probably in 1720.

Seven years later, when the first of the extremely detailed OS maps was published, the area through which the Holloway and Hornsey Roads ran appears as entirely built over, or designated for building. It was in this newly urbanised district, which came to be known as Lower Holloway, that George Grossmith's famous Mr Pooter, the incarnation of the suburban clerk, had his fictional home. Development runs right up to the Islington boundary; that is, to the south side of what was still, just, called Stroud Green Lane. The north side, which is in Hornsey, is unbuilt for the moment, though it would not be for long. The new railway lines, of course, figure on this map, and Crouch Hill station. There are some brand new detached houses, and plots laid out for more, ascending Crouch Hill – where there is also, now, a brick works which might surely have deterred some buyers, since brick kilns notoriously smelt.

The Stapleton Hall complex, with its gardens and its farmyard, is still, just, untouched, though a new and rather grand house has appeared nearby, standing in its own ornamental garden, on a piece of the left-over common land by the side of the lane. But between Stapleton Hall and Crouch Hill station a brand new short road has appeared, leading to a footpath over one railway, under another and hence to the fields all the way up the hill. It was to be called, logically, Mount-pleasant Road and had been planned since 1863, but the covenant for it was not signed till late in the autumn of 1868, just as the OS map was being prepared. It appears, from documents that have come to rest in the London Metropolitan archives, to have been the result of a long drawn-out negotiation between Joshua Lucas, who, as we know, owned much of the land round there, and several other people who had acquired the rights to small bits and pieces of 'waste' abutting the lane. These included the proprietor of the Japan teahouse (which would disappear under the road), a speculative builder called Hodson who was to become very active in Hornsey in the next thirty years, and a William Henry Cox. This person, described as 'of Guildford, in the County of Surrey, gent.' owned a lot of land immediately to the north. I conclude that he had already made a tidy profit by selling strips of this to the railways.

The ebullient Henry Cox, whom we met in Limpsfield arguing both with his neighbours and with the squire about his right to take over pieces of waste and divert watercourses, was by that time in his late eighties. This had not diminished his zeal for combat, as his archive shows, but I do not suggest he was personally involved in Stroud Green. However, he had a lawyer brother, and a nephew in the same profession, and the family owned other properties in Surrey besides Henry Cox's own place in Limpsfield. Cox being a common name, I cannot prove that the William Henry Cox of Guildford in Surrey, who must ultimately have made such a good thing out of land he had acquired at Stapleton Hall, was related to the colourful and like-minded Henry Cox of Limpsfield, also in Surrey, but I would not be surprised if he were.

Under new government regulations, guarantees now had to be given as to the surface and drainage of a new road, and Lucas had to get permission from the Local Board to divert two footpaths across his estate – though I suspect that one of the diversions related to further plans he had in mind. Mountpleasant Road got constructed, if rather slowly. But there, for the time being, matters rested. Rather too many houses had been built in the previous decade; they had not all sold or let easily. Indeed, some roads remained chronically uncompleted and unpaved as the cash flow of speculative builders dried up. Some houses only a few years old were already slipping down the social scale into multi-occupation by fly-by-night tenants. The planned genteel suburb of Lower Holloway was turning into a dingy urban area faster than anyone had foreseen. Landowners hesitated. For a few years more Stapleton Hall and its surroundings were reprieved. A local resident, referring to this time, was to write nostalgically at the end of the century: 'I can remember the flowering hedgerows of the rich meadows in Stroud Green, when the newly opened High Barnet branch of the [Edgware, Highgate & London] railway ran through fields from Finsbury Park . . .'[5]

Charles Turner's cows still grazed undisturbed, and he figured on the census of 1871 as 'farmer of 120 acres, employing 8 labourers'. The amount of land was reduced, but the size was still significant and the number of employees would indicate an active dairy farm. (The Prowses, he now aged sixty-six and figuring as a music publisher, were still there too in Stapleton Hall itself.) However, it is a measure of the changing Hornsey landscape, and of attitudes changing with it, that public indignation was altered in tone. Complaints received by the new Parks Authority were not now about old footpaths being diverted but about the nuisance caused by these rights of way through the park to the surrounding pastures: '. . . cattle [are] being driven through the Park day and night, to the danger of people in the day time and the detriment of roads at all times. The Park, owing to its having to be kept open continually, is frequently used at night for immoral purposes.'

The fact that immorality had undoubtedly been taking place for centuries, probably more comfortably and discreetly, on the same site when it was wooded, had evidently not occurred to the complainant. But it is possible that ladies of the night from Islington were taking their customers up to the convenient park on the new horse trams, just as others did from Camden Town to Hampstead Heath at the same period.

In 1874 old rights of way through the park were cancelled, and after that it was closed at night by wrought-iron gates. I don't know what accommodation Charles Turner and his cows made with this state of affairs, but I suspect that he managed to profit rather than lose by it. After 1878 the gravelled roads and paths within the park were gaslit, and in 1879 playing football in the park was banned for anyone over thirteen. Needless to say, the park was nicely planted with suitable shrubs and there were plenty of keepers to keep everyone in order.

That same year, the weekly *Seven Sisters and Finsbury Park Journal* was started by an ambitious printer. Its headquarters was in Stroud Green Road. In its late-December number a correspondent extolled 'old-fashioned Dickensian Christmases' (Dickens himself had died only nine years before), and suggested 'a walk out of London on Boxing Day . . . Nothing more invigorating than the open road . . . the fresh, bleak air blowing on you from the Hertfordshire hills or through the Middlesex lanes . . . lots of rustic scenery out beyond Edmonton and Southgate. Then there are the capital hostelries on the roads – hostelries with swing signs and sanded floors – places built when George III was king.' There was also a wistful reference to the tracks over stiles that had, till recently in Hornsey itself, led to stretches of the New River. Already, even as a rural habitat was being destroyed month by month and respectability ruled, nostalgia for a lost, less controlled world was thriving.

In the same edition many shops were advertising 'Christmas wares', as if this were rather a new idea, brought about by increasing prosperity; but also anxieties were expressed for the poor in what was turning out to be a particularly cold winter. There were suggestions that a local soup kitchen should be started. Dickensian London had evidently not yet quite passed away.

Chapter XIV

Passionate Hornsey

The founding of a local paper in the newly self-conscious area of Finsbury Park was an accepted sign of Progress. Other supposed signs were eagerly hailed by the paper itself. Someone calling himself an Old Resident was soon writing an approving piece on the urban growth of the last few years: 'This is no longer the outlying suburb of a large metropolis, but a great centre destined to become – and that most rapidly – a great metropolis of itself . . . One must almost go to the Western states of America to see a progress so rapid.' This rather overwrought account went on to list as unequivocal gains bazaars (large shops), halls, public baths, concert rooms, bicycle clubs, cricket grounds, young men's associations, 'self-improvement' groups, literary and dramatic clubs and magic lantern shows. 'Where once the New River pursued the noiseless tenor of its way, streets and thoroughfares are now to be found, inhabited by tens of thousands of people. A vast, teeming population has arisen, brought here by a system of rapid communication by rail from all parts, by several lines of continuous trams and buses, pretty well filled all the day long.'

A week or two later the same writer, or another like him, was extolling the fact that 'Numerous new shops are about to be opened in Finsbury Park and the influx of enterprising traders should be to our neighbourhood an encouraging sign of the times. This week the building operation in connection with three handsome shops adjoining Crouch Hill station is expected to be almost completed . . . The addition of shops to the row of houses in Seven Sisters Road . . . is an important work.'

In fact shops being built out over the front gardens of existing private houses is not usually a sign of progress but rather of insidious social decline. However, the rising population of the district was almost entirely composed of what were known as 'the commercial classes'; they probably did not think in the same terms as the more traditional inhabitants. To the new population all the clutter of urban living, including the numerous new clubs and entertainments, were a sign that they themselves were attaining a level of civilisation and prosperity unknown to their mainly working-class parents and grandparents. This was just before the beginning of the 1880s. In under twenty years the population of Hornsey had risen from eleven thousand to thirty-seven thousand, most of that increase having been in the last ten years, It was to double again by the end of the century. London, like all expanding cities everywhere, has been steadily fed by an influx of people born in remote rural spots: the birthplaces stated on the successive census forms, particularly of domestic servants, are testimony to this. It is therefore perhaps worth remembering that in the decade 1871 to 1881 the population of Taynton, like so many other villages, actually shrank by over a hundred, or nearly one third.

It is not over-fanciful to imagine a boy, one of the brightest at the small school in Taynton, who knows that profits are diminished on the farm where his father is head cowman and that everyone is worried. He ponders his own future and by and by he finds a job as a shop-boy in Burford. He is paid little: Burford is now an economic backwater too, but he is quick and willing. After several years he confides in his employer his desire to try his luck in London, where he has never been. His employer, who thinks highly of him, has a brother-in-law who is a market gardener and has London connections. Wheels turn. Someone is extending his fish and green-grocery shop in the Seven Sisters Road, and is looking for an assistant, a strong boy who won't be too particular to sleep on the premises. So our boy makes his way, with delight and trepidation, and with a borrowed train fare, to the newest suburb of the city that is now the biggest in the world.

At first he is not sure he will be able to cope with it: the gaslights everywhere in the streets so bright that you cannot see the stars, the flaring naphtha lamps on the cheap stalls, the mixture of smells, the incessant noise of wheels and hooves, the incessant voices mostly in a raucous London accent that is strange to him, the visual assault of handbills and advertisements pasted up every-where, the sooty dirt, the sense of never being alone . . . But he is young, he gets used to it and then comes to like it. He begins to take a pride in the Finsbury Park area, so full of people not after all very different from himself. He enrols for evening classes in accountancy. He buys a cheap suit on the instalment plan, a stiff collar and a bowler for Sundays instead of his cloth cap. He watches other tradesmen. In the job he looks for next he will hope to better himself. He has become an inhab-itant of Hornsey. By and by he feels he would never now live anywhere else . . .

Like all local papers, the *Journal* was sustained from the first by advertisements, both commercial and personal. One has the impression of mass nest-building and a constant preoccupation with Getting On, or at any rate Getting By: 'How to purchase a house for 2 guineas a month . . . A plot of land for five shillings per month . . . A "coal saving" iron stove . . .' 'Board (or Partial) and Residence Finsbury Park (15 mins from City) is offered by private English family to gentleman desiring comforts of a domesticated house.' 'Washing wanted by a well-experienced laundress . . .' 'German and Music lessons by a German (Hanoverian) lady, 7 years experience. Terms 1/6 an hour, 19 Perth Rd . . .' '12 Stapleton Hall Rd, furnished apartments for gentleman, bicycle not objected to.' 'Ennis Rd. off Stroud Green Rd, to let, unfurnished breakfast parlour and 1 or more bedrooms, Use of kitchen.' The family who owned, or more likely rented, that fairly new house clearly needed to bring in some more income without delay.

These last three addresses were (and are) on the north side of what was now definitely Stroud Green Road, which had not been built over at all ten years before. A glance at the revised Ordnance Survey map of the 1880s indicates a staggering change. Although there are still fields not far off, up at Mountpleasant above the smoke and the railway lines, all the immediate area of Stroud Green, including the Stapleton Hall site, has become densely urban. In 1881, as if to confirm its changed nature, it even acquired its own station at the intersection of the Tottenham & Hampstead Junction Railway and the Edgware, Highgate & London one. The way to the station was up the new Stapleton Hall Road. A road? Where a short side lane used to run into the stockyard?

So had Charles Turner the farmer disappeared from this blighted scene, now that his cows could no longer cross the park? No, in fact he hadn't. The census taken the year the station opened shows him still there, with his wife Dinah and one living-in female servant, but he is now not a farmer but a 'hay salesman'. This was a key occupation on the edge of a great city for which hay was all-important for transport. The petrol engine was only just being invented, and the first motor cars would not appear in the London streets for another fifteen years. Capitalising, no doubt, on a lifetime's contacts, Charles would have bought hay wholesale from the farms still existing further out and sold it on to the numerous stables, carts, costermongers and cab drivers of the area as well as to the select number who kept a carriage. Indeed he had one of those next door to him. The Prowses, now well into their seventies and marked 'retired', still employed a coachman and his wife, a groom and his wife, a gardener and another female servant. In the Victorian world where all nice homes had a piano, the music publishing business was doing as well as the hay trade.

There was, however, one significant change. In the new Stapleton Hall Road the Turners were now listed as occupying Stapleton Hall itself, while the Prowses were living in 'Stroud Green House'. This was the detached house standing in its own garden that had been built on a bit of old common land by the time of the 1871 map. It was a large and elegant residence with domed loggias, though a surviving print of it may make it look more palatial than it really was. On the mid-1880s map it was still there, though it was to disappear in the 1900s when Stroud Green Road became more densely built and less socially desirable. 'Prowse Terrace' replaced it.

There were several reasons for the Turners' shift. One was that Charles Turner, who had started off as Lucas's tenant farmer, had for some time owned the freehold of the whole of the Stapleton Hall complex of buildings. Presumably Lucas had sold this to him once the adjacent fields had been laid down to houses. One may well surmise that, settling into his declining but still vigorous years, buying and selling hay, serving on the Hornsey Local Board and living comfortably on his accumulated savings, Charles Turner and his wife had no more need for a farmhouse and yard and preferred to occupy the rather more imposing part of their freehold property. This would certainly be true – but the more salient fact is that, by 1881, the old farmhouse, its yard and the several farm buildings on the far side of the yard were no longer there. The laying out of Stapleton Hall Road had swept them away.

The Hall itself remained, as did the big old barn on the other side, now edged by Mountpleasant Road. But the actual farm that was the subject of more than one nostalgic picture had been reduced to rubble and dust, its Jacobean origins ignored, its ancient timber taken away as useful props, its weatherboarding perhaps recycled for various lowly uses in the houses that were being built along the paved road where the farmyard used to spread.

I don't know the exact year in which this transform-ation happened; for this particular bit of road-building no documentation seems to have survived. It must have been before 1881, but probably only two or three years before. No mention of Stapleton Hall Road occurs in the Local Board minutes till late in 1879. What the coming of the road meant was that the east side of Stapleton Hall, instead of abutting on to its ancient conjoined twin house, now stood right by the pavement of the new road, which had been plotted (no doubt at Turner's down-to-earth wish) to run right past it. Indeed, this newly exposed gable end wall of the Hall, stripped of its centuries-old support, had had to be rebuilt and strengthened. Inside the house today one can see that work has been done on that wall, including a rebuilding of the chimney.

In 1886 William Prowse died. I suspect it may be no coincidence that in the same year the Turners, their long-term neighbour having gone, finally left their old neighbourhood. They were not to move far: just up the hill to Mountpleasant, to Womersley House. This imposing residence had been built a generation before by the usual 'linen-draper', who in this case was Peter

Robinson, founder of the West End department store.

One of the many local clubs, enthusiastically started in those years for the upwardly mobile inhabitants of the burgeoning area, was the Stroud Green Conservative Association. In 1886 the Association had been looking without success for suitable premises. In May the *Hornsey & Finsbury Park Journal* announced: 'A few days ago . . . it became known that Mr Charles Turner, of Stapleton Hall, was about to leave that residence for Womersley House, which we understand he has purchased, and that the premises he intended to vacate would be let.' The Conservative Association put in for it. A meeting was held, and evidently a lease was at once agreed since it was noted that Charles Turner (who was a lifelong Tory) was 'acting very generously toward his new tenants. By a small outlay for the lengthening of one of the apartments [rooms] an excellent billiard room would be provided. Another fine oak panelled room will serve for the studious, and there are numerous other apartments for games, smoking . . .' The grounds too were said to be 'large and well-planted, there is space for two, if not more, lawn tennis courts, without much interference with the flower garden. A pride of the grounds is a splendid weeping willow which, if it had to be removed, would, we have heard, become the property of a Rothschild, but such a loss is not now to be feared.'

Why any member of an international banking family of enormous wealth should be thought to have a claim on a tree in a now-suburban garden is, today, rather obscure, unless this is an oblique reference to a splendid Rothschild garden then in Gunnersbury – another select district which would presently be engulfed by London. Can the Stapleton Hall tree have been one of the numerous willow trees in England allegedly grown from cuttings taken from Napoleon's grave on St Helena, where ships passed homebound on the India run? Or do we have here some vaguely anti-Semitic jibe of a kind that was becoming current in London then, with an influx of poor Russian Jews into the East End?

Given the extensive premises, great plans could now be made for the club, including 'Ladies' days' and garden parties. There was also a note of warning: 'As the club will be social as well as political, it is intended to keep the character of it as high as possible, the indiscriminate admission of members without regard to their "club-bable" qualities being a mistake more easily made than rectified.' In other words, the founder members, mostly the prosperous tradesmen now settled along the Stroud Green Road and in villas in new roads leading off Crouch Hill, were determined to preserve their hard-won status as people who enjoyed tennis courts and garden parties. The lower-class people now beginning to crowd some of the district on the southern, Islington side of Stroud Green Road must be kept at bay.

I think it must have been at this time that Stapleton Hall received another makeover. The 1820s porch had probably become rickety and anyway hopelessly out of date. Solid was what late-Victorian buildings were required to be, and what was now added to the front façade was a version of a pillared mid-Victorian enclosed porch with a slight hint of Egyptian tomb about it. (Flinders Petrie was then engaged on his works on the Great Pyramid, and Egypt was much in vogue.) A stone vase was added on each side, and the Georgian windows lost their fine panes to standard late-Victorian sash-glazing. The stuccoed front was covered in a thick coat of grey cement, incised at ground-floor level to represent stone blocks. It was perhaps at this time too (or possibly a few years earlier when the farmhouse was pulled down?) that the famous board carved with the Drapers' initials, for so long and so repeatedly attributed to the Stapleton family, was removed from wherever it had originally been and enclosed in a somewhat amateurish frame.

The front view of Stapleton Hall c.1911, with the farmhouse gone and the Conservative Association in occupation. Comparison with the top picture on p.197 will show that the configuration of the windows is still the same, though the Georgian small panes have been replaced by late nineteenth-century glazing and the porch by a heavier one. The weather-cock house that used to stand on top of the farmhouse has been installed on the end of the Hall roof.

The club seems to have flourished, throughout its early years, in the way intended. Two years after its founding a summer fête was held. An expected conjuror did not turn up (ill) but as 'the club numbers among its members artistes quite capable of the task, it was announced that a musical entertainment would be given'. The current Conservative MP, a member of the family that manufactured Stephens Blue-Black Ink, came with his wife and made a tour of the house and gardens. There was 'a nigger minstrel entertainment . . . a burlesque lecture . . . ventriloquial entertainment . . . From 8.0 pm the marquee was cleared for dancing . . . ground illuminated . . .'

Happy, innocent days. In that decade there was little crime in the area. The theft of a purse on a tram was denounced as a 'scandalous outrage'. A man found 'swearing in front of females' in a railway carriage at Finsbury Park was fined at Highgate Petty Sessions. A furious letter to the *Journal* from a father living in one of the roads between Stroud Green station and the park described how his daughter had been followed home by a young man 'making indecent propositions to her. Upon her telling me of this, I rushed out in pursuit, but the cowardly fellow had gone. It would have gone hard with the miscreant if I had caught him . . .' And further remarks on the lines of 'sound thrashing' and 'police'.

Dinah Turner died in January 1891, aged eighty-two. She had been taken down to the classic seaside resort of Bournemouth the previous week 'it being hoped that the change would have a beneficial effect', but it did not. She was brought back home for burial, not in the parish churchyard in which her husband's forebears lay and which was now closed, but in Highgate Cemetery. She had been born in Yorkshire, so I must suppose that when young Farmer Turner courted and married her, around the time the railways were beginning to bring people to London from distant regions, she was employed in domestic service in some substantial Hornsey house. In her long life, ending as mistress of Womersley House, she had come quite far in another way. The *Journal* recorded, 'A great deal of sympathy is felt for the bereaved husband, who is fast approaching eighty years. [In fact he was five years younger than she was.] Mr and Mrs Turner were devoted in their attachment to one another . . . She was of a retiring disposition, but very benevolent in a quiet way.'

Charles Turner had at one time been a churchwarden at Holy Trinity, Stroud Green, which was built on a greenfield site just beyond the railway lines in the 1870s.[1] But in recent years the Turners had preferred a larger, classically Gothic church, St Mary's, which had been established earlier off the Hornsey Road. Holy Trinity had acquired a vicar who was 'high' and given to elaborate vestments, and I rather think Charles Turner may have disapproved of that. The passions aroused by the Oxford Movement sixty years before were still bubbling away in Stroud Green, as in Burford. So the funeral service was held in St Mary's, before the cortège made its way to Highgate with five mourning coaches. The flag of the Stroud Green Conservative Association was flown at half mast.

The land on which St Mary's was built in 1861 had been given by a local man, who had found himself the fortunate possessor of a couple of fields off the Hornsey Road just at the time when they could be sold for building. Inside the church, several of the handsome William-Morris-inspired stained-glass windows were given as memorials by families who had enjoyed similar good fortune, including the Turner family. Charles Turner died eighteen months after his wife, and they are commemorated together in a window depicting Faith, Hope and Charity, under intricate Gothic canopies, giving to the poor. All the participants, including the poor, are very fair-skinned with ethereal tendrils of

Pre-Raphaelite hair. It is not an unattractive piece, but sheep (or cows) safely grazing in a biblically green pasture, beside the still waters of the New River, might, one feels, have been more appropriate.

The clerics in charge when I visited (one a woman and the other from Africa) were rightly proud of their church and of their success in holding together a congregation, though their modernised form of service would probably have appalled the Turners. Neither of them, unsurprisingly, had had any idea that one window commemorates the last dairy farmer in the district.

Meanwhile, what had been happening round Hornsey village itself, at the other end of the old parish?

In the 1870s old Hornsey, and the neighbouring settlement at Crouch End, being further from London than the Finsbury Park area, did not undergo the same rapid urbanisation. Large and sometimes quite grand detached houses went on being built at Crouch End, and up at Muswell Hill, to the end of the decade. Photos of Hornsey village at the time show old cottages, stables and well-known rural inhabitants – if now rather self-consciously posed. Before the 1880s, Harringay House still stood in its extensive private park between Hornsey and Tottenham. Edward Chapman, with whom the Vestry had got so annoyed, had died in 1869, but it is a measure of how desirable the property continued to be that it was subsequently let, in succession, to two further wealthy City bankers.

However, there were other pressures on Hornsey and even on the more distant districts of Tottenham and Wood Green, besides the money-making designs of speculative builders. As early as 1850, when the Great Northern line was still being built, the idea was floated that the workers of London might live further out if both rents and railway fares were low enough. The whole concept of commuting was being tentatively invented.

The kind of man who had always, till then, needed to live within an hour's walk, at most, of his place of work would be induced 'to exchange the dirty suburb for the pure and invigorating atmosphere of the country.'[2] 'Dirty suburb' by this time indicated Islington or Camden Town. It may be remembered that Bob Cratchit, the underpaid clerk in Dickens's *A Christmas Carol*, lives in Camden Town and goes back and forth to the City on foot.

Once the Great Northern line was open and a station was built at Hornsey – to the disgust and concern of the special committee set up by the Vestry – the idea of planned cottage estates far out of town became more concrete. Like the Model Dwellings being built in London at the same time, it was envisaged that the distant homes would be for clerks and artisans; that is, not the poorest classes but those with a degree of respectability and aspiration. The railways were obliged by Parliament to run a certain number of third-class coaches in which the journey cost much less than in first or second, but really cheap, early morning workers' fares did not come in till the 1880s.

Hornsey and Tottenham were both suggested as suitable sites for the determinedly rural-sounding 'cottage estates', since in the 1850s land there cost only a fraction of the price nearer London. However, as the promoters of Finsbury Park were also discovering, the very suggestion of a new scheme sent the asking price for land upwards. In the event, most of the suburban development that followed the coming of trains and the opening of stations was the result of ad hoc private enterprise.

The deep-seated paradox of the suburb, everywhere, is that it is started as an attempt to secure a romanticised and tamed version of country living (clean air, space, gardens, known neighbours) but that its very success ends up by transforming it into crowded townscape. The trains that opened up the glorious possibilities of working in the City while living among fields, were soon so well used that they destroyed those same fields by bringing population to them. Twenty years after the station consisting of two wooden platforms had been opened at Seven Sisters Road in 1861, with only a handful of passengers each day, the traffic there had become enormous. That emblematic figure, the season ticket holder, had appeared. In 1867 there were 2,500 of these using the line, and 6,500 by 1874. By 1882 there were more than twice as many, and the numbers were growing exponentially.

By the 1880s other pressures were also coming. The attempts to create purpose-built estates for those with modest means had resulted in the formation of the British Land Company. This was set up as part of a laudable attempt to control and regularise the use of land, though in the end its operations became more or less indistinguishable from those of commercial companies. In 1880 (the same year in which Canon Richard Harvey finally retired as vicar of the greatly altered parish) Harringay House and its land were sold to a William Hodson, a builder from Hackney who had already been party to the building of Mountpleasant Road and probably Stapleton Hall Road as well. He sold on the Harringay House estate the next year to the British Land Company, who also owned land at Crouch End. The *Hornsey & Finsbury Park Journal*, which had been so proud ten years earlier of the burgeoning suburb around the park, now sounded a note of dismay. Evidently it, in its turn, was now discovering that a suburb with meadowland and picturesque cottages just up the road is one thing, and a suburb with other suburbs spreading far out beyond it is very much another: 'The doom of Hornsey is settled. Not much longer will it remain the quiet and secluded village of which everyone has heard . . . protestations come too late now. Hornsey is to be given to the builders.'

So the tight grid pattern of streets that would soon cover the Harringay House grounds (what is today known as the Harringay ladder) began to be constructed. On the OS map of the mid-1880s the plan is laid out, though only the first few streets to the north, towards Turnpike Lane, have houses. On this map one remaining loop of the New River encircles a piece of garden in which Harringay House still stands. The idea was to sell it like that, but no wealthy gentleman buyer appeared. In 1885 the House, which had been so valuable a generation before that the owner had received substantial damages when the railway came within sight of it, was now, by the success of that railway, rendered near-worthless. It was pulled down, the river was aligned in a canal, and the grid of streets was extended to cover the site.

In Crouch End too, in the 1880s, old, big houses were being dismantled, along with their gardens. By the mid-1890s the hamlet where several lanes met had been magically transformed into a modern town centre, complete with clock tower. And up and over the Mount-pleasant ridge that separated Stroud Green from Crouch End, houses began to march, often bigger and nicer ones than those round Stapleton Hall – since the 'air' was considered better up there and the views over London fine – but houses all the same. No industry, beyond all the building trades and such services as printers and laundries. Commuting had done away with the traditional need for local factories and workshops. By 1896 a writer in the periodical *London* rather sadly concluded: 'The parts which are not yet turned into streets are surveyed and planned for future operations. Rural Hornsey has become a thriving modern suburb, and considers itself an eminently respectable middle-class community.'

The population of the old parish, even without a part to the south which had been hived off to Stoke Newington, was now about sixty thousand and rising. It was effectively part of London, and it was only through the intransigence and determination of local people that it avoided being included within the area of the LCC. The result was a cat's cradle of interlocking and denied responsibilities for highways, sewage and the like. One dispute, over who should lay a storm drain in the Stroud Green Road, where the old floods had returned, revived the eighteenth-century battles over highways between Islington and Hornsey, and actually went as far as the House of Lords. In 1903 Hornsey became a municipal borough in its own right, with its own corporation.

A snapshot view of Hornsey as seen by a stranger, is provided in Arnold Bennett's *Hilda Lessways*, which was published in 1911 but is supposedly set rather earlier. Hilda, trying to visit her mother who is very ill in a Hornsey boarding house, arrives in London and takes another train from King's Cross. We seem here to be in the London of doom-laden railway viaducts that had been turned into an archetype by the French engraver Gustave Doré:

> Often [the train] ran level with the roofs of vague, far-stretching acres of houses – houses vile and frowsty, and smoking like pyres in the dark air. And always it travelled on a platform of brick arches. Now and then the walled road received a tributary that rounded subtly into it, and this tributary could be seen curving away, on innumerable brick arches, through the chimney pots, and losing itself in a dim horizon of gloom . . .

So much for the 'journey among cornfields' enthused over by the *Illustrated London News* in 1852. Because of the universal burning of coal, London murk and London grime were then inseparable from the arrival of houses, however jaunty the intentions of the architect and however bright red the brick, which was one more reason why the desirable habitat rapidly became less so.

Hilda at last arrives, and finds that her mother has died. The next day she waits on Hornsey station for an elderly relative:

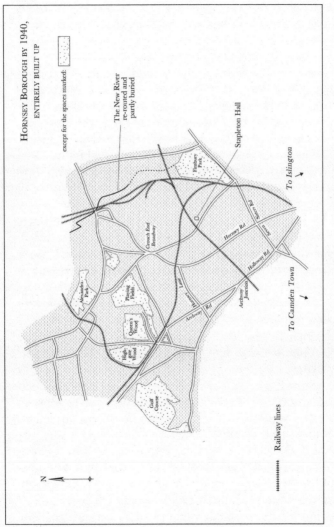

HORNSEY BOROUGH BY 1940,
ENTIRELY BUILT UP
except for the spaces marked:

The New River
re-routed and
partly buried

Stapleton Hall

Finsbury
Park

Crouch End
Broadway

Alexandra
Park

Playing
Fields

Queen's
Wood

High-
gate
Wood

Golf
Course

Hornsey Rd

Seven

Seven Rd

Holloway Rd

Archway
Junction

Archway

Archway Rd

To Islington

To Camden Town

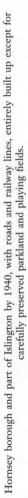

Railway lines

N

Hornsey borough and part of Islington by 1940, with roads and railway lines, entirely built up except for carefully preserved parkland and playing fields.

She had waited over half an hour, between eight and nine, and in that time she had had full opportunity to understand why these suburban stations had been built so large. A dark torrent of human beings, chiefly men, gathered out of all the streets of the vicinity, had dashed unceasingly into the enclosure, and covered the long platforms with tramping feet. Every few minutes a train rolled in, as if from some inexhaustible magazine of trains beyond the horizon . . . Less frequently, but still often, other trains thundered through the station . . . and these trains too were crammed with dark human beings frowning in study over white newspapers . . . Train after train fled downwards with its freight towards the hidden city.

Meanwhile the Stroud Green Conservative Association, in its oasis of a garden, continued to do well. There were more annual garden parties, and some winter 'smoking concerts'. These seem to have been more proper than the term might suggest, since the repertoire of songs included 'The Ash Grove', 'On the Road to Mandalay' and nothing more daring than 'A Lass that Loves a Sailor'. A high point was reached for the Association in 1900, when a new MP for Hornsey, a Captain C. Barrington-Balfour, was welcomed at Stapleton Hall. The previous MP, 'Inky' Stephens, had retired, and Barrington-B. had apparently been adopted without opposition. Hornsey was then, and for many decades after, a safe Conservative seat, which was just as well for Barrington-B. as he seems to have been a nonentity. He in turn was to retire, 'taking the Chiltern Hundreds', seven years later. The *Journal* (firmly Conservative itself in 1900) recorded: 'The appearance on the platform of the gallant officer was a signal for a remarkable outburst of enthusiasm. The Stroud Green piper, whose performance on the memorable Mafeking

Relief night gave so much pleasure, played "Cock o'the North".' (Barrington-Balfour was from minor Scottish aristocracy and his wife was a daughter of the Earl of Antrim.) There was a brief skirmish about the retiring member, who had been rumoured to be a 'pro-Boer', a viewpoint then widely regarded as akin to treason. This, said the chairman, was 'absolutely false'. ('Hear. Hear') 'He was retiring after thirteen years because he wished to live the life of a country gentleman.' The great English aspiration. The chairman was responded to by the vice-chair, Mr H.T. Tubbs JP, a name we shall hear again.

I wonder if our imaginary young man who left Taynton, Oxfordshire in the 1870s to seek his fortune in London would by now be a member of the Stroud Green Conservative Association? He might be, if, as I think, he 'bettered himself' through a series of jobs and was by now, say, manager of a large hardware store stocking the new electrical goods – perhaps Sandilands in the Stroud Green Road, whose owner had himself been born a countryman, near Limpsfield in Surrey. He might even have married the owner's daughter, and be occupying a snug house in Stapleton Hall Road, with one polite gentleman lodger in the first-floor back to help with the rent. But I would prefer to think that he was drawn, rather, to the Liberals (known darkly in the Stroud Green Association as the Radicals) whose chief mover till his death in 1897 had been a wine merchant and chairman of the Local Board, Henry Reader Williams.[3] Born in Wapping, he had come a very long way in life. He occupied a castellated Gothic mansion on the other side of Hornsey called The Priory, and was deeply involved in various philanthropic works and in trying to ensure that in the borough's development adequate open spaces were preserved. He is usually credited with saving the last remnants of the Great

Forest – Highgate Wood and Queen's Wood – from the hands of builders, though the true story seems to have been rather more complex and his role in it more equivocal.

By the early years of the twentieth century the *Journal* was affirming that 'The Hornsey [of today] is very different from the Hornsey of 1880'. Cycle clubs, flower shows and improving talks still figured, but disorder, crime and signs of poverty were more in evidence than in the paper's first jubilant years. There were complaints of fights in tram queues outside Finsbury Park station each evening, and also 'insufficient police protection . . . periodical outbreaks of burglary. At first they were annual during the holiday season and the early winter, but now frequent . . . soon to be perennial.' There was a bag-snatching at Crouch Hill station. The occasional beggar was arrested in Stroud Green Road, where there was also a permanent Mission to Poor Children providing twice-weekly free meals. An address in Finsbury Park no longer seemed to promise a vibrant new life. Advertisements of houses for rent or sale in Stapleton Hall Road made only the modest claim that they were 'well built', and, judging from the columns of Rooms to Let, lodgers were ubiquitous there. Yet at the same time, on the far side of the borough, where the Priory estate was now being laid out on the grounds of what had been the grand Williams mansion, there were 'tasteful residences' advertised for rent or sale at a higher price, all with 'bathroom, h and c'. With no mention of the steepness of the ascent, they were said to be 'a few minutes, walk from Muswell Hill', which was regarded as the acme of elegance. One may recall Hilaire Belloc's rhyme on the fictional Charles Augustus Fortescue, who achieved a very desirable life merely by Doing the Right Thing:

He thus became immensely Rich,
And built the Splendid Mansion which
Is called 'The Cedars, Muswell Hill',
Where he resides in Affluence still

To be Charles Augustus Fortescue was certainly the quiet dream of many of the members of the Stroud Green Association.

In 1906 an official guide was published entitled *Healthy Hornsey*, extolling 'the bracing qualities of the air' and the area's 'wholesome amusements', its paving, sanitation, gas and electricity, planned telephone exchange ('quite a necessity of civilisation'), trees et cetera, and the fact that 'we have today a municipal borough within seven miles of Charing Cross, and yet inhabited entirely by the middle classes . . . The men of Hornsey belong to London. They pour out of their front doors in the morning, and the evening sees them return in their thousands by train or tube or tram or bus.' (The line to Moorgate had opened in 1903, and the Piccadilly Line Tube had reached Finsbury Park in 1906). 'Between 10 am and five at night Hornsey, except for shop-keepers, is a town of women.'

It is clear what had really happened. The relatively new developments over Crouch Hill, Mountpleasant and down the other side, all the way to Alexandra Park, still had a metaphoric shine upon them. But the areas further east and south, including Finsbury Park itself, bordering as they did on Islington and Stoke Newington, had turned, in less than a generation, into despised inner London. Stapleton Hall itself had become an outpost, green and genteel still but on the edge of poorer areas both across Stroud Green Road and further down it toward Finsbury Park station. The name Seven Sisters Road, once proudly incorporated into the title of the local paper, now had a tainted, faintly intimidating quality. The haunting name had in fact been taken prosaically from a group of seven pine trees, by now long vanished, that were a landmark in Tottenham when the road was laid out, but various colourful historical myths had been woven around them.

This suggestion of something murky or tragic connected with 'seven sisters' was exploited in literature. Arnold Bennett perceived in the line north from King's Cross, with its endless viaducts and cavernous stations, a kind of Infernal Way with death at the end of it. Compton Mackenzie, too, made the Seven Sisters Road stand for the classic outer London area by which one might be fascinated or repelled in equal measure. Mackenzie's *Sinister Street*, published in 1913, immediately preceded his *Guy and Pauline* with its idyllically rural setting. It is Guy's friend Michael Fane who is the central character in *Sinister Street*: a rich, talented young man in energetic quest for experience, understanding, sexual passion, sin and religious revelation.

Having taken a decision that these things might be better sought elsewhere than in his accustomed Cheyne Walk and Oxford settings, Michael then takes a cab – to hitherto unknown London, and more specifically to Hornsey: 'strange suburbs had always seemed to him desolate, abominable and insecure. He always visualised a draughty and ill-lighted railway platform, a rickety and gloomy omnibus, countless Nonconformist chapels and infrequent policemen.' However, a sexually ambiguous, monkish figure met years before at a schoolboy retreat in a Benedictine abbey has given him an impression of the Seven Sisters Road as something both darker and more exciting, imbued with 'sly and labyrinthine romance', some kind of gateway to Avernus, the classical Underworld. Michael's expectations are high:

That he had never yet been to the Seven Sisters Road gave it a mystery . . . a nightmare capacity for suggesting that deviation by a foot from the thoroughfare itself would lead to obscure calamities. Those bright yellow omnibuses on which he had never travelled, how he remembered them from the days of Jack the Ripper, and the horror of them skirting the Strand by Trafalgar Square on winter dusks ... Even now their painted destinations affected him with a dismay that real people could be familiar with this sinister route.

Hornsey had several public libraries by this time. What the more literate section of the population thought about having one of their main roads depicted in this apocalyptic manner is not recorded.

But after a lengthy and expectant ride through almost-as-sinister and unknown Camden and Kentish Towns 'Michael was disappointed by the Seven Sisters Road. It seemed to be merely the garish mart of a moderately poor suburban population.' He drives back along the Camden Road and finally settles for lodgings in a decayed crescent that appears to be the setting for a number of Walter Sickert's dark pictures, where he attempts unsuccessfully to befriend a prostitute.

Sinister Street was the book that made Compton Mackenzie's reputation. It was enormously successful, seeming to speak for a whole generation of clever, questing aesthetically aware young people – the generation that, the very year after its publication, was to be hustled down into the Avernus of the First World War.

It was not, after all, the Seven Sisters Road that was the way into hell.

Yet the suburban ideal, that had shone so brightly and continued to shine in the more select parts of Hornsey borough, was itself now coming under attack, and the attacks would intensify in the post-war years as suburbs sprawled ever further out, swallowing Edmonton and Finchley, ballooning into what became known as

Metroland. Already, in 1908, the *Journal* had reported at length on a lecture given to the Mountview Literary Society (Mountview was the name bestowed on a long road running near the top of the ridgeway) on 'The Narrowness of Suburban Life'. With an irony that one feels may have been lost on some of his audience, the speaker, a Mr Harrison, said that many thanked God that they were not as other men and women were, but belonged to the great, unprejudiced middle classes. Continuing in the same taunting vein he remarked that because the men went out first thing in the morning to catch 'their' train and did not arrive back home until the evening, the evening meal was often rushed if the wives, after a day at home, wanted to get out to a concert or a talk – 'but how many of the men knew how deadly dull was a suburban road on a winter afternoon before children coming from school enlivened it for a few minutes? The milkman was often the only sign of life to be seen . . . Was it a wonder women went shopping, ostensibly to buy necessities . . . but really to experience the sensation that they were part of the living world?'

He painted a picture of wives repetitively 'calling' on one another, of conversation bounded by gossip, scandal, class distinctions and 'the merits or otherwise of cooks and housewives and the talents of their respective children'. The effect of such a life, he went on, was narrowing, 'limiting ideals, interest and sympathies'. Suburban wives were cut off from the knowledge of life as it was lived by those less fortunately placed, and so 'did not long for a time when all men would have equal opportunities'. He did not add women to this remark. He might have pointed out that, only a few days before, the neighbouring Muswell Hill Wesleyan Literary Society had debated whether ladies should have the vote and decided against it, but possibly he did not wish to inflame his already uneasy audience further by entering the then-vexed Women's Suffrage Question.

'Mr Harrison concluded by saying he had not by any means exhausted the subject, and he hoped he had not exhausted the patience of the hearers. He expected there were some who were, metaphorically speaking, thirsting for his blood.'

I expect there were.

Chapter XV

WHERE WE CAME IN,
AS THE PARSONAGE HOUSES DECLINE

We are, with the three houses, back now in the twentieth century where we started. *'This is where we came in'*.

The phrase is now falling out of use, but it is still resonant to those old enough to remember the great age of cinema, with its boast of 'continuous programme', its B-pictures and newsreels entirely filling the gap between one showing of the main feature film and the next; and also its long evening queues snaking all the way round the sides of the huge picture palaces that had appeared in every provincial high street and suburb. From the 1920s to the end of the 1950s ordinary people seeking after-work entertainment, daydreams, a warm place to hold hands and rather more, or just a temporary escape from the family, the chilly bedsitter or the rain, did not go for any timed showing of a film or even necessarily for any particular film. They just 'went to the pictures'. They joined the queue, shuffling gradually forward as other people, who had seen the whole programme round from whatever arbitrary moment they themselves had entered, left the cinema in ones, twos or groups. The man in charge of the door would call out 'Four in the two-and-sixes now . . . Two in the one-and-nines . . .

And another one-and-nine . . .' and so gradually, piece-meal, the cinema was entered. By a momentary flash of the usherette's torch the newcomer stumbled over knees into his seat and began watching, through a haze of cigarette smoke, what was running on the screen at whatever stage it had reached.

The cinema, pronounced 'ky-nee-ma', began as a short, flickering Special Show in London music halls and on seaside piers, but soon extended its range. It gained ground quickly in places like Hornsey, where people were neither too poor to afford it nor rich enough for other distractions. Before the First World War several cinemas had already started up in the borough; their twice-weekly changing programmes were advertised in the *Hornsey Journal*. The Scala in Stroud Green Road opened in 1914, but two years later it was functioning only at week-ends. So many men were now fighting in France. The early flush of enthusiasm for patriotic volunteering was past, and conscription had come: there was a chronic shortage of labour for civilian jobs. There were tram conductresses now on the Seven Sisters run; and it may be supposed that even the bored suburban wives whom Mr Harrison had pilloried in his evening lecture a few years before were now winding bandages, knitting 'comforts for soldiers' or even working as VADs in the Royal Northern Hospital on the Holloway Road. The columns of the *Journal* were full of local boys who had been 'offered commissions' – clerks and shopmen who were elevated to the ranks of Officers and Gentlemen to plug the gaps left by the escalating slaughter at the Front, which wiped out even more young officers than Other Ranks.

Our young man from Taynton who came to Finsbury Park to seek his fortune would now be well into his fifties. Too old to fight, perhaps he had a son as energetic as himself who went to war and made the great jump into another social class – if he survived. There were lengthy weekly lists in the *Journal* headed 'Our Honoured Dead'; and also a vendetta against a Presbyterian minister from Crouch Hill who dared to be a pacifist – a 'broken reed'. Clearly this was even worse than having been a pro-Boer.

The cinema took rather longer to have its effect on towns outside London, but once the war was over it began to penetrate even remote and provincial places. It is significant of Limpsfield's determination to remain a village that it never developed a cinema (nor yet the Working Men's Institute that one grumpy Oxted socialist thought it should have) but Oxted itself had a picture house by 1929. It was, and is, an impressive, Tudor-replica building near the station, specialising today in arthouse films.

There was no question of Taynton, which did not even have a pub, having a cinema of its own. But Burford's relationship with the age of the cinema was also problematic, and typical of that unique miniature town. To find the cinema, we have to transport ourselves back to the sixteenth century, when Edmund Harman's father-in-law, Edmund Silvester, merchant of Burford, built himself a handsome stone house not far from the bridge. It later came to be known as Falkland Hall and, like most of the old houses in Burford, passed through various vicissitudes. At one time it was part of the Bear Inn, but once the coaching age was over and Burford's time of social and economic eclipse set in it was divided into tenements. In 1888 the Salvation Army acquired the main hall downstairs, where the Silvesters and the Harmans had once feasted: Burford, rather surprisingly for such a rural place, always had a strong Nonconformist tradition; sects such as the Plymouth Brethren flourished there. A Burford Recreation Society was founded in Falkland Hall in 1904 (choral singing? Ping-pong? Possibly whist drives?). After the First World War, when the inevitable war memorial with too many familiar names was erected halfway up the High Street, a memorial fund was also started. It was this that paid for a weekly cinema show in Falkland Hall from the early 1920s to the 1960s.

In the mid-1930s, when resplendent Odeons and Rialtos were spreading through the land, there were fears that two old shops near the top of the hill would be bought and pulled down for this purpose. The Sharpe sisters, who sold china and glass there, and also shoes, wished to retire, but as they belonged to the Plymouth Brethren they wanted to avoid being replaced by a cinema, which represented worldliness and probable sin. They managed a private sale to an antique dealer from a prominent local family of Quakers, and the cinema scheme was seen off.

Meanwhile, how was Taynton vicarage faring?

W.P. Leonard Hand, who had rescued the old registers and papers from the parish chest, moved on with his family after twenty-two years and was succeeded by the gentlemanly and scholarly bachelor William Emeris. With Emeris's arrival in Taynton the minutes of the now-only-annual Vestry meetings, which he always kept in person, take on a higher tone. Prayers were said at the start, and the church accounts were formally presented. It was soon decided that the sum for which the church was insured should be increased. 'The Vicar also called the attention of the meeting to the need of a few slight repairs to the fabric of the church.' However, he revealed that the churchwardens' expenditure in the previous year had been about £12, and that the balance in hand was only seventeen shillings, one penny and one ha'penny. It is from this time on that the chronic financial problem of running the parish begins, insidiously, to make itself felt, though for the moment the problem was perceived as relating only to the fabric of the church: choked gutters, ominous cracks in the south wall that must be 'carefully watched', and the need for coal for the ageing boiler (installed in the 1860s).

Between 1910 and 1915 an Inland Revenue valuation was carried out on houses all over England. It was an exercise in setting the rates and, incidentally, a way of disposing finally of the remains of the tithe system on which church finance had originally depended so much. How such a comprehensive survey was completed even as civil servants were disappearing in droves into the trenches of France is something of a mystery, and it is not a well-known set of documents, but it provides an extraordinary close-up view of English domestic life just at the edge of present-day memory. What could be more evocative than the word-picture of Taynton schoolhouse in which the schoolmistress and her mother lived, and which was owned by the Rhys-Wingfield family who descended from the Dynevors? It comprised '3 bedrooms, a sitting room, a kitchen, pantry, wash-house and a garden with privy'. The gross value, along with that of the similarly stone-built school itself, was estimated at £876. Or there is the all-purpose shop next door, which also belonged to the Wingfields and was let on a yearly rent of eleven pounds, fifteen shillings and tenpence:

A semi-detached house with 2 attics, 4 bedrooms, room used as shop, sitting room, large beer cellar, bakehouse (1 oven), flour room over, bread store, back kitchen, a cold store, and outbuildings comprising a stable (loose boxes and 1 stall), loft over, disused pigstye etc. Coal shed with loft and hovel adjoining a small kitchen garden. Off-beer licence.

'Etc.' must, I think, in this case cover another privy, no doubt very similar to the wooden-seated one over a deep pit, belonging to the cottage on Ashdown Forest I had wanted to adopt as a child.

'Hovels' and pigsties seem to have been numerous in Taynton, though one senses, from the number marked 'disused', that the long era of rural working-class pig-keeping was now drawing to its close. The rural working classes themselves still occupied the village, if in smaller numbers than before. By the end of the First World War twelve young men from the parish lay dead in foreign fields, including two Pittaways. Four Wingfields from Great Barrington had been killed, among them the heir to the estate, and two more would die in the Second World War, leaving that village in the doldrums for two generations.

The Taynton vicarage of course, cuts a rather different figure in the IR Survey from the cottages round about: 'House counting top floor and attics, first floor: 5 bedrooms. Study, Bathroom H and C. WC.' (So modern plumbing had now made its way in, probably under the Hand family in the 1870s, the time when terraced houses in towns were being provided with one modern lavatory apiece, usually halfway up the stairs, and even bathrooms were becoming quite common.) 'Ground floor: Drawing room, Dining room, Library, morning room, Entrance Hall, Kitchen, Servants Hall, Scullery, Larder and outside WC. Back garden with lean-to greenhouse, yard with stable and loft, harness room and traphouse, a woodhouse and dairy, fowlhouse and woodshed, and orchard with 2 cowsheds and stable, 3 pigstyes and shed and small fir plantation. Gross value £900.' The condition of the house was said, like that of most of the buildings in Taynton, to be 'old but fair'.

Nine hundred pounds, hardly more than the school and its adjacent dwelling-house, does not sound very much for such a large place with so much land. However, the time when an influx of monied middle-class people would transform life and property values in remote villages such as Taynton still lay in the hidden future. Emeris had lived comfortably in the vicarage, but he had been moved by his Bishop to take charge of Burford in 1908. Two briefly staying vicars succeeded him; then, in

1915, the year when the IR Survey was completed, the living was taken on by a James Ledhi Sloane. It is instructive to compare the Survey's summary of an apparently desirable large house with another description of it given by Sloane only seven years later. A Bishop's Visitation was made in 1922 – the same year, as it happened, that the meetings of the Vestry finally ceased, the last vestiges of its powers and duties having passed to the Parish Council. In the Visitation, Sloane was asked 'Is the House of Residence suitable for the residence of the incumbent? If not, in what respect is it unsuitable?' his reply was this:

> House insured for sum of £6382, but it would not fetch more than £1000 at a sale . . . Lawns and gardens absurd for income of joint parishes, house old patched-up place involving constant expense. A lot of rooms with only a few any use. 3 living, 6 bedrooms (2 no manner of use), 3 large attics quite useless, 2 kitchens, large stone-floored pantry, stable, dairy buildings, hen-house and another building.
>
> I was informed up to 1914 the average dilapidation was £8 per ann. It was £200 in 1914, £160 last year, it would have been £360 only buildings were ordered to be demolished . . . £140 is estimated for five years hence.

This is the cry of an underpaid man. When Thomas Lewes had been nearing the end of his long life in the vicarage in 1870, *Crockford's*, the directory of Anglican clergy, had stated that his annual stipend for the two parishes was a little over the £300 then generally considered adequate for a respectable life, but he also received £222 in tithes from Great Barrington, and he owned land in the area which brought in an annual rent of rather more than £60. Both he and Leonard Hand could afford to employ curates. By the 1920s, however, the tithing system had disappeared and the value of ill-managed ecclesiastical stock that had been given in lieu had fallen, as had the value of land. But most significantly the cost of living, which had been remarkably stable for most of the nineteenth century, had begun the relentless rise that was to characterise it in the twentieth. Vicars without private incomes (which advantage was also becoming much less common than it had been in times of late-Georgian and Victorian industrial prosperity) were finding it a struggle to pay their way. Gone was the 'portly parson' of the counting rhyme, with his large household of servants, exchanging succulent dinners with the local gentry. Many of these had been impoverished too by death duties and (like the Wingfields) by the multiple deaths of those who should have inherited. As the 1920s turned into the 1930s things did not get any better. The Church began the perpetual scrabble for money that would characterise its activities later in the century, for the value of stipends was constantly eroded by inflation.

A particular cry from the heart came in the late 1930s from the vicar of Asthall, a thinly populated but widely scattered parish on the far side of Burford, where the annual stipend seems to have been only £361 – and ten pence. After enumerating a few other small grants, which were more than consumed by the need to pay rates, run a car and contribute to the pension of a previous incumbent, the vicar wrote:

In addition to all the other necessary outgoings, there is scarcely enough left for the bare necessities of life, especially in view of the increased cost of living. In consequence my wife has to do without domestic help and I am compelled, for lack of funds, to give home tuition to one of my boys, now of school age, since we cannot afford to pay school fees. I have no private means.

This was still a time in which no middle-class parents, however impoverished, were expected to send their child to the village school. The vicar's son must not speak with the accent of the cowherd's son, it would handicap him for life. Essentially, the Asthall vicar's problem was still the same as that of the Rev. Quiverful in *Barchester Towers*. He has a family of fourteen which he can only just afford to feed and clothe, but he must in addition contrive to 'bring them up as ladies and gentlemen'.

By the end of the Second World War, by which time four more hard-pressed vicars had come and gone in the vicarage at Taynton, the income on offer, jointly with that of Great Barrington, was only £535 a year. This was by then worth a fraction, in real terms, of the comparable income received by Lewes a hundred years before, or indeed by Emeris fifty years before (and he had had significant private means). From 1947 a further annual grant was made of £118, but it was noted in pencil on the back of the document relating to this that the benefice had recently lost £74 per annum through the nationalisation of the railways under the post-war Labour government. In the nineteenth century railway shares had been 'a good sound investment'. By the mid-twentieth century this had long ceased to be the case. Such mismanagement of assets had dogged the Church of England for some time and was to continue to do so.

By 1953 the total income from Taynton and Great Barrington, including a grant as a 'stabilization measure', was still only £535 in all. It was boosted slightly in the next few years, mainly with money donated by two elderly ladies, connections of the Rhys-Wingfields, who were evidently trying to keep a resident vicar in place. By 1955 the annual income reached the princely sum of £621, but that year the last resident vicar of the two parishes, a Mr Walker, left, and the benefice was declared vacant.

That same summer Taynton church itself was listed as being of Special Architectural Interest.

* * *

From then on and into the present, as with parishes all over England, Taynton has been looked after by a series of priests also attached to other parishes, an itinerant lifestyle for the modern clergy with multiple and often conflicting responsibilities. Since 1938 the number of clergy in England has been reduced to considerably less than half. But the decline in the number of traditional vicarages still in use is far greater, and this tells one more about the Church's reaction to the relative poverty of its incumbents than it does about the realities of funds and maintenance costs.

It may be said that even before the Second World War, and certainly after, the Church of England was trying to make a virtue of necessity by deciding that a modest life-style was becoming to a vicar: what has been called a 'proleier than thou' philosophy set in. The modern clergyman – or 'clergyperson' – should, in the opinion of certain people, live in a very ordinary house 'like anyone else', regardless of the fact that a clergyman has a special social and cultural role to fulfil and that his neighbours on the Council estate may not actually want him, or her, to be just like them. As a result, the large, traditional vicarage has been seen as a burden irrelevant to 'today's Church'. Out of some thirteen thousand vicarages and rectories in existence at the start of the twentieth century, today probably fewer than five per cent have been kept in use.

It is true that after the First World War vicars all over England were, like James Ledhi Sloane, complaining about the draughty, dilapidated, expensive inconvenience of their accommodation. But this complaint was taken at face value and became a kind of diocesan mantra, a settled pretext for summary sales that went on for decade after decade, long after the tide of public opinion, in the world outside the Church, had turned in favour of restoration and the revaluing of the past. These large, old and often beautiful houses were sold off, time and time again, not even as substantial assets to be realised but simply and short-sightedly to 'cut expenses'. Alternative solutions that would have kept the freeholds in the Church's possession – renovation, division into flats and village meeting rooms, the use of part of the gardens as communal parish space – were not even examined. This process continued long after general property values began to rise in the 1950s and '60s, and many of the 'inconvenient old places' disposed of then for a few thousand pounds were sold on again after a very short period for much larger sums. Meanwhile the inadequate monies that had been raised by sale were spent, not on the creation of well-designed modern parsonage houses, but on shoddy little brick boxes as anonymous as possible. This procedure has been called by a knowledgeable observer 'the most remarkable, continuous and wholesale divestiture of valuable assets ever undertaken by any institution'.[1]

The vicarage in Taynton, with its gardens, orchard and paddock, was sold in 1957 for £3,000, which was then about six times the price of a small car. The buyer was a Mrs Graham, she who ran the place for the next ten years as a bed-and-breakfast establishment. It was stipulated in the conveyance document that 'neither the property conveyed nor any part thereof shall at any time hereafter be used as or for a place of amusement hotel tavern inn or public house nor shall any spirituous or fermented liquors at any time be sold in or upon the same property or any part thereof'. Evidently bed and breakfast (which Mrs Graham augmented in summer with cream teas on the lawn) did not quite count as an hotel, though how the prohibition on the sale of alcohol was to be enforced in perpetuity was not clear. Nor is it obvious how the Church, having rid itself of the place, thought it could continue to insist that 'no act deed matter or thing shall at any time be suffered or permitted in or upon the property . . . which may be or become a nuisance annoyance or disturbance to the Minister for the time being conducting the congregation attending divine service'.

After five hundred years, and maybe much longer, the Church was casually giving up its traditional site in Taynton, on the one bit of raised ground out of the way of the Windrush floods. But it was as if neither its bishops, its commissioners nor its lawyers really understood what they were doing, or faced the fact that gone does mean gone.

This again is where we came in. My cousins, the Milners, never affluent, bought the property from Mrs Graham in 1968 for an amount they could just afford, and sold it thirty-nine years later for a sum that enabled them to buy several desirable smaller properties. During the years they lived in Taynton with a family growing up and a varying retinue of helpers and lodgers, the village was gradually but surely changing around them. The last of the old inhabitants, those with family names on the war memorial, died. One by one the old cottages were renovated: discreet extra gables and garden rooms were added to them, all in the approved Cotswold stone and style so that after a few years the modern additions blend entirely with the old. The cottage gardens, for so long full of cabbages, potatoes, washing lines, pigsties and privies, now have beautifully mown grass. The lovely, artless clumps of snowdrops, crocuses, daffodils and blue-bells that come up every spring are in fact as carefully nurtured as the later lilacs and roses. By the time my cousins finally decided to leave, with their roof in serious need of repair, their grandchildren's toys and bikes littering the drive, and their coke-consuming Aga over which the house agent's glossy brochure enthused as a quaint and charming feature, they were themselves the last representatives of a time that had gone.

They embodied in many ways a remark made by a

perceptive observer of parsonage houses in 1964: 'The grown-up children of a parsonage often unconsciously cultivate in their own homes a reminder of every vicarage and every rectory, whereas the layman destroys this atmosphere within a few weeks of buying a parsonage house'.[2] The newest owners of what has been called, since 1957, the Old Vicarage, are of a different world and generation. They have removed some of the late-Victorian clutter of rooms, rescued the attics from their primitive state, installed a modern kitchen, turned the old one into an elegant formal dining room, and have spent a great deal on restoring the house to a genuine beauty, with fine traditional materials. Part of the garden has been relaid as the tennis lawn that was there early in the century; there are hunters in the stable and a groom to look after them.

Substantial money is concealed today within the doors of even the smaller village houses. The stone and timber of the buildings have been immaculately preserved, but the fabric of centuries-old rural life has been lost, and this has happened up and down England: it is useless to mourn or to apportion blame. There is, of course, no shop in Taynton now, no post office, no school. There are, however, a few advantages. When the new rich of Taynton got together in the summer of 2010 to organise a village fête in the best of old-fashioned traditions, the sum raised was a remarkable £11,000. Six thousand of this went to the Specially Interesting but perennially needy church, where the carved faces of long-ago villagers continue to look down from the cornices, eternally quizzical about what they are required to witness.

Chapter XVI

Stapleton Hall and the
Manor House in need of rescue

Week after week, for the whole of the twentieth century and on into the twenty-first, the *Hornsey Journal* has recorded the affairs of its populous urban district, holding fast to its old name and roughly to the boundaries of the old parish even after Hornsey was at last engulfed, in 1964, by Greater London and by the new, large borough of Haringey.[1]

To sit all day in a newspaper library with a succession of leather-bound broadsheet volumes before you, turning pages through the weeks, months and years, is to feel both the copious persistence of daily life and its transience. The brown, friable edges of the sheets shed a sprinkling of crumbs as if partaking in mortal dissolution. Even the commercial advertisements that are the paper's staple tell of the inevitability of change. The horses of the livery stables in Stroud Green Road are sold and motor hearses take their place. Cinemas rise, flourish, decline and become bingo halls, nightspots, offices or centres of religious cults. Department stores squeeze out individual shops and extend themselves with plate-glass grandeur, then wither slowly into obsolescence themselves. Teashops appear, multiply, grow into brash cafeterias, and are replaced by smaller coffee-houses which in turn are replaced by doner kebab shops. 'Sunlight' Laundries, drapers and wool shops become second-hand car dealers; Fifty-Shilling Tailors, rubber goods shops; Greek barbers, betting shops.

You could write a complete social history of the twentieth century simply out of the pages of the *Hornsey Journal*, although the sense of having under your hands a vast wealth of information but most of it disposable and ephemeral, might, in the process, overwhelm you.

Letters about car accidents and about motor traffic using residential roads 'never intended for the purpose', about chronic high unemployment and about 'the Modern Girl', merge gradually into concerns about 'the refugee problem', the extension of the Piccadilly Line northwards from Finsbury Park, the dangers of Socialism, and eventually into items about underground bomb shelters, gas masks, blackout curtains, barrage balloons, evacuation, the putting-down of pets, numerous hasty marriages and 'a crusade against evil'. In January 1939 a Mrs Bridget Hitler of Priory Gardens (a suburban cul de sac on the edge of Queen's Wood, with its own neat entrance to what was then still Highgate railway station rather than a tube station) was summoned for non-payment of rates. She was, the paper stated, 'the wife of Mr Alois Hitler, Herr Hitler's half-brother'. She was summoned again on 1 September that year, but there were weary smiles in Highgate Court when it was announced that the summons could not be served.

War was declared on 3 September, though it was almost a year before the bombing began in earnest. Hornsey, with all its railway lines and sidings as targets, was heavily affected, especially the south of the borough, including the Stroud Green Road. Whole runs of houses were reduced to ruins by bombs, and many others, among them Stapleton Hall, had general blast damage. Elsewhere, the assault was more sporadic, with little destruction in Hornsey village itself except near the station. But several houses were wiped out just off suburban Priory Road, below Muswell Hill, and others in Crouch End. The Harringay ladder, being near the main line north, had some hits too. Later, towards the end of the war, the pilotless rockets began coming over. A V1 landed early one morning on a corner of Stapleton Hall Road just at the bottom of the hill up to Mountpleasant. It damaged Holy Trinity church beyond repair, partially demolished twelve houses and killed fifteen people. For years afterwards, a collection of prefabricated temporary homes occupied the spot. At least you could hear and see the V1s coming. The V2s that succeeded them were undetectable until they exploded. One fell just on the Islington side of the Stroud Green Road near the crossroads with Crouch Hill, taking out more houses and lives.

By the time the war was over the spectre of unemployment that had haunted the 1920s and '30s had disappeared from the pages of The *Hornsey Journal* as if it had never been, to be replaced by indignation about a 'crime wave' and about the genuine and acute housing shortage all over London. There were plans for blocks of flats off the Stroud Green Road since 'the Ministry of Health does not approve of building houses on the larger vacant sites'. Already, the notion that small, individual houses somehow embodied the 'unhealthy' poverty-stricken past was taking its ideological grip on areas such as Finsbury Park, while the local paper lamented – though for quite other reasons – that the country was in for 'five years of Socialist rule': what would America think of their Marshall Plan loan being used to 'bolster up schemes of Socialism' such as the nationalisation of the railways? Meanwhile, the huge demographic change that was on its way to districts such as Hornsey was apparently unpredicted by anyone.

Even before the war there had appeared the occasional reference in the paper to Cypriot inhabitants, typically in connection with some domestic fracas or with a restaurant selling meat only passed for animal consumption. By the 1950s, the number of citizens of Greek Cypriot origin settling in the area, mainly as industrious corner-shop and café owners, had become enormous. For the rest of the century other waves of immigration followed: African, Caribbean, Indian and Pakistani and, most of all, Turkish and Kurdish. Various other Middle Eastern nationalities arrived too, and the end of the century brought Bosnians and Albanians. For a time, the Stroud Green Road became an unofficial venue for those seeking employment, with battered, anonymous white vans coming by each morning to pick up men hanging hopefully about on corners.

In 1990 a large mosque was built just south-east of Finsbury Park station, near to where the old Arsenal football ground still lay and where, long ago, a cornfield had varied the smooth vistas of green pastures that provided hay and milk for the metropolis. By the 2000s, with the advent of terrorist attacks, 'the Finsbury Park mosque' had become a shorthand term for the aspect of modern London that many citizens found the most disquieting. Yet meanwhile, in the side streets not far up the Stroud Green Road that had once been contemptuously scheduled for demolition, house prices continued to rise and rise, inexorably making much of Hornsey too expensive for the very section of society for which it had been built.

Up until the Second World War, the Stroud Green Conservative Association seems to have maintained a distinctive presence in the area, though a gradually diminishing one.

In the Inland Revenue survey made in the First World War the house is described as an 'Old, detached cement-rendered house ... Ground floor 3 rooms (one had recent addition which enlarges it, making a billiard room to take 2 tables). Kitchen in rear and scullery (which is now club bar). First floor, 4 rooms (medium size) and lavatory. Attic, 3 rooms in rather poor order.'

The gross value of the site was estimated at £1,550, but out of this the house itself was valued at only £200 – a portent of the thinking that would come near to destroying it later in the century. The lease, originally taken out for twenty-one years in 1886, had been renewed in 1907, and the current freehold owner was said to be a Mrs Tubbs. As a Mr H.T. Tubbs JP was vice-chairman of the association in 1900, when the new MP was welcomed with a rousing rendering of 'Cock o'the north', one may guess that after Charles Turner's death the Tubbses, as prominent members, had bought the property from his daughter, probably on favourable terms. One of them was an executor to Turner's Will.[2] The Tubbses owned other properties nearby and were a thriving local family: several households of them lived up the hill in or around select Hornsey Lane. Typically for that prosperous era, the older members had done well in such trades as brewery and wholesale drapery; and the census for 1901 reveals that by then some of the younger generation were becoming solicitors and chartered accountants. Other well-regarded local families who frequented the Association were the Harlings (the Rev. W. Harling was the minister at the Hornsey Road Methodist church) and the Sandilands, who owned a big electrical supply and repair shop and advertised regularly in the *Journal*. After the First World War the same names are still present at 'the revival of the children's party' in January 1922 for 180 young guests – 'brilliantly illuminated by means of the electric light – coloured bulbs, Chinese lanterns et cetera, all provided by Mr A.E. Sandilands of Stroud Green Road ... It was after midnight before the revels ceased.'

Yet with the passing years and with newer suburbs endlessly uncoiling, out beyond Finchley and Edmonton, towards Barnet and Chingford, the social character of the area was insidiously changing. The generation who had started the Association with such firm intentions of preserving its select character were gone by the 1930s, and most of their kind no longer wanted to make the environs of Finsbury Park their home. When one of the last 'old stagers' of the Association, himself the deputy editor of the *Hornsey Journal*, with a son working for Sandilands and a daughter married to a Harling, died just before the Second World War, it must have seemed the end of an era. Significantly, young Mrs Harling lived further out in polite, salubrious Potters Bar. Already, half a dozen years before, a general appeal had gone out in the Conservative Party for more members for Stroud Green – yet I came to realise, when trying to trace the Association's later history through Conservative Party central archives, that in practice, as time went by, the Association has less and less contact with the Party as such.

MPs came and went, often transient grandees para-chuted into what remained (till eventual rearrangement of constituency boundaries) a safe Conservative seat. But after the First World War there are no reports of triumphant visits to Stroud Green. Indeed, by the late 1930s the Conservative political headquarters for Hornsey was established in Crouch End. The Young Conserva-tives, which in the mid-decades of the century constituted a fashionable Middle England mating organisation, flour-ished in Crouch End also in Highgate and Muswell Hill, but Stroud Green was by this time off all socially aspirant maps. In the 1950s it lost its railway station that had been proudly opened in 1881. The Tottenham & Hamp-stead Junction Railway (as was) continued to run a few trains in a low-key, little-advertised way through Crouch Hill station, but the Edgware, Highgate & London line through Stroud Green was declared redundant. In any case its track from Highgate northwards had been taken over by the Northern Line tube extension. The section of embankments and cuttings from Finsbury Park to Highgate gradually became smothered in trees, bracken and brambles and disappeared from maps, not to be rediscovered and reinvented as an urban 'green parkway' for another thirty years. Creepers began to drape the fine brick viaduct that crossed Stapleton Hall Road a little to the north of the Association's house and garden.

One must suppose, since the Association remained solvent and was now being run by a board of directors, that it continued in a quiet way as a social club, but the hundred-odd members apparently went in for little political activity at either national or local level, and in the summer of 1962 they had a shock:

> Members of Stroud Green Conservative club [*sic*] were unaware, till they were told by the *Journal* this week, that Hornsey Borough Council will be asked next Tuesday to give consent to an outline planning application for the demolition of the club's leasehold premises, Stapleton Hall . . . and its redevelopment by unnamed developers for residential purposes . . .
>
> The owner of the premises is Miss Tubbs, who lives abroad, and the lease has just over two years to run.
>
> A few months ago Miss Tubbs' agents told the club that she wished to sell and that they could have an option to purchase. The club offered £6,000 – they could not go higher – and a valuer had called at the premises.
>
> 'We have heard nothing since', said Mr F.R. Jordan, the club secretary . . . 'Miss Tubbs has been very good to us', he added, 'and it is possible that this application was not made on her behalf.'
> (*Hornsey Journal*, 20 July 1962)

Six thousand pounds was a realistic figure for such a house at that time, if it was regarded simply as a 'period property' rather than a unique survival. Large but shabby eighteenth-century houses in Islington were then selling for about that amount. The value of old houses was just beginning to be appreciated. The obsession that bricks and mortar were a declining asset, which had gone unquestioned during the first half of the twentieth century, was on the cusp of tipping over into the belief that they were an automatically increasing asset – the notion that has dominated public thinking ever since.

Miss Tubbs was presumably the daughter, if not the granddaughter, of the original vice-chairman of the Association, and evidently, in the tradition started by Charles Turner over seventy years before, she continued to be good to it. The Council did give planning consent for demolition and a block of flats but, late in the year, Miss Tubbs intervened, and instead of selling to the developers accepted the Association's offer to purchase, probably for rather less than the six thousand earlier mentioned. One of the directors of the Association told the newspaper: '"This means that the oldest club – in fact the oldest building – in Hornsey has been preserved". He felt that it would not be in the club's interest to disclose the price, at least not at present.'

Not a trace of this make-or-break moment in the house's long history appears in the Conservative Central Party's records: clearly it was not their affair. Nor does any record of it seem to have survived in local authority archives, possibly because, three years later, Hornsey Council was swallowed up into Haringey. The London Metropolitan archives admit to no evidence either.

Yet in spite of the directors' satisfaction, and the apparent assumption that the club would continue in the same way into the long future, not much more than twenty years later another major event occurred in Stapleton Hall's varied and wayward existence. It was once again up for sale, and once again modern flats on the site were proposed.

Fortunately by this time, the mid-1980s, accepted views had changed and it was not being suggested that the house itself should be demolished. The Hornsey Historical Society, with some very well informed members, was now in existence. Stapleton Hall had been carefully surveyed and its much-altered structure analysed. Haringey had listed it as being of local significance, and an enlightened planning officer now contacted the Society for further guidance. Letters kept by one of their members[3] show that representations were made to the newly founded English Heritage organisation, and, in the summer of 1986, the house was nationally Listed Grade I, as an exceptional survivor from the distant past in such an improbable setting. This meant that an initial plan to fill its one-time garden with an unrelated tall block had to be abandoned by the would-be developers and a more sensitive scheme devised.[4]

It was exactly one hundred years since Charles Turner had leased the place to the Conservative Association. How, I wondered, had the Association fared, or failed to fare, in the twenty years after its successful purchase from Miss Tubbs?

An appeal in the local paper for old Conservatives who might remember the place in club days produced nothing. Evidently, too many years had passed. Eventually I did locate, on a local website, someone who recalled it – but what he recalled came as a surprise:

I can remember Stapleton Hall as the Conservative Club from '76 onwards until its sale in approx '86.

It was a very down-at-heel address with no sign or notice board that I can recall. It had a badly lit muddy car park on one side which was always full of vans and pick-up trucks as it was frequented for the most part by builders and labourers at all hours of the day. There was a modern prefab extension to the side which housed two full-sized snooker tables. It was basically a drinking club with no official events that I can recall and definitely not open to all-comers. Sir Hugh Rossi, MP at that time, was almost certainly never there . . .

Another blogger had similar memories:

It was essentially an annexe of the pub, you could watch people walk from the Stapleton to the club (pub hours were different then) and later in the evening/morning you would hear them leaving. It was definitely a case of a funny knock on the door and wink-wink to gain entry – I tried a couple of times, to no avail.

The freehold would have been quite a valuable asset I suppose. I do remember it took quite some time for the development plans to be agreed and a sale to go through – they had 5 or 6 very large trees of 100 years or more which people wanted to protect – during the application process some trees died mysteriously, the fence was allowed to collapse etc. In the end it [the garden] was all levelled and the two blocks west of the original building were built over it.

How the organisation which had for so long prided itself on its middle-class tone, and which was still suffi-ciently in touch with its origins in 1962 to get prefer-ential treatment from the surviving Miss Tubbs, had transformed itself in a decade into an out-of-hours drinking club for building labourers, I cannot pretend to know. Another blogger mentioned that the 1970s had been, socially, the lowest point for Stroud Green Road, with muggings and burglaries blamed locally on Niger-ians living in 'drug refuges'. At this time, too, the dere-lict railway line, not yet done up as a green walkway, was a hiding place for illicit activities. Possibly a dwindling band of aged Conservatives, demoralised by their circumstances, had sold the place on. But the point about the rising value of the Stapleton Hall freehold is valid. Someone, or two or three people, must eventually have made a good deal of money out of the sale.

The buyer in the 1980s was a company called Lovell Homes, which must at that point have acquired the house's Deeds or Land Registry papers. But Lovell Homes have since been subsumed into another corporation and then into an international conglomerate. Enquiries in that direction have produced no one able to give me any account of the transaction, or of the architectural firm responsible for carrying out the substantial work on the building that followed.

The company, however, once it had been made to understand the restrictions under which it would have to work now that the building was nationally Listed, seems eventually to have taken its responsibilities to heart. Its brochure for potential flat-buyers referred (with the customary well-intentioned inaccuracies) to the house's ancient lineage, and threw in an elusive 'stane-staple' from the Domesday Book to add lustre to a triumphant final sentence – 'You are looking at virtually seven hundred years of Middlesex history.'

The house was refurbished, with due attention to the display of some of its ancient timbers, two flats were installed on the ground floor, two on the first floor, and a larger one on the attic floor. On the one-time garden in front of the house, which had latterly become the muddy car park with big old trees, another block of the same height and dimensions was built at right angles to the old house, and another at right angles to that. The ensemble now facing on to Stapleton Hall Road thus formed an open-sided square, which was landscaped with grass and paving and a wrought-iron gate. On the old Hall the cement front was left in place, painted white to look like stucco, and the same treatment was given to the heavy late-Victorian porch, which was not replaced as it might have been. But the new wings were built of yellow London stock brick, matching the flank wall of the old one, and were given similar mansarded tiled roofs. An old miniature bell tower, from the crown of a roof, was rescued and reinstated, and twelve paned sash windows were installed throughout. The brochure enthused: 'You'll sense a Georgian feel in the courtyard, tinged with later echoes.'

What must be the one survivor of the lost garden is a convoluted fig tree, sustaining a cramped existence between a wall and a railing on the west side of the property.

But currently the whole place looks pleasant and well maintained. A few years ago the tenants formed a company to buy the property, and are now joint free-holders. Even if most passers-by never realise that the eastern side of this neo-Georgian development is actually centuries old, Stapleton Hall could have fared a great deal worse. As I go past it on an early winter's evening when curtains are not yet drawn, on a bus which allows a sideways view into the lighted rooms, I can catch a brief but clear impression of roof beams. Once again, this is where we came in.

In the 1970s, when Stapleton Hall was a drinking club for lorry drivers, the Manor House in Limpsfield was derelict.

The school, with its pupil numbers diminishing and its image demoded, had shut down in 1969. Occasionally, over the intervening years, I who had been an unhappy child there in the early 1950s would find myself driving along the A25 under the North Downs. Several times I made a brief, compulsive detour down Limpsfield High Street. As the familiar buildings came into view, high wall, pink bricks and contorted fire escape prominent, a

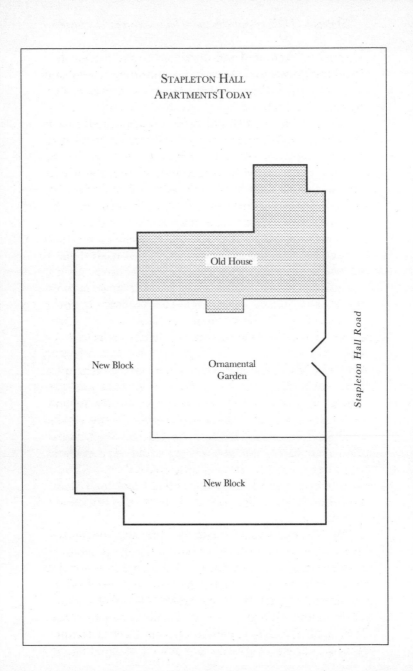

STAPLETON HALL
APARTMENTS TODAY

Old House

New Block

Ornamental
Garden

New Block

Stapleton Hall Road

miasma of sickening dread unrelated to my present life would invade me, to be followed at once by a triumphant wave of relief, as when waking from a bad dream. I've escaped! I'm free!

At long intervals, I would suffer an actual nightmare about being back in the place, and it figured in incidental ways in the novels and short stories that I wrote. Then, one autumn, I saw with amazed delight that the whole place was empty and had a 'For Sale' notice on it.

A side door in a yard was not properly secured. I got in easily, and wandered around up and down the intimately known corridors, stairs, classrooms and bedrooms, all now emptied except for a few piles of rubbish, and silent except for a storm of rain which broke outside, hammering in a remembered way on the dirty glass roofs of lean-tos, dripping into a familiar puddle halfway down a dark passage. I thought, then, that I would never, ever return. From that time on, the nightmares ceased.

The buildings were sold to a developer, but they remained empty for years. Others too found their way into the derelict and darkened place. Broken window glass and the occasional empty bottle began to litter the downstairs floors, and once or twice fires were started which fortunately smouldered out before they could set the whole agglomeration alight, leaving only charred boards and a smell of old bomb sites. Birds entered and built nests, their droppings adding white spots to the thickening layer of dirt.

The developers had bought the grounds too, apparently with large-scale development in mind, though they were eventually to sell them on. Their intention for the house itself was to demolish the ugly pink-brick wing, and also the collection of one-storey, twentieth-century constructions stretching out at the back, and to retain the original house along with its early nineteenth-century kitchen quarters. This, like a number of buildings in

Front view of Manor House School, derelict and up for sale c.1970. The flank wall of the house on the left of the photo is readily recognisable from the drawing of 1821. The neo-Queen Anne building with tall chimneys on the right was added by the Misses Lyon at the end of the nineteenth century. The developers initially planned to keep it, but demolished it when their repeated applications to insert a large number of flats into it were refused.

Limpsfield, had been Listed (Grade II) by the local authority in a well-intentioned if not very well-informed way as early as 1958, when public concern about the cavalier post-war destruction of old houses was beginning to make itself felt. The developers also planned initially to keep the neo-Queen-Anne block, which had been built adjoining the main house in 1897 by the Misses Lyon to accommodate their exclusive school of twenty-odd pupils.

The developers' first proposal was for conversion of the buildings into sixteen oddly shaped flats, mostly quite small. However, the planning committee for Tandridge District Council considered that such a density would be 'too high for this locality', and in July 1970 a modified application for twelve flats was granted. That same summer someone from the County Architect's department visited the place. Like his predecessor in 1958, he took the building at face value to be Georgian, and merely commented 'The original part undoubtedly fully merits its statute-listing [*sic*].' His brief report to what was then known as the Council's Historic Buildings and Antiquities Office does not mention the kitchen quarters with their puzzlingly ancient beams. Perhaps he did not even discover this part of the house, for he did not apparently enter the buildings at all, though in his official role he would have had ready access. His report concludes 'The proposed alterations are mainly confined to the interior, and it would seem unlikely that objection would arise from the purely architectural and antiquities angles [*sic*]'. How he thought that he could make such a judgement merely by viewing only the outside of the buildings is not clear. Had he peered in through the glazing on the front door beneath the porch, he would have seen the large old central fireplace which indicates an origin much earlier than the eighteenth century. And even a brief sortie inside this main house would have revealed the graceful eighteenth-century staircase as worth preserving too. The chance to make a proper architectural and historical assessment of this complex building, and to rehabilitate it properly, was there – and it was lost. The fireplace is now buried in the partition wall of a bathroom; the lovely flights of stairs have been replaced by unsuitable and rickety modern ones.

In these circumstances, the subsequent conversion had little chance of being done to the standard that the house warranted, but in any case it was put off for half a dozen more years. The developers and their 'agents' (possibly all the same two people) would say that the delay was due to the Council procrastinating in accepting details of the planning application. But Council's record for the early 1970s shows that numerous and repeated applications were also made to build unrealistically large numbers of often unsuitable houses in the grounds. All were refused, and meanwhile the fate of the Manor House itself was in abeyance. By May 1975 the Chief Executive of the Council was writing to the developers:

As you know, Manor House, Limpsfield, is a statutory Listed Building, and for some time the Council have been very concerned about its continuing deterioration. They have refrained from taking positive action because it was confidently expected that the problem would be solved by the exercise of the planning consent which had previously been granted for the conversion of the Manor House into flats.

This has not materialised, and you will, I am sure, be aware of your statutory obligation to take such action as may be necessary to ensure the proper preservation of this building.

Further mutual reproach followed, including threats from the Council to take the necessary action themselves and bill the developers. In June the developers' agent wrote to say that a builder had now been instructed to 'secure the building against trespass forthwith, boarding up windows where necessary and preventing entry to the property'. This letter ends, somewhat naively one may think, 'I fully agree with your concern and must thank you for bringing it to my attention', which would seem to indicate that until then the house had been effectively abandoned. It has been suggested to me that the developers, baulked of their original sixteen flats, and also of their plans for houses in the grounds, may have hoped the place would degenerate to a point at which they would be allowed to pull everything down.

Representations continued from the Council, who found the boarding-up inadequate, but by the late 1970s matters were at last moving. At about the same time the developers, perhaps realising when they were outmanoeuvred, sold off much of the school grounds to the huge Wates company. Somewhere along the line, too, the idea of keeping the neo-Queen-Anne building had been scrapped; only the Listed original house and the kitchen quarters were retained. The number of flats to be created was reduced to seven: the kitchen quarters were to be divided off as a separate house to be called Bell Cottage, after the belfry put on the roof about 1880 when the place was an army crammer belonging to the eponymous Mr Bell. Everything else – cheap bricks, wooden classrooms, iron fire escapes, plywood false timbering, fetid sculleries, prefabricated huts, old stone walls, remnants of long-forgotten stables, tennis courts, the static-tank swimming pool – all were swept away. The Manor House returned to the size and silhouette it had in its days when it was a home for a wealthy gentleman and his family.

Today, a doorway that I recall as having been part of a windowless passage leading from the day girls' cloakroom to the forbidden front hall is the side entrance to the house, the point of access for most of the flats. It was probably the main door when Marmaduke Mills reconstructed his two old cottages into one substantial dwelling around 1740, before anyone gave it a fashionable stucco facelift and a porticoed porch facing the road. An ancient bow window from a funny little attic that used to look down on a squalid interior yard now surveys flower beds and a driveway. This leads up to the new estate of well-designed modern houses ('Stanhopes') for which the Wates organisation finally got planning clearance. Most of them form a loose square round a green expanse which is the shadow of the one-time tennis courts and swimming pool. A beech hedge at least a hundred years old still runs past them.

In Philippa Pearce's classic book *Tom's Midnight Garden*, a child discovers that night transforms a backyard with dustbins into the vanished grounds of a big house, but the reverse may also be imagined. If I were to sleep in one of the flats in the Manor House today, would I be jerked away by the echo of a jangling school bell, a blur of high-pitched voices, feet hurrying over bare floors, and find my moonlit view from the staircase's arching window blocked by three storeys of brick? Not a ghost person but a ghost building.

I have, till now, kept off the possibility of supernatural happenings in any of my three houses, not having much inclination to believe in such things. I know that the Misses Lyon, the Strongs, Marmaduke Mills, Parsons Lewes and Stiles, Edmund Harman, Charles Turner, the Lucas dynasty and all the rest were as real and intricately attached to their lives and their homes as we are today: I do not need to seek them as disconsolate shadows. However, I offer the following pieces of thought-provoking information . . .

When researching into the Manor House I was introduced to the current occupant of a one-time gardener's cottage in the grounds whose family had long been tenants of the Leveson-Gowers. He remembered the girls' school in its final years, and also the long period when the buildings stood empty. His own children used to like to creep into the derelict rooms from the overgrown gardens and explore, but this seemed greatly to distress their dog. It refused to go in with them, and would sit outside growling as if in warning. This behaviour persisted, and the family eventually began to wonder if past children had been unhappy within those walls, and if the dog was somehow picking up this accumulated emotion.

Old vicarages, benefiting from great continuity of occupation, are proverbially haunted and the one at Taynton is no exception. When the Milner children were young one of them, Cathy, used to sleep in a small bedroom situated approximately over the kitchen. She would complain of hearing noises below in the night: chairs being moved on the stone floor and sometimes feet. Her mother would briskly assure her 'Oh, it's just the dogs moving around and flumping down by the Aga.'

Years passed, Cathy grew up, and the night came when I was in the house alone with my sick cousin. I had been offered Cathy's old room to sleep in but it seemed to me rather remote and lonely: I rationalised my feeling by deciding it was too far away from my cousin, who might need me in the night. I brought my bedding downstairs to his small sitting room. I slept fitfully, aware of the man a few feet away from me whose life was nearing its end – and aware too that the Aga in the kitchen next door might need feeding with more coke in the night, and that I was not confident of my skill with that redoubtable kitchen museum-piece. The kitchen itself was entirely quiet, the dogs quiescent in their baskets.

What I heard several times that night seemed to come from overhead, in the direction of the room where I could have been sleeping. It was exactly as Cathy (and others) had described: furniture moving, and at one moment tramping feet. She had heard it as from one floor above, I from one floor below, but the elusive sounds were unmistakable.

A more striking piece of testimony came from one of Cathy's brothers. In his teens he slept in the attics, and was up there one summer day revising for an exam. He thought he saw pass down the side of the room what he took to be a friend from abroad who was staying in the house, dressed up in some way. He said 'Don't be an idiot, Alain—' Then he looked up, and it was not Alain (who turned out to have been down the garden at the time) but an elderly man in 'something like a white robe – maybe a surplice', who was there just for a moment then no more.

Such oddities in the old vicarage were no secret, but nobody talked about them much. The family line was that they were quite harmless and that you couldn't do anything about them anyway.

It had not occurred to me that I might hear any such tales about Stapleton Hall. Of my three houses, it was the one that seemed to have undergone such physical vicissitudes as would have wiped out any delicate ghostly imprint. It is only a part of its one-time self; and the total transformation of its surroundings from cow pastures to busy inner city streets must, I vaguely assumed, have laid multiple, shattering new impressions over the older ones.

It took me a while to get inside the original part of the building, but eventually I and an accomplice from the Hornsey Historical Society made contact with the tenant of one of the two ground-floor flats. We were welcomed by her one winter afternoon, and admired the chunks of very old blackened oak apparent at various points in her irregular walls. We also noted to our satisfaction that the sitting room fireplace and its gable-end wall had clearly been rebuilt (when the road swept past, shaving off the farmhouse shortly before 1880), and the fact that the eighteenth-century window apertures were unrelated to the basic beam frame of the house's construction. Outside this tenant's flat, in the ceiling of a narrow hallway containing the stairs (early Victorian) leading to the upper floors, there was a massive beam that was clearly part of the main structure of the house, and there were other very old, heavy timbers upright at the stairhead which may have been moved from their original setting. Her own front door too was thick and ancient.

She was young, cheerful, matter-of-fact. She said she'd had trouble at first with rats and hornets (old-fashioned nuisances not likely, today, to impinge on the inhabitants of modern flats) but now was very happy in the place which had 'a nice feeling'. She knew nothing of its history but she ventured, quite unprompted, that she had wondered if the house might be haunted? There was, she said, a lot of creaking and sometimes bumping on the hall floor at night, and often in the morning she found her old-fashioned door-chain undone when she was sure she had done it up before going to bed.

It did not seem to worry her.

My three houses have all been survivors. E.M. Forster, writing of the deaths of houses being like those of men, said that some go 'with a tragic roar, some quietly . . . while from others . . . the spirit slips before the body perishes' (*Howards End*). Part of Stapleton Hall fell with a roar for road-building; the Old Vicarage has been quietly vacated by the Church spirit that lived in it for centuries; the Manor House was, for a time, both abandoned and perishing – yet all three have, against the odds, been saved. Their lives continue.

Of the three, I feel that while both the Old Vicarage

and Stapleton Hall have in different ways reached some state of quietude and completion, the Manor House is still a hostage to fortune. Since its origins in 'two old cottages' it has undergone more physical and social transformations than the other two, but it is still semi-disguised and undervalued. As I write, it is the subject of some dispute between those notionally responsible for its structure and those who have chosen to make it their home. It is my hope that its story is not yet fully told, and that in its unwritten future someone will rescue it from its present botched state and restore it to its true self with the knowledge and care that it deserves.

I end, as I began, with Margaret Harding, she who was the wife of George Harding the parish clerk of Limpsfield in the mid-eighteenth century, and who used a few tempting blank spaces on the rag-paper pages of a no-longer-used register to write riddles and practise her flowing, loopy signature. She was probably rather proud of her literacy, something to which most wives in her station of life did not yet aspire.

She was from the Mills family. Her husband (whose name she variously spells Harding, Hardin and Harden, just as she sometimes puts an extra 't' on the end of Margaret and sometimes not) seems to have inherited the job of clerk from his father-in-law. The number of Millses in and around Limpsfield at the time makes it difficult to be sure about this, but if I am right then she was a sister of Marmaduke, the blacksmith and builder of the house. What is certain is that she would have known the remains of the two old cottages on the site above the high road that was once called Joane-atte-Wells, and would have known Elizabeth Lone and Nicholas Constable who were currently in possession. She would have seen Marmaduke's fine new house go up around the old chimney stack in about 1742, and I expect she visited the house, for its successive tenants would have been known to her as well.

I have not found her baptism which, judging from when she was married, was probably before 1714, in the reign of Queen Anne. Some pages of the baptismal register for that period are so rubbed at the edges that a number of entries are illegible. But I do know that at the end of April 1733 she became the wife of George Harding, weaver, also of the parish of Limpsfield. It was a suitable match, for weaving was then still an established and prestigious trade, though over the next two generations it was to decline with the coming of industrialised looms. The couple's first child, a daughter, was baptised only five months later, a not unusual timetable in those days and one which no doubt most people accepted with a circumspect smile. Perhaps the wedding might have been a month or so earlier if Lent, when weddings traditionally did not take place, had not supervened.

She had another daughter in 1736, who did not survive, and then a son in 1737. Three more daughters followed in 1739, 1742 and 1744, but at least one of these died in 1748. It was a common enough pattern for the time: I hope her losses did not quench Margaret's spirits.

On 25 December 1734 – Christmas Day, in fact, which was then more of a religious festival than a time for self-indulgence – she wrote a sober couplet:

Lord God Give me Wisdom to Direct my Ways
I Beg not Riches nor yet Leangth of Days

– but her other messages are more teasing:

Joyne these too Lettres Cunningly and you may know
my name then – [ink blot]

> *. . . This Book shall my name have*
> *When I am Dead and Laid in grave*
> *When Groady worms my Body has eat*
> *then you may see my name Compleat . . .*

She was to be laid in Limpsfield churchyard in 1756. The burial registers for that era do not give ages, but she was probably, judging from her childbearing record, not yet fifty. Her realism about not praying for length of days was justified.

I like to think that death would not have fazed her. I see her tripping down the muddy high street in home-woven linen petticoats and cap, a child or two at her side, admiring the shiny new coach pulled up by the Bull Inn, bobbing a curtsey to a passing Gresham, dropping in on her brother in his forge. With her goose-quill pen (borrowed, no doubt, from her husband while he was out of the way in his weaver's workshop or arranging things in the church) she achieved her own tiny stake in immortality. Clever Margaret Harding.

Notes

Chapter II: Any Boarding School

1. A survey of all properties in Britain was undertaken by the Inland Revenue between 1910 and 1915. The quality of the information varies from one district to another, and that for Limpsfield is not good, but the presence of bathrooms and lavatories (undifferentiated) is indicated in the Manor House report.

2. Lady Benn, daughter of Maurice, Lord Hankey, who then lived in Limpsfield. Quoted in an undated cutting from a local newspaper.

Chapter III: Letters and Deeds

1. The building lease system (peculiar to Britain) was the means by which a huge number of our houses came into existence in the eighteenth and nineteenth centuries. The ground landlord would lease a parcel of land to someone prepared to invest in developing it with a building or buildings – often, in towns, rows of terraced houses. The developer or his heirs would profit from renting out the houses, but at the end of a set term of years, typically ninety-nine years but sometimes fewer, the land plus the houses would revert to the ground owner. That, at any rate, was the theory.

2. Marmaduke was not a name commonly found in blacksmithing circles. I suppose that the fact that it was a Gresham family name had made it popular among the villagers of Limpsfield.

Notes

Chapter IV: Bombs and fantasies

1. For this piece of information, and a number of others concerning the past of Stapleton Hall, I am indebted to John Hinshelwood of the Hornsey Historical Society.
2. *The Victoria County History*, vol. VI, p.147.
3. This should read 'south-west end'. Such a mistake does not inspire confidence.
4. An early twentieth century correspondent to the *Hornsey Journal* quoted the advertisement in full but attributed it only to 'a periodical of May 1682'.
5. For sources see Hornsey Historical Society Bulletin 51, *Stapleton Hall, Stroud Green; the Myth Exposed* by John Hinshelwood.
6. As reported on 9 June 1759 in a news-sheet *The Universal Chronicle or Weekly Gazette*.

Chapter V: London's countryside, where houses get facelifts

1. See Chapter IV, note 5.
2. The present Archway Road, which is the start of the A1 Great North Road branching off from Holloway Road and bypassing Highgate village, was not opened till 1813.
3. Thomas Edlyne Tomlins, *Perambulation of Islington*, 1844.
4. Credit for the New River traditionally goes to Sir Hugh Myddelton, MP and alderman, whose statue stands today in Elizabethan dress in the centre of Islington, but contemporary accounts attribute the inspiration for it also to a Mr Inglebert whose contribution was never formally recognised.
5. 'Harringay', spelt sometimes thus but with variants, was an old name for an area north of London, of which the name 'Hornsey' is supposed by some people, but not by me, to be a corruption. Once Harringay House had been built *c*.1790, this name and spelling

286

became mainly concentrated on that particular seat and its grounds. The name 'Haringey', spelt thus, only entered general use when, in 1965, it was formed as a Greater London borough out of three Middlesex municipal boroughs, Hornsey, Wood Green and Tottenham. To add further to potential confusion, the architects of the new borough at first tried to insist that it should be pronounced Ha-*rin*-gey.

6. Ken Gay, *From Forest to Suburb*.
7. It was customary then for expensive or minority interest books to be financed by subscribers, who would be listed in the front of the book as a sign of respect and a marker of status. The system is still occasionally used today.
8. This story was repeated from one antiquarian to another, and a mid-nineteenth century one (Tomlins, as above) confused the issue further by unearthing a medieval reference to a 'Stapeled-halle' in some unspecified place just north of London which could have been Hornsey. Tomlins was, however, scrupulous enough to point out that this was not so much a proper name as a descriptive term for a house grand enough to have a secure fastening – staple – on the door rather than just the latch-and-catch ordinarily in medieval use.
9. S. Lewis, *The History and Topography of the Parish of St Mary, Islington*, 1842.

Chapter VI: Into Oxfordshire and the more distant past

1. Kathryn Hughes, *Guardian*, 27 November 2010.
2. A rector holds the benefice in his own right. Traditionally, in the days of tithes, he had the right to the lot and to any land attached to the benefice. Many rectors were therefore quite well off. A vicar, however (the word is related to 'vicarious'), is standing in for a rector, and in the past the rector was quite often someone leading a life unconnected with the parish,

sometimes attached to an Oxford college or to one of the great public schools or not in Holy Orders at all. Vicars, therefore, only enjoying a portion of the parish revenues or a set stipend, tended to be less well remunerated.

3. According to Frank Hansford-Miller, *A History and Geography of English Religion*, vol III.
4. I am indebted to Anthony Jennings, *The Old Rectory*, for this and other insights.
5. Sir Thomas More is the best-known example.
6. The Rev. William Charles Emeris.

Chapter VII: Edmund Harman's legacy and the house he lived in.

1. This hitherto overlooked fact has only been noticed in the last twenty-five years, when a local researcher named Michael Balfour made a careful study of the *Inquisitio post Mortem*, a mixture of inquest and probate assessment that followed Harman's own death. See *Edmund Harman, Barber and Gentleman*, Tolsey paper no. 6.
2. With the advent of a younger generation this has now been remedied. Twenty years ago a visit to Great Barrington felt like falling into a time-warp, with cottages in a state of dilapidation by then unknown elsewhere in the Cotswolds, and a village pump still standing among rank grass.

Chapter VIII: 'The spiritually comatose base of the Church of England'

1. A small book that is still sold in Taynton church, *A slight History of the Church and Village*, compiled by a Mrs Mollie Purefoy in the 1960s, apparently without reference to the Churchwardens' Book, states, after consultation with the College of Arms, that the Royal arms 'may be of any date between 1714 and 1801'.

2. Ronald Blythe, author of *Akenfield*.
3. Information from Mollie Purefoy's book, as cited above. The source of this startling piece of information was presumably, by then, already lost.
4. Terms such as 'carpenter' and 'stonemason' could cover anyone from a journeyman to the head of a large firm, since there was no general word then for building contractor.
5. *Chronicles* I, 19: 4 and 5.

Chapter IX: Back to Surrey, with Jane Austen

1. There were two young sons, Charles and John. Charles, who should have inherited, was lost at sea in 1750 when his brother was still only fifteen.
2. Since the stonemason Strongs of Taynton had, by the eighteenth century, developed London connections and were less in evidence in Oxfordshire, it occurred to me to wonder if the well-to-do Limpsfield Strongs, with their progeny of clergy, were a branch of the same family. Unfortunately, no such satisfying pattern emerged but, thanks to the help of a friend in the genealogical business, I am able to say that the Clement Strong born in Wandsworth, who rented the Manor House for forty years, came from a line of distinctively named Protestant Strongs living in the City of London and before that in Exeter, Devon. In other words he, like very many eighteenth century gentry 'of independent means', derived, several generations back, from ordinary stock.
3. William Cobbett, *Rural Rides*, 1822–26.
4. See her quoted in the epigraphs of this book.

Chapter X: Limpsfield changes, slowly but inevitably

1. Less well known than her children's books about theatre life and stage schools is an autobiographical novel she published in 1965, *Away from the Vicarage*,

depicting the life of herself and her sisters as girls in a clerical household in the 1920s.

2. *The House by the Thames*, 2006.

3. The ground landlord is written down, mistakenly at that point, as Leveson-Gower. The land had indeed been manorial property and soon would be again, but at that time Charles Stanhope owned the freehold.

4. This discovery was made by speculatively putting the Morton Daniels, with their full names, into an internet search. The internet is often unreliable on genealogy, possibly because of a desire of people in distant corners of the world to associate themselves with grand families, but more idiosyncratic and specific information is likely to be true.

5. Various commentators and writers of guidebooks have created confusion between Mountstuart and his nephew, Lord Elphinstone, also a Governor of Bombay at a later date, and also, briefly, an occupant of Hookwood House. They are buried together just outside the north side of the church, but it is Lord Elphinstone, not his uncle, who lies in lifesize marble and peer's robes in a rather crowded corner inside the church, petrified lilies in his hand.

6. Indeed, buildings are only summarily indicated on both maps: the church is a mere cross and the rectory an unrealistic square. On a plan of two other parcels of land being sold there are shown a couple of 'messuages' which had in fact been pulled down twenty-five years before. Testimony to this effect, taken from an aged inhabitant of Limpsfield, is attached to the Bill.

7. A note in the Manor House School newsletter published at the outbreak of the Second World War reads 'During this term Mr Hancock [who appears to have been the father of a pupil] made further interesting discoveries of ancient timbers, Norman bricks, and eventually he showed us a second staircase,

in the old part of the Manor House.' This is presumably the same person whose views on the house were cited later in the century by local historians Kay Percy and Peter Gray.

8. See Note 4 above. The Dent family wealth makes them readily traceable.
9. Today the institution is shut down and the building has been converted into expensive flats.
10. It was the presence of this fountain that made me able to identify him.
11. Annie Laura Saunders.

Chapter XI: Taynton Vicarage grows, but Burford does not

1. H.J. Dyos, *Victorian Suburb*.
2. Payne's Farm today is part of Swinbrook parish.
3. Sources vary slightly, but this seems to be the correct date.
4. Noted by a later vicar, William Emeris.
5. Testimony of Phillip Lee, the last quarry owner.

Chapter XII: The dynamic Railway Age. And its dark heart

1. Roger Braiser in *Limpsfield Ancient & Modern*.
2. Quoted ibid.
3. Now in Bruce Castle Museum.
4. The persistent notion that the Hall and the farmhouse were one and the same building has led to some unrealistic published interpretations of the various censuses.
5. I am indebted to John Hinshelwood for this recondite information about Joshua Lucas's other house.
6. In the census for 1841 ages were only stated to the nearest five years.
7. In *A Christmas Carol*, 1843.
8. Neither of the two churches has survived. Both had ended up too unfashionably near a large railway

viaduct and the industrial works that railways attract. The 1830s church, having become more or less abandoned, was pulled down, all but the old tower, in 1927, and in 1968 the bigger, newer one followed it into oblivion. Its congregation was merged with that of another church in a different, more salubrious part of the district, whose main building had itself been destroyed in the blitz of the Second World War. Thus the long existence of Hornsey as one parish came to an obscure end.

9. On this point, see Malcolm Stokes in *People & Places*.

Chapter XIII: Cow Pastures become Finsbury Park

1. The description of the visit to Sir George Grey, with accompanying quotation from 'The *Observer*' of the time, comes from Hugh Hayes, *A Park for Finsbury*, to which I am also indebted for a number of other points in this chapter.

2. Famously, at the same period, Sir Thomas Maryon Wilson, the lord of the manor of Hampstead, was making repeated attempts to build houses on Hampstead Heath, one of his devices being the pre-emptive erection of a carriageway on a viaduct over a marshy site. The Heath was saved for posterity: the viaduct still stands, as part of a network of footpaths.

3. Quoted by R.O. Sherington in *The Story of Hornsey*.

4. A pub called The Hornsey Tavern was opened in the Seven Sisters Road, but it was not the same place.

5. Sherington, *The Story of Hornsey*.

Chapter XIV: Passionate Hornsey

1. The present church dates from rebuilding after bomb damage in the Second World War

2. Quoted from 'The Railway Times' in *A History of London Transport*, T.C. Barker and Michael Robbins.

3. I don't think there was any connection between him and the Stapleton Hall wine merchant called Williams

of the 1840s, similarly a local public figure. It has been pointed out to me that Nonconformist, liberal wine merchants were, for some reason, much in evidence in Hornsey.

Chapter XV: Where We Came In, as the parsonage houses decline

1. Anthony Jennings, in *The Old Rectory: The Story of the English Parsonage*, 2009.
2. Anthony Bax, in *The English Parsonage*, 1964.

Chapter XVI: Stapleton Hall and the Manor House in need of rescue

1. See Chapter V, note 5 for the Harringay-Haringey question.
2. For this piece of information I am indebted to Roy Hidson in *People & Places*.
3. Bridget Cherry, who collaborated with Nikolaus Pevsner on *The Buildings of England*.
4. The Listing description reads: 'Circa early 17th century with later additions, including early 19th century façade. Timber frame, stuccoed; steeply pitched plain tiled roof to parapet. 2 storeys, small bays. Entrance almost centrally placed with projecting solid-sided pilastered porch. Square-headed windows; sashes, plate glass. Barn stack to left of centre. Interior with substantial chamfered and stopped beams, parts of original roof-structure, broad timber floor boards etc.' Whoever viewed the house for its Listing was diligent (unlike the architects who viewed the Manor House *c*. 1958 and 1970). He or she noticed that the overall construction is oddly off-centre, but probably did not realise that this might be because the whole corpus of the building was once a much larger T-shape, and that one side of the T had been lopped off when Stapleton Hall Road was driven through.

Sources and Bibliography

Writing a book such as this, I have made extensive use of unpublished and mainly untranscribed documents which, along with other primary sources, have come to rest in a variety of different archives, listed here in alphabetical order:

In the archive library of Bruce Castle Museum, Haringey, I have consulted some census material, maps, some copies of the periodical *London* Vol. V for 1896, the Vestry minutes of the parish of St Mary Hornsey from 1834 to 1896, the minutes of the Hornsey Local Board from 1868 to 1880, and the minutes of the meetings of those promoting the Tottenham & Hampstead Junction Railway in 1863. I have also been able to see original pictures that the Museum holds relating to Stapleton Hall.

At Colindale Newspaper Library (a branch of the British Library) I have been able to browse at will across a great many years of the *Hornsey Journal* and its predecessors – an aid to study which is soon likely to be withdrawn. I have also found there more fleeting newspapers such as the *Croydon Chronicle & East Surrey Advertiser* (1868), *The Village Searchlight* (published in Oxted for a few months in 1898), the *Reigate & Redhill Gazette* for 1907.

In Finsbury Library (Local History section) I have been able to read the Vestry minutes of the parish of St Mary Islington from 1662 to the end of the eighteenth century, and also to consult maps.

In Gloucestershire Archives I have been able to handle and look at the original parish registers of baptism, marriage and burial for Great Barrington (1547–1687), also to consult the 'Great Barrington Charities Notebook' (1821–1893), and assorted nineteenth-century diocesan communications regarding the joint parishes of Barrington and Taynton.

In the Hornsey Historical Society's archive in the Old Schoolhouse in Hornsey I have been able to browse the Middlesex Photographic Society's historic collection, also to consult some twentieth-century copies of the *Hornsey Journal*, some incidental papers relating to the mid-twentieth century Hornsey Conservative party, some correspondence between members of the HHS and the local authority relating to the Listing of Stapleton Hall in the 1980s, and also a copy of the Will of Joseph Lucas (1739–1807).

In Lambeth Palace Library I have read documents relating to the financial situation of vicars and their vicarages, in Taynton and other nearby parishes, in the first half of the twentieth century, and diocesan correspondence regarding the eventual dissolution of the joint parishes of Great Barrington and Taynton; also the conveyance of Taynton vicarage in 1957. I was in addition usefully introduced to the Church of England database.

In the London Metropolitan Archive I have consulted estates conveyances and planning documents relating to the area near Stapleton Hall in the last quarter of the nineteenth century, also Middlesex Bomb Damage Maps of World War II.

In the National Archives at Kew, west London, (till recently known as the Public Record Office) I have accessed census material and also the Inland Revenue Surveys c.1915 along with their attendant maps.

In the Oxfordshire Record Office I have been able to see the original Taynton registers of baptisms, marriages and burials from 1538 until the present day, the

Churchwardens' account books (1724 to 1877), the 'Vestry Book' (1807–1923), and the Taynton Land Tax Assessments from 1785 to 1831. Also various boxes of miscellaneous papers from the parish chest, as retrieved by a vicar in 1873, including a few indentures, Deeds, Wills and conveyances mainly relating to gifts, various Church Rate assessments from 1667 up to the 1840s, many eighteenth- and nineteenth-century legal documents relating to the Poor Rate and to rights of settlement, maintenance orders for bastardy, removal notices, receipts, letters, declarations, militia notices et cetera, et cetera.

In the Surrey History Centre, Woking, I have been able to consult the original baptism, marriage and burial registers from 1674 onwards, the Limpsfield Manor Court Rolls from the mid-sixteenth century to 1922, the Limpsfield Parish Rates for 1651–52, the 'Church Book' (rates 1811–1825), the Limpsfield Parish Clerk's accounts (1814–1837), the Land Tax Assessments from 1780 to 1832, the Poor Rates (1836–9 and 1840–1848), and the parish accounts from 1760 to 1941. Also bundles of Deeds and ancillary material relating to Stanhopes *alias* the Manor House, deposited in the archive by the Leveson-Gower family. Also the Peter Gray collection of documents, donated by Kay Percy, which contains the Cox papers; and another recently donated collection of documents relating to the Manor House School between the 1920s and the 1960s.

Although not strictly speaking an archive, the resources of the London Library have, as ever, allowed me to browse at will through copies of *The Times*, the *Illustrated London News* and *Punch* for the mid-decades of the nineteenth century.

The British Library has been able, in their invaluable way, to supply copies of certain books unobtainable anywhere else – including a select compilation of church records, privately published in 1949 by a Limpsfield rector and otherwise unknown.

The list of printed sources which follows cannot mention every book which has contributed over the years to my interest in the history of place, but aims to include those which have direct bearing on my Three Houses:

Adams, Christine, with Michael McMahon, *A Lifetime in Building*, 2009

Austen, Jane, *Emma*, 1815

Balfour, Michael, *Edmund Harman, Barber and Gentleman*, Tolsey Paper No.6, Burford, 1988

Barker, Paul, *The Freedoms of Suburbia*, 2009

Barker, TC and Robbins, Michael, *A History of London Transport*, 1963

Bax, Anthony, *The English Parsonage*, 1964

Bennett, Arnold, *Hilda Lessways*, 1911

Brayley, Edward, *History of Limpsfield*, 1878 (and in Local History Reprints, 1996)

Bryson, Bill, *At Home*, 2010

Cave, Lyndon F, *The Smaller English House*, 1981

Cobbett, William, *Rural Rides*, 1822–26

Davenport-Adams, WH, *A guide to the History, Antiquities and Topography of the County of Surrey*, 1860

Denford, Steve, *Hornsey Past*, 2008

Dickens, Charles, *A Christmas Carol*, 1843

Dyos, HJ, *Victorian Suburb*, Leicester, 1974

Gay, Ken, *From Forest to Suburb*, HHS occasional paper no.4, 1988

Gray, Peter (editor), *Limpsfield Ancient and Modern*, Limpsfield History Group, 1997

Gretton, RH, *The Burford Records: a Study in Minor Town Government*, Oxford, 1920

Gretton, Mary Sturge, *Burford 1920*, 1925, revised 1944.

Hansford-Miller, Frank, *A History and Geography of English Religion*, vol. 3, privately published, 1990

Hardy, Thomas, *Under the Greenwood Tree*, 1872
—*The Woodlanders*, 1895

Hayes, Hugh, *A Park for Finsbury*, published by the Friends of Finsbury Park, 2001

Hill, Rosemary, *God's Architect: Pugin and the Building of Romantic Britain*, 2007

Hinshelwood, John, *Stapleton Hall, Stroud Green; the myth exposed*, article in HHS Bulletin 51, 2010

Hoskins, WG, *The Making of the English Landscape*, Leicester, 1955

Jay, Elizabeth, *Faith and Doubt in Victorian Britain*, 1986

Jennings, Anthony, *The Old Rectory: The Story of the English Parsonage*, 2009

Knight, Caroline, *London's Country Houses*, Chichester, 2009

Knight, Frances, *The Church in the Nineteenth Century*, 2008

Lewis, S, *The History and Topography of the Parish of St Mary's*, Islington, 1843

Louis, Keith, with Horsford, Anthony, *St Peter's Church, Limpsfield: a Brief History*, published by the parish council, 2009

Lysons, Daniel, *The Environs of London*, vol. 3, 1795

Mackenzie, Compton, *Sinister Street*, 1913
—*Guy & Pauline*, 1915

Middleton, John, *A View of the Agriculture of Middlesex*, 1798

Moody, Raymond, *The Ancient Boundaries of Taynton*, Tolsey Paper No.5, Burford, 1985

Moody, Raymond and Joan, *The Book of Burford*, Buckingham Press, 1983
—*A Thousand Years of Burford*, Hindsight of Burford, 2006

Mount, Harry, *A Lust for Window Sills*, 2008

Nelson, John, *The History, Topography and Antiquities of the parish of St Mary, Islington*, 1811

Oliphant, Margaret, *The Curate in Charge*, 1875

Palmer, WT, *Odd Corners in Surrey*, 1951

Parker, Eric, *Highways and Byways of Surrey*, 1909

Parker, Rowland, *The Common Stream*, 1975

Pemberton, W Baring, *William Cobbett*, 1949

Percy, Kay, *Limpsfield Explored*, published by Tandridge District Council, 1975

—with Gray, Peter, *Limpsfield Revisited, A guide to the village and conservation area*, privately published 1986

Pratt, EA, *A History of Inland Transport and Communication in England*, 1912

Purefoy, Mollie, *The Book of Taynton* c.1968, re-issued by the parish council c.1990

Sherington, RO, *The Story of Hornsey*, 1904

Schwitzer, Joan, *Buried in Hornsey, The Graves of St Mary's churchyard*, published by HHS, c.1995

Schwitzer, Joan (editor) *Lost Houses of Haringey* published by HHS, 1986

—*People and Places: Lost Estates in Highgate, Hornsey and Wood Green*, published by HHS, 1996

Steer, Charles (editor) *Extracts from the Rector's Book, Limpsfield*, privately published, 1949

Streatfeild, Noel, *Away from the Vicarage*, 1965

Tomlins, Thomas Edlyne, *Perambulations of Islington*, 1842

Townley, Simon (editor) *Burford, buildings and people in a Cotswold town*, Phillimore in association with the Victoria County History, 2008

Trollope, Anthony, *The Warden*, 1855

—*Barchester Towers*, 1857

—*Framley Parsonage*, 1861

—*The Last Chronicles of Barset*, 1867

White, Jerry, *Campbell Bunk: the Worst Street in North London between the Wars*, 1986

Williams, Raymond, *The Countryside and the City*, 1985

Winstanley, RL, with Hughes, David (editors) *The Diary of a Country Parson, the Revd. James Woodforde*, Folio Society, 1992

Anonymous works:

Healthy Hornsey, an official municipal guide, published by the *Hornsey Journal*, 1906

Letters of Lord Chesterfield to his Son (editor and Preface unattributed), 1929

Manor House, Limpsfield, planning requirements for development of Manor House grounds, published by Tandridge District Council, 1977

Titsey Place and Gardens, current house guide, unattributed or dated

General works of reference:

Crockford's Clerical Directory, various late 19th century dates

Kelly's Directory for Surrey, 1870

The Post Office Directory, Surrey, 1870

The Survey of London (St Pancras part II) vol. XIX, 1938

The Victoria Country History, Middlesex, vol. VI, 1980

The Victoria County History, Surrey, vol. IV, 1967

Acknowledgements

When one sets to work on a defined area, one usually finds quite soon that there are one or two local people whose interest and help will prove invaluable. With my houses in three quite different locations, I have been lucky to find in each place one or several people whose willingness to share their own knowledge or experience has been crucial to my research.

In Oxfordshire, it was my good fortune to be closely related to the previous owners of the Old Vicarage in Taynton, Anne Milner and her family. The present owners, Charles and Alexandra Lloyd, have also shown a kind interest in my research. But the lifetime local knowledge of Raymond and Joan Moody of Burford, freely offered, has been of great additional help to me. So has been the expertise of David Clark of the Oxfordshire Buildings Record, who generously made time to visit the interior, and particularly the roof timbers, of the one-time 'parsonage house'. I am grateful as well to Charles Moore, of The Rectory Society, and to his colleagues Christine Bland and Alison Everington for supplying me with back-numbers of its Newsletter.

In north London, several members of the Hornsey Historical Society have been most generous with their time and interest, especially Peter Barber, Joy Nichol and, above all, John Hinshelwood, who has not hesitated to share his own copious research-findings in return for some slight input from me on the exact configuration of the Stapleton Hall-Farm complex. It was in his company that I finally managed to enter the oldest part of the building and so verify our suppositions – thanks also to Kate Walsh, who welcomed us in.

In Limpsfield, the two local historians to whom I would particularly have liked to talk have passed into history, along with so many others in this book – but I have been most fortunate to find, among the recent and present occupants of the Manor House and the Stanhopes housing estate, a pool of interest and enthusiasm for my research. With their help, I have had the strange experience of visiting almost every corner of the Manor House in its present (dis)guise. Thanks especially to Maureen Bunn who welcomed me and introduced me to others, to Vicki Dean and to Carolyn Rayner and her late husband Peter who kindly lent me material, also Sylvia Bancroft-Hunt, Angie Ellingford, Nicky Hill, Richard Hudson, and Mr and Mrs Frank Skinner. Also to Limpsfield residents Keith Louis, Brian and Betty Shearing and Mr and Mrs Bell for help and information.

The Planning department of Tandridge District Council supplied me with documents relating to the Listing of the Manor House and to the 1970s plans for the building's redevelopment. My thanks to Piers Mason.

Other people have given incidental and sometimes invaluable help and/or advice, either with research, with suggestions or snippets of information, or by reading through and commenting on the book before its final journey into print. My grateful thanks, therefore, to Anthony Adolph, Clare Baines, Roger Cazalet, the late Christopher Elrington, Penny Hoare, Malcom Holmes, Daphne Mackay, Jeremy McIlwaine, Sharon Pettle, Christopher Phipps, John Richardson, Mike Shaw, Gavin Stamp, Nicholas Tindall, Colin Thubron, Gordon Wise and Robin Woolven.

From the archive centres listed under Sources & Bibliography I have received great help, sometimes going

Acknowledgements

beyond the ordinary. Especial thanks, then, to Mark Aston of Finsbury Library, to Val Crosby, Deborah Hedgecock and Clare Stephens of Bruce Castle archive, to Lynda Haynes and others of the Oxfordshire Record Office and, most of all, to Mike Page, Jane Lewis and others of the Surrey History centre for their understanding approach to my demands.

Extract from 'An Arundel Tomb' by Philip Larkin taken from *The Whitsun Weddings* © The Estate of Philip Larkin and reproduced by permission of Faber and Faber. Extract from *Howards End* by E.M. Forster (Penguin Modern Classics) © E.M. Forster 1910; reproduced by permission of The Provost and Scholars of King's College Cambridge and The Society of Authors as the Literary Representative of the Estate of E.M. Forster.

Every effort has been made to trace and contact all holders of copyright in quotations and illustrations. If there are any inadvertent omissions or errors, the publishers will be pleased to correct these at the earliest opportunity.

Index

A40 (road) 74, 77, 187
Adelaide, South Australia
    152–3
agriculture: depressions and
    depopulation 168, 169–70,
    223; developments in
    168–9
Albert, Prince Consort 191,
    211
Alden, Francis ('Francis of
    Bicester') 99
Alexandra Palace 54
All Souls College, Oxford
    80
Amwell, Hertfordshire
    64
Ancient Corporation of
    Stroud Green 49, 51
Anglicanism *see* Church of
    England
Anne, Queen 29, 283;
    Queen Anne's Bounty
    125, 157
Archway (London) 36,
    286*n*2
Arsenal football ground 57,
    263
Ashdown Forest 2–3, 5, 251
Asthall, Oxfordshire 115,
    188, 254–5

Aubrey, John 6
Austen, Jane 135, 138, 184;
    Emma 135–7
Australia 152–3

Baker, William 115
Balfour, Michael 288*n*1
Bankside (London) 81, 149
Barber-Surgeons, Company
    of 85
Barker, Frederick Raymond,
    vicar of Taynton 126–7
Barnet 264
Barrington Magna *see* Great
    Barrington
Barrington-Balfour, Charles,
    MP for Hornsey 239–40
Barringtons (paper
    manufacturer) 169
Bastardy Act (1733) 113
Battersea Park 210, 211
Bayley (Limpsfield
    churchwarden) 148
Bede, Venerable 5–6
beggars 115
Bell, Alex Mounterie 163,
    164, 165–6, 277
Belloc, Hilaire, 'Charles
    Augustus Fortescue'
    241–2